THE CONSERVATIVE TRADITION IN AMERICA

by
Charles W. Dunn
and
J. David Woodard

ROWMAN & LITTLEFIELD PUBLISHERS, INC.

ROWMAN & LITTLEFIELD PUBLISHERS, INC.

Published in the United States of America
by Rowman & Littlefield Publishers, Inc.
4720 Boston Way, Lanham, Maryland 20706

3 Henrietta Street
London WC2E 8LU, England

British Cataloging in Publication Information Available

Library of Congress Cataloging-in-Publication Data

Dunn, Charles W.
The conservative tradition in America / Charles W. Dunn and
J. David Woodard.
p.   cm.
Includes bibliographical references and index.
1. Conservatism—United States—History.   I. Woodard, J. David.
II. Title.
JC573.2.U6D85   1996   320.5′2′0974—dc20   95-26196   CIP

ISBN 0-8476-8166-1 (cloth: alk. paper)
ISBN 0-8476-8167-x (pbk.: alk. paper)

Printed in the United States of America

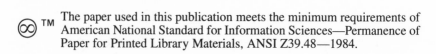

The paper used in this publication meets the minimum requirements of American National Standard for Information Sciences—Permanence of Paper for Printed Library Materials, ANSI Z39.48—1984.

Contents

Preface

Conservatism, once at the periphery of American politics, now occupies a central and strategic position in the seat of political power. The 1994 election confirmed a realignment of American politics along conservative lines in the general electorate, but in the halls of academe conservatism remains a neglected subject, on the fringes of the curriculum and outside the door of the faculty lounge. Many academics are politically liberal, and few scholars in the social science disciplines take conservative intellectual positions seriously.[1]

Students in the classroom, by contrast, are very interested and supportive of conservative ideas. Unfortunately, their enthusiasm is often keener than their acquaintance with the thought to which they have such a fervent devotion. Many present-day converts to American conservatism are astonished to discover that it has a long history that predates the election of Ronald Reagan in 1980.

We have written this book primarily for our students and colleagues and also for anyone interested in a survey of the ideas and traditions of American conservative political thought. Not since the 1950s, when Clinton Rossiter's *Conservatism in America* appeared, has a comparable survey of conservative thought been published. Our survey approach necessarily means that important ideas are given briefer attention than the reader, or the authors for that matter, would like. Each of the sections of this book could be greatly expanded and still not do justice to the ideas associated with the topic. We have included an expanded bibliography in the hope that the serious reader will independently pursue related books on subjects of interest.

We have found conservatism to be a complex subject. Although commonly considered an ideology, many of its best-known adherents do not believe it is; conservatism is not easily defined, and its principles often appear in conflict. Its evolution in American history has been long and meandering and is likely to remain so given the present dialogue in Washington.

Today, some conservative adherents would say that there is no significant conservative tradition in America. Here we will argue otherwise, believing that the ideas of conservatism were forged in the crucible of history and experience in reaction to hostile ideas and unfortunate events.

Unlike communism, with its *Communist Manifesto*, conservatism has no coherent tome of principles; it did not spring—fresh and sparkling—from the chambers of the human mind. Heterogeneity, rather than homogeneity, typifies its history. Conservatism is composed of a diversity of groups and a complexity of ideas. Its future is hotly debated; some argue that it has finished its course, while others believe its best contributions lie ahead.

In the first chapter, "The Emergence of Contemporary American Conservatism," we examine the reasons why conservatism moved from backstage to center stage on the American political scene. We survey major currents of conservative thought since World War II. Chapter 2, "The Problem of Defining Conservatism," discusses various definitions of conservatism, noting how they are alike and different. Conservatism is defined and placed in the context of American political culture. "The Ten Most Important Beliefs of Conservatism," the third chapter, sets forth the fundamental principles of conservatism as accepted by most of its advocates. The next two chapters explore the tradition of American conservatism. Chapter 4, "The Classical Roots of Conservative Thought," examines the non-American roots of American conservatism, covering such subjects as classical and modern political thought, the Enlightenment, and utopian ideologies. Chapter 5, "The Historical Development of American Conservatism," shows how conservatism developed since America's founding. The sixth chapter, entitled "The Competing Conservative Traditions in America," presents the political, economic, and religious past of American conservatism. The final chapter, "The Directions of Contemporary American Conservatism," contemplates the present state of conservatism and its prospects in light of changing conditions.

Our work is a summary of conservative thought; the lists of canons, principles, and definitions are not advanced as an ideological blueprint. Many individual conservatives might wish to add to the information we present here, and some might well take exception to some of our statements. We accept responsibility for any errors in our presentation and invite constructive criticism. Conservatives argue among themselves as to the proper ranking of their values and will disagree on the practical application of their principles. One need not adhere to every conservative idea to be known by that label. These qualifications aside, we believe that the ideas in this book constitute the core meaning of conservative thought.

Note

1. Stanley Rothman, "Academics on the Left," *Society*, Vol. 23, No. 3., March/April 1986, pp. 44–49. For a conservative analysis of this problem see T. Kenneth Cribb, "Conservatism and the American Academy: Prospects for the 1990s," (Washington, D.C.: The Heritage Foundation, 1989). See also: Everett Carl Ladd, Jr. and Seymour Martin Lipset, *The Divided Academy: Professors and Politics* (New York: McGraw-Hill, 1975).

CHAPTER ONE

The Emergence of Contemporary American Conservatism

In the United States at this time [1950], liberalism is not only the dominant but even the sole intellectual tradition. For it is the plain fact that nowadays there are no conservative . . . ideas in general circulation.

LIONEL TRILLING[1]

A s World War II ended, liberalism stood as the foremost ideology in American politics. Louis Hartz wrote that "America represents the liberal mechanism of Europe functioning without the European social antagonisms."[2] A fluid class structure, unbounded opportunity, and acquisitive individualism stood out as hallmarks of Hartz's analysis of liberalism's dominance. Conservative emphasis on community, authority, deference, and the sanctity of tradition appeared out of place.

Acknowledgment of a large role for the national government in American life became a widely accepted truism after the New Deal. President Franklin D. Roosevelt announced in his 1932 inaugural address that "the money changers [have] fled from their high seats in the temple of civilization."[3] The ostensible creators of the Great Depression, finance capitalists and advocates of private markets, relinquished their position to the priests of a new order, government officials with a vision for management.

An entire generation, marked by the unforgettable collapse of the national economy and the successful mobilization against German and Japanese aggression, accepted the idea that government should set the economic agenda and care for the welfare and security needs of society. Conservatism's "last rites," pronounced by Lionel Trilling in 1950,

seemed appropriate for an era of optimism about a glittering and bounti-
ful liberal future.

But this was not to be. Sweeping cultural changes, a worsening economic condition, and the national traumas of Vietnam and Watergate
eroded the liberal confidence in a strong national government in less
than three decades. The results of the 1994 midterm election concluded
a trend that began with the election of Ronald Reagan in 1980 and
continued with a conservative triumph in a repudiation of liberal postwar expectations.

Today, liberalism is in retreat; conservatism outlived its last rites. After
the election of Ronald Reagan in 1980, no thoughtful political leader
could profit among voters by willingly accepting the label of "liberal."
The 1994 midterm election results stand as a benchmark testimonial
to the defeat of New Deal liberalism. Conservative and Republican,
synonymous with victory in that election, signaled the acceptance of the
traditional ideas of personal responsibility and a smaller national government. For the first time in forty years a new political party won in
the House of Representatives, creating the potential for reshaping the
American legislative agenda for the next quarter century.

Causes of Conservative Resurgence

Why did the liberal solutions fall out of favor with the electorate and
allow conservatism to take center stage in American political life? Some
say that liberal ideas lacked wide acceptance; others believe that failed
policies led to a rejection of liberalism as a guide for political action; still
others think that the interruption in liberal leadership is temporary.

Here we want to explore this dramatic turnaround in political outlook
and cultural attitudes by presenting the conservative political view of
the good society. The conservative ascendancy is best understood by
examining its major premises, the incidents that changed American culture, and the ideas of prominent writers associated with the conservative
movement.

Most writers agree that the genesis of the conservative renaissance is
found in the events of the 1960s. The Kennedy and Johnson administrations raised hopes that poverty, racism, and chronic unemployment associated with business cycles would disappear through liberal legislation

and Supreme Court decisions. Some groups, disappointed that government action did not bring immediate and far-reaching results, resorted to street protests and violent confrontations.

On college campuses, middle-class youths became outspoken critics of American life, protesting the war in Vietnam, parading for civil rights, and seizing campus buildings to demand changes in university rules and policies. The youth revolt took the form of unconventional clothing, socially conscious rock music, the widespread use of illegal drugs, and uninhibited sexuality.

Black Americans, seen as special victims of American society, received much sympathy with their plight from artists and intellectuals in the best of circles. "Radical chic" was in style. Tom Wolfe chronicled the new fashion, typified by "the [Black] Panther women trucking on into the Bernsteins' Chinese yellow duplex, amid the sconces, silver bowls full of white and lavender anemones, and uniformed servants serving drinks."[4] One writer commented at the time, "Should these various people have their way, society as we know it, in all its imperfections but also in all its glories, would be replaced by a desert inhabited by the nihilistic and the bored rich."[5] Conservatives had an alternative vision of the postwar world.

The idea of conservatism is distinctive: it emphasizes political stability as the forces of change slowly become integrated into time-tested institutions. During the liberal ascendance of the postwar era, the themes of state rather than federal action, fiscal responsibility, decreased government spending, and a reduction in governmental regulation of the economy sounded anachronistic. The New Deal, Fair Deal, New Frontier, and Great Society endorsed government as the positive force that ameliorated wrongs and expanded the freedom of the individual. When freedom became indistinguishable from anarchy, many people who supported the liberal emphasis on individual rights looked for an alternative vision for society. Even as the liberal ethic flowered, the conservative alternative blossomed.

The intellectual and philosophical resurrection of contemporary conservatism began in the 1940s with the publication of several books. First, Friedrich von Hayek's *The Road to Serfdom* (1944) presented a bulwark for conservative economics against the high tide of state-managed economic policies. Milton Friedman later incorporated competitive free-market principles and government noninterference in the economy in his popular book *Free to Choose* (1976). Second, University of Chicago professor Richard Weaver's *Ideas Have Consequences* (1948) traced the decline of Western culture since medieval times and foreshadowed a later University of Chicago professor's best-seller, Allan Bloom's *The Closing of the American Mind* (1987), which critiqued liberal cultural excesses in academe and the society at large. Third was Peter Viereck's *Conservatism Revisited* (1949), featured in *The Times* of London as "the most intelligent summary of conservatism, based itself on the principles of British statesman Edmund Burke."[6]

Between 1950 and 1953, eight books appeared that had themes compatible with the works of Hayek, Weaver, and Viereck. They included Russell Kirk's *The Conservative Mind*, now in its seventh edition; Eric Voegelin's *The New Science of Politics*; William F. Buckley, Jr.'s *God and Man at Yale*; Gertrude Himmelfarb's *Lord Acton*; Leo Strauss's *Natural Right and History*; John Hallowell's *The Moral Foundations of Democracy*; Whittaker Chambers's *Witness*; and Robert Nisbet's *Quest for Community*. Each of these books discussed the role cultural traditions play in the stability of a society.

In 1955 Clinton Rossiter's *Conservatism in America: The Thankless Persuasion* won the Charles A. Beard Memorial Prize and announced to the academic world that being to the right of center was intellectually respectable.[7] When released, Rossiter's book created a stir; some critics considered it a defense of the mainstream or moderate center of American politics rather than a statement of purely conservative principles. Regardless of this debate, the book contributed to the growing attention given to the ideological origins of public policy.

New conservative journals of opinion, such as the *National Review, Modern Age,* and the *Intercollegiate Review,* arrived on the literary scene during the 1950s. Conservative think tanks, including the American Enterprise Institute, the Center for Strategic Studies at Georgetown University, the American Security Council, the Hoover Institution, and the Foreign Policy Research Institute at the University of Pennsylvania, began to offer alternative visions for the American experience. Prior to the creation of such centers, new ideas in American politics remained almost exclusively the domain of liberals in such places as the Brookings Institution.

Revived interest in two classics also occurred. Alexis de Tocqueville's *Democracy in America* and Edmund Burke's *Reflections on the Revolution in*

France emphasized custom and order as the protectors of social morality and fit the needs of a nation wondering about its values after achieving economic abundance.[8] The themes of respect for cultural tradition and fear of human tinkering with proven institutions permeated these works. Collectively they had much to say about current problems. Viereck and Kirk applied Burkean principles to the contemporary debate on the Cold War, comparing Communist excesses to the revolutionary indulgences in France that had alarmed Edmund Burke. Conservatives later used the same logic to draw parallels between the excesses of the New Left of the 1960s and those of the Jacobins of the 1790s. The depravity of human reason unchecked by tradition, conservatives argued, produced such dictatorial monsters as Stalin and Napoleon.

Richard Weaver and Leo Strauss traced conservative thought back to the classical ideal of Plato's "ordered society," with its sense of noblesse oblige. To conservatives, American society placed too much emphasis on rights and not enough on responsibilities. They argued that change had to be gradual and consistent with society's foundations. Classical scholars, such as Weaver, Strauss, and, later, Allan Bloom, contended that America's hurricanelike changes in civil rights for minorities, the women's revolution, and the street confrontations with government authorities that characterized the 1960s and early 1970s caused the nation to lose its cultural anchor and drift in a sea of relative values.

Political seeds of conservatism budded alongside these intellectual works. In the postwar years a consistent chorus in the Congress rejected the liberal themes. Senator Everett Dirksen's regular bickering with presidential social welfare legislation made him a national figure. Senator Barry Goldwater's *The Conscience of a Conservative* (1961), which frontally challenged American liberalism, sold millions of copies.[9] Also on drugstore shelves were the writings of William F. Buckley, Jr., James J. Kilpatrick, and M. Stanton Evans, which contributed to the discussion of conservative ideas in the general populace. Buckley's *Up From Liberalism* (1959), Kilpatrick's *The Sovereign States* (1957), and Evans's *The Liberal Establishment* (1965) added to the philosophical resurgence of contemporary conservatism.[10] Their commentary in news magazines and newspapers and on television formed a cornerstone for the conservatism of the 1980s and 1990s.

Conservative Cycles

According to Arthur M. Schlesinger, Jr., the political cycle is a continuing struggle between conservative values such as the sanctity of private property, the maximization of profit, and the free market and liberal values such as equality, freedom, social responsibility, and public regulation of property and profit. Schlesinger contends, "The roots of this cyclical self-sufficiency doubtless lie deep in the natural life of humanity."[11]

The cycle of liberalism, which began with Franklin Roosevelt in 1932, dominated American politics and public policy even during Republican administrations. President Eisenhower, for example, made little effort to reverse the tide of liberal New Deal policies and President Nixon had little success in changing the social welfare agenda of the Congress. Before 1968 the Republican Party generally represented white-collar voters and the Democratic Party, blue-collar voters. Ten years later the parties represented two ideologically different sets of upper middle-class voters: "The Republicans came to represent the more conservative wing of the traditional middle class and the Democrats the more leftist wing of the liberal middle class, or the 'new class.' "[12]

The political success of Ronald Reagan supplanted the liberal and Democratic ethic of public supervision with one emphasizing private and local initiatives. The 1994 midterm election brought these ideas to the legislative halls of Congress, but the jury remains out on their continued dominance of public policy over several decades as Roosevelt's New Deal did. Both President Ronald Reagan in the 1980s and Speaker of the U.S. House of Representatives Newt Gingrich in the 1990s quoted Roosevelt because they saw themselves as the same kind of harbinger for a new political era.

Should the conservative cycle be abbreviated, its internal tensions may be a major cause. Some conservatives who wandered for forty years in the postwar wilderness resent freshmen congressmen, upstart academics, and think-tank activists. Longtime philosophical conservatives may also resent the popularizers who write weekly news columns and host radio talk shows.

For some, the term conservatism conjures up a unity of ideas said not to exist in fact. To illustrate, consider that Barry Goldwater did not even merit a mention in the index of the seventh edition of Russell Kirk's *The Conservative Mind*.[13] Even after Ronald Reagan's election in 1980, some conservatives criticized his administration because it failed to adhere to a strict agenda of economic, social, and foreign policy items. They targeted "moderates," such as senior advisors James Baker in Reagan's first administration and Howard Baker in his second.

With no master plan to guide and unify American conservatism, haphazard development and setbacks marred its progress. The low point came in the 1964 presidential campaign of Senator Barry Goldwater, when the outspoken conservative carried only six states in the electoral college; yet even this defeat had a silver lining. The Goldwater campaign demonstrated that: (1) a significant segment of the American public reacted favorably to the conservative message; (2) conservatives could organize and capture control of one of the two major political parties; and (3) the political infrastructure built by conservatives in the early 1960s could be used as a launching pad for political success. Ronald Reagan first gained national political notice when he spoke for Goldwater in 1964, an appearance in which he seemed a more reasonable conservative advocate than the Republican presidential candidate.

Shared traditional values held conservatism together during the turbulent postwar era. These values emphasized local control, a sense of morality, and respect for tradition. The disposition toward religion among many conservatives caused them to adopt an emphasis on the limits of man's power of reason. "We know," wrote Edmund Burke, "and it is our pride to know, that man is by his constitution a religious animal . . . religion is the basis of civil society."[14] At the turn of the century, mainline Protestant religious establishment figures appeared as "the Republican Party at prayer." Eighty years later religious leaders, such as Jerry Falwell and Pat Robertson, worshipped at the Republican altar. In the years after World War I the rise of the Social Gospel movement and the response by fundamentalists to the attack on the traditional authority of the Bible led to a split in American Protestantism.[15]

By the 1970s the debate over abortion, "together with a number of other issues that divide the public along much the same lines— pornography, homosexuality, school prayer—the question of public morality and its relation to government policy has provided a continuing source of tension between religious liberals and religious conservatives."[16] The decade after the sixties witnessed a rise in public concern about cultural values and the future of American society.

Ronald Reagan's candidacy in 1980 won endorsements from many conservative religious groups, including the Moral Majority, the Eagle Forum, and the Religious Roundtable. The Christian Coalition and other conservative religious groups undergirded Republican victories in the 1990s. People who believed the Bible to be God's word and literally true usually favored increased defense spending, a tougher policy with Russia, opposition to abortions, and prayer in public schools.[17] From conservative ideological circles came supporters associated with the American Enterprise Institute, the Hoover Institution, and the Heritage Foundation. Many Catholics abandoned their traditional loyalty to the Democratic Party to embrace the Republican platform, especially the plank opposing abortion. White evangelicals and white Catholics have been moving away from the Democratic Party since the 1960s.[18]

According to conservatives, the merger of ideological and theological strands of thought reveals a truth about American politics. For cultural conservatives, federally funded sex education classes, homosexual rights, abortion, the Equal Rights Amendment, and the abolition of school prayer violated sacred principles derived from the Judeo-Christian heritage of the Western democracies. One writer summed up the theological differences this way: "Conservatives tend to believe, liberals to doubt."[19] When the sea of faith recedes, conservatives argue, the body politic faces nihilism in all its stark despair. Tocqueville recognized the important affinity between religion and democracy in America when he wrote of the role that churches and other private voluntary organizations play in affirming the community ties on which American democracy depends. Traditional values served as an umbrella under which various religious groups could unite, and religion played an important role in the maturation of political movements.

Religious conservatives took for granted school prayer at athletic events and pastoral sermons at baccalaureate services until they suddenly had the rug of religious security pulled from beneath them. Since many of these people believed in America's Christian origins, they saw these actions as hostile to the very core of their national experience. In the 1970s the debate on the origin and purposes of America heated up, with most liberals arguing that the nation had only a nominal Christian heritage that had been superceded by a respectful tolerance for social and religious pluralism. Conservatives contended that the distinctive character of the Judeo-Christian tradition explains why the American republic developed as it did. They believed that liberal social policies erode the very foundation of the country.

The 1963 Supreme Court decision against official prayers in public schools kindled the fire of debate on religion in public life. Subsequent cases asked whether creation science could be taught alongside evolutionary theory in the public school classroom. Could the Ten Commandments be posted on public school classroom walls? Is secular humanism a religion that denies God and holds to relative, rather than absolute, moral standards? Could it be taught in textbooks and public school classrooms in place of Christianity? Could public school students meet for religious purposes in public school buildings if the meetings did not interfere with school activities? Could the Catholic Church have its tax-exempt status revoked because of alleged lobbying activities against abortion? Could a religious school have its tax-exempt status revoked because its religious convictions forbid interracial dating and marriage? These, and a long list of other religious issues, made their way into the courts between the 1970s and 1990s. Millions of Americans, influenced by these debates, petitioned the judicial, legislative, and executive branches of government for differing interpretations of the Constitution.

In 1964, while campaigning for the presidency, Lyndon Johnson said, "We're in favor of a lot of things, and we're against mighty few." Support for Great Society programs, including Medicare, Medicaid, the food stamp program, legal assistance for the indigent, economic revitalization for distressed areas, and medical research, rested on the belief that economic growth facilitates funding. Such illusions, no less than the programs they spawned, became the first casualties of the Vietnam War.

In the decade of the seventies public confidence in government as an equitable economic arbitrator shook when the economy languished. Running against Gerald Ford in 1976, Jimmy Carter devised the "misery index," defined as the addition of rates of inflation and unemployment. In 1976 the misery index stood at 12.5 percent; by 1980, when Ronald Reagan ran against Carter, it had reached nearly 20 percent. Reagan cited this poor economic performance as evidence of Carter's lack of leadership: "In Reagan's campaign and presidency, the principal accusation against Democratic predecessors and rivals [was] that they were guilty of pessimism."[20]

Liberal public policies, once accepted uncritically, faced new challenges. Do not public housing projects and highway construction programs destroy the community and the integrity of local neighborhoods? The Great Society programs not only failed those to be helped, they also turned the intended beneficiaries against the programs. School busing also outraged the people it was designed to help. In the seventies busing for purposes of integration became the most controversial political issue in the country. One of the heartbeats of conservative thought is its assumption that the community is central to the definition of the individual. African Americans and others attacked the injustices of housing programs and busing decisions, because such actions forcibly evicted them from their neighborhoods to achieve racial balance.[21] These controversies publicized liberal assumptions and expanded alternative policies that favored conservative values.

Both a social and an economic impulse undergirded Reagan's victory in 1980. While supply-side economics occupied the headlines, the social agenda galvanized individual allegiances to Reagan and the Republican Party: anti-abortion, for school prayer, against school busing, opposed to pornography, against government regulation of private and religious schools, hostile to employment quotas, and opposed to the Equal Rights Amendment. Republicans favored tuition tax credits for parents of children in private and religious schools and strict school discipline. Supreme Court decisions in the 1960s and 1970s added momentum to this agenda. The Court's opposition to school prayer and support for abortion, for example, aroused a large and vocal opposition among the conservative public.

To conservatives, the equal rights impulse and the homosexual movement undermined traditional cultural values that had stood the test of time. Many Americans believed that social experimentation would destroy proven values. An appeal to a simpler past, when Americans had confidence in themselves and what they stood for, had immediate acceptance during the 1980s. Entering the decade of the nineties, the administration of President George Bush either openly supported Reagan administration policies or only quietly demurred from them. Continuity rather than conflict was the norm.

Neoconservatism added momentum to the right-wing resurgence. It is a movement made up, in the phrase of Irving Kristol, of "liberals who had been mugged by reality."[22] Many of its adherents were once active supporters of the New Deal; some even thought of themselves as liberals until they reacted against the events of the 1960s and the overextension of liberal public policies that characterized the time. They number among their ranks Irving Kristol, who helped found the highly regarded journal *The Public Interest*; Jeane Kirkpatrick, who became ambassador to the United Nations under President Reagan; Harvard University professor Edward Banfield, author of *The Unheavenly City* (1974); and former Harvard, and later UCLA, professor James Q. Wilson, author of numerous works critical of liberal public policies.

Some prominent intellectuals also shifted from ardent advocacy of liberal politics to conservative values, such as anticommunism and a smaller role for the federal government. The most dramatic example of such conversion from liberalism to conservatism was Norman Podhoretz, whose book *Breaking Ranks* typified the shift to new values. Podhoretz would subsequently edit the highly regarded neoconservative journal *Commentary*.[23]

Aside from being disenchanted with employment quotas, affirmative action, pornography, and other perceived excesses of liberal public policies, neoconservatives reacted to the weak position of modern liberalism on communism. The staunch anticommunist position, of course, was not new to conservatism. During the late 1940s and early 1950s, several writers developed the conservative position of strident opposition to communism. Among the most prominent works were Whittaker Chambers's *Witness* (1953) and James Burnham's *Containment or Liberation* (1953).[24] Anticommunism had immediate appeal to Catholic intellectuals from Eastern Europe, whose homelands were under communist domination.

Neoconservatives want to reverse the agenda of government, turn away from grand governmental schemes, and reform America by relying on the private sector, the market mechanism, and traditional institutions, such as the family and local community. They argue that efforts to promote equality in the sixties threatened individual freedoms in the eighties. Neoconservatives also decry the oppressive encroachment of government bureaucracies on the spontaneous exercise of free-market capitalism. They prefer that local communities solve their own problems without national government interference.

Conversion from liberalism to conservatism is the distinctive mark of neoconservatives. The failed idealism of liberalism preceded their acceptance of conservative social theory. Many neoconservatives are college-educated adults who were raised in liberal homes, attended fashionable institutions of higher learning, and sampled the values of the sixties. Their attitude remains antiestablishment, but the values that they reject are liberal, not conservative.

The New Conservatism

By the 1980s conservatism underwent a metamorphosis in self-image. During the 1940s and 1950s, and even in the 1960s, it had a more negative tone, carping about governmental policies but offering few alternatives. The conservative looked at himself as the last sentry of sanity against the majority view of state dominance. Still, conservatives offered few specifics to contradict the prevailing liberal climate of state activism, cultural pluralism, and equal rights.

The conservative renaissance rested on a belief that the first task of government should be the protection of national life. Consequently, conservative policymakers urged that military programs receive greater funding priority than at any time since the Vietnam War. Stronger national defense, a priority of conservative policymakers in the decade of the 1980s, assisted the demise of Soviet communism and proved necessary for the war against Saddam Hussein in 1991. Conservatives emphasize defense for several reasons. First, it was believed that the Soviet Union had gained an advantage over the United States in the seventies. The United States was the "second most powerful military nation," according to Ronald Reagan in the 1980 election. The defeats the Pentagon suffered in Vietnam were but a prelude to skepticism about new weapons systems and the accusation of an exaggerated Russian threat that greeted military planners on Capitol Hill. Second, the United States military enjoyed a technological advantage—better bombs and radar, faster planes and missiles; but the seventies revealed an erosion of technological dominance that favored Japan and other Pacific Rim nations. To remain a world leader, the United States needed a renewed commitment to research and development of high-tech weaponry.

Early in the Reagan administration attention to Pentagon projects gained favor, but when a number of expenditures for items such as coffee pots and hammers became subjects of investigative media stories, the military realized that priority funding came at a price. These stories seemed to discredit the newfound fascination with exotic military weapons, until the 1991 Iraqi war confirmed the conservative devotion to the military. The Patriot and Cruise missiles and laser-guided bombs proved that the American military remained the standard for comparison in the world. Since Iraqi weapons came from the Soviet Union, their destruction by American technology was especially sweet. President Bush basked in the sunlight of Reagan administration defense initiatives as he led the nation in defeating Iraq, then the world's fourth largest military power. The long shadow of Vietnam-era pessimism about the military receded in the bright sunshine of a Bush-led victory in the Gulf War.

Gradually, conservatism took on a more positive cast with an agenda of reducing social spending, emphasizing traditional values, reshaping the tax code, and rebuilding national defense. Through the 1970s and 1980s more Americans characterized themselves as moderates than either liberals or conservatives, but whereas in the early 1970s liberal and conservative responses to survey questions were given in equal numbers, by the end of the eighties, "conservative responses outstrip[ed] liberal ones by a ratio of about 4 to 3."[25] The conservative view shifted to a positive and majority conviction as it became energized to fight within the political realm. For example, rather than just being against Keynesian New Deal economics and big government budgets, conservatives gradually developed constructive policies of their own that emphasized supply-side solutions and market alternatives.

In the Reagan administration implementing these conservative ideas had the highest priority. The 1980 Republican Party platform declared that "the family, the neighborhood, the community, and the workplace [were] vital alternatives in our national life to ever-expanding federal power."[26] The policies emerging from such conservative think tanks as the Heritage Foundation and the Manhattan Institute found widespread acceptance in mainstream America. They confirmed the rhetoric Ronald Reagan had preached for years—an enhanced, vital free market, uninhibited by government intrusion, excessive taxes, or regulatory burdens. The economic results of such an approach were spectacular: the 1980s "have seen the longest, or perhaps second-longest, expansion in the entire history of the American business cycle."[27]

At the end of the Reagan administration, even some liberals embraced conservative capitalistic ideas. The era of national renewal emphasized

traditional values, the dignity of work, love for family and neighborhood, faith in God, a belief in peace through strength, and a commitment to protect freedom as a unique legacy of America. George Bush
said in his inaugural address, "We know how to secure a more just and
prosperous life for man on earth: through free markets, free speech, free
elections, and the exercise of free will unhampered by the state."[28]

The new regard for conservatism went beyond economic indicators.
If conservatism was to be successful in reaching those outside its philosophical foundations, it had to develop new slogans and symbols. The
social agenda gave energy to the new conservative legions. Abortion,
banning school prayer, leniency in handling criminals, job quotas, riots
and violence on campuses and in cities, pornography, and the Equal
Rights Amendment could be visualized quickly and clearly by the
masses. In the malaise of the Carter era Ronald Reagan said, "I am
deeply concerned with the wave of hedonism, the humanist philosophy
so prevalent today, and believe this nation must have a spiritual rebirth,
a rededication to the moral precepts which guided us for so much of our
past, and we must have such a rebirth very soon."[29] Reagan was the
"Great Communicator" because he reached and soothed the anxieties
of Americans concerned about the future. He offered an alternative view
of tomorrow based on the values that worked yesterday.

The Reagan presidency deeply influenced the American conscience.
To many Americans, identification with the Reagan presidency was like
marrying a popular cause, one that changed the way people thought
about their government and its role in their lives. A *Washington Post* poll
in July 1988 found that more than half—52 percent—of the respondents
believed that the country was better off because of Reagan's presidency;
only one-third said they were worse off, and 13 percent said his tenure
made no difference.[30] Continuing to follow a generally conservative
agenda, President Bush enjoyed a level of popular support higher than
that of his predecessor and the highest of any president at comparable
times in his presidency. Both Reagan and Bush helped change the way
most Americans thought about the federal government, the Republican
Party, and the conservative political ideology.

The 1990s

The interruption in this generally conservative renaissance came in 1992
when Bill Clinton won the presidency as a "New Democrat," promising

an administration consistent with popular conservative themes. Within four months of his inauguration the disapproval rating of the new president soared and there emerged an almost visceral level of mistrust and dislike for him, a rejection not just of him as a leader or politician, but as a person. Much of the aversion seemed to be based on cultural issues, such as homosexuals in the military, abortion, and doubts about the president's character. These controversies, breaking early in his administration, set the tone for his first two years in office. Then the 1994 midterm election delivered an enormous setback to the ideals of liberalism and the Democratic Party.

Conservative radio talk shows, popularized by irreverent hosts such as Rush Limbaugh, prospered during Bill Clinton's presidency in the 1990s. President Clinton's positions on abortion, feminism, homosexuality, and other moral issues became their cannon fodder. No liberal talk show even came close to rivaling Rush Limbaugh's audience ratings. While conservatives often decried liberal dominance of the print and electronic media, they reigned almost unchallenged on radio both nationally and locally.

From the 1940s through the 1990s, conservative authors wove a common thread into the conservative quilt, undergirding and strengthening its fabric. The list of books in Table 1-1 is suggestive of the growing influence of conservatism in the last half of the twentieth century. Three books, among many, illustrate this common thread during the 1990s.

First, *To Renew America*, a best-seller by House Speaker Newt Gingrich, critiqued American history, offering lessons to be heeded if America is to regain lost luster.[31] Restoring the family, reviving community, reducing the power of government over American lives, and rekindling the American spirit of creativity and quality loomed large in Gingrich's prescriptions. Gingrich believes in the exceptional nature of American culture, made so by divine providence and human ingenuity.

Second, William J. Bennett's best-seller, *The Book of Virtues*, unearthed a gold mine of great moral stories in the conservative tradition.[32] Covering such subjects as self-discipline, compassion, responsibility, friendship, work, courage, perseverance, honesty, loyalty and faith, his book reveals the quality of character that conservatives claim must be restored in the personal lives of Americans. Moral education, Bennett argues, is the key to restoring not only personal character but also to reviving national greatness.

TABLE 1–1
Selected Books Molding Contemporary American Conservatism

Decade	Year	Author	Title
1940s	1944	Friedrich von Hayek	*The Road to Serfdom*
	1948	Richard Weaver	*Ideas Have Consequences*
	1949	Peter Viereck	*Conservatism Revisited*
		Ludwig von Mises	*Human Action*
1950s	1951	William F. Buckley, Jr.	*God and Man at Yale*
	1952	Eric Voegelin	*The New Science of Politics*
	1953	Russell Kirk	*The Conservative Mind*
		Leo Strauss	*Natural Right and History*
		Robert Nisbet	*The Quest for Community*
		Whittaker Chambers	*Witness*
	1955	Clinton Rossiter	*Conservatism in America*
	1957	James J. Kilpatrick	*The Sovereign States*
	1959	Harry Jaffa	*Crisis of a House Divided*
1960s	1961	Barry Goldwater	*The Conscience of a Conservative*
	1962	Milton Friedman	*Capitalism and Freedom*
		James Buchanan and Gordon Tullock	*The Calculus of Consent*
	1965	George J. Stigler	*Essays in the History of Economics*
		Forrest McDonald	*E Pluribus Unum*
1970s	1970	Edward Banfield	*The Unheavenly City*
		Willmoore Kendall and George Carey	*The Basic Symbols of the American Political Tradition*
	1972	Irving Kristol	*On the Democratic Idea in America*
	1975	Thomas Sowell	*Race and Economics*
	1976	George Nash	*The Conservative Intellectual Movement in America Since 1945*
	1978	Harvey Mansfield	*The Spirit of Liberalism*
	1979	M. E. Bradford	*A Better Guide Than Reason*
		Norman Podhoretz	*Breaking Ranks*
1980s	1980	Milton and Rose Friedman	*Free to Choose*
	1981	George Gilder	*Wealth & Poverty*
		Herbert Storing	*The Antifederalists*
	1982	Michael Novak	*The Spirit of Democratic Capitalism*
	1983	George Will	*Statecraft as Soulcraft*
	1984	Richard Neuhaus	*The Naked Public Square*
		Charles Murray	*Losing Ground*

TABLE 1–1 (Continued)
Selected Books Molding Contemporary American Conservatism

Decade	Year	Author	Title
	1987	Allan Bloom	*The Closing of the American Mind*
		E. D. Hirsch	*Cultural Literacy*
1990s	1991	Shelby Steele	*The Content of Our Character*
	1992	Dinesh D'Souza	*Illiberal Education*
	1993	William Bennett	*The Book of Virtues*
	1994	M. Stanton Evans	*The Theme Is Freedom*
	1995	Newt Gingrich	*To Renew America*

Third, *The Theme Is Freedom*, by M. Stanton Evans, presents a compelling case for America's Christian heritage, arguing that no society can survive without a solid religious foundation that provides absolute standards for moral and educational development.[33] Evans argues that the historical record refutes two liberal myths: (1) that our liberties stem from secular doctrines and (2) that religious absolutes endanger freedom.

No discussion of the 1990s would be complete without noting congressional and constitutional changes. The Contract with America, which defined public policy debates during and after the 1994 midterm election, offered a positive conservative prescription for America's policy ills in the Congress. Reforming welfare, balancing the budget, reducing the size of the national government, and returning power to state and local governments highlighted this agenda. The Supreme Court, dominated by a narrow conservative majority, attacked such liberal icons as affirmative action, separation of church and state, and national control of public policy through the commerce clause of the Constitution, inciting long-awaited cheers from a previously silent conservative audience.

Conclusion

American conservatism emerged in the 1980s and 1990s as a viable alternative to post–World War II liberalism; it was not an isolated event. The popularity of the New Deal and Keynesian economic policies began to wane in the seventies when government policies triggered stagflation. Federal initiatives in education, health, and employment raised the standard of living for most Americans but led to bureaucratic stupor and the specter of socialized regulation.

Conservatism, dormant during the postwar years, flowered when liberalism began to wilt in the heat of the social and economic turmoil during the sixties and seventies. In 1979 the Reagan campaign commissioned a poll about the values and aspirations of the electorate and found that Americans regretted the loss of values in society, particularly those associated with business ethics and traditional meanings. The next year the Connecticut Mutual Life Insurance Company found that the values of the nation's leaders—in business, the news media, government, science, education, and law—conflicted with those shared by the public. The gap between rank-and-file Americans and their leadership elites was as much as 30 percent on such fundamental issues as abortion, pornography, and homosexuality.[34] The conservative Reagan revolution strategically appealed to values emphasizing an "era of national renewal," one that would "revitalize the values of family, work and neighborhood."[35]

A diversity of economic, political, religious, and social opinion resurrected traditional conservatism. The causes of its rebirth were interrelated, but conservatism's turnaround in the 1980s and 1990s would have been impossible without the philosophical foundations provided in the forty years after World War II. The turbulent change of the sixties hastened the appeal and visibility of conservatism in the general public. The neoconservative impulse contributed an essential momentum to push society to consider the traditional conservative agenda.

Five conclusions about conservatism are evident from this review of the literature. First, philosophical and intellectual discourses on conservatism preceded popular and political treatises. Second, a wide variety of political, economic, social, and religious writing contributed to its development. Third, political success required several decades of maturation as various philosophical ideas gradually penetrated the public mind. Fourth, no master plan directed the rise of conservatism. Contemporary American conservatism is heterogenous, not homogenous. No one strand of thought and no single writer, leader, or group presided over the resurrection of conservatism from the dead. Fifth, to achieve political success in the future, candidates vying for conservative support must carefully walk through disparate conservative ideas.

Notes

1. Lionel Trilling, *The Liberal Imagination* (New York: Viking, 1950), p. ix.

2. Louis Hartz, *The Liberal Tradition in America* (New York: Harcourt, Brace, 1955), p. 16.

3. James MacGregor Burns, *Roosevelt: The Lion and the Fox* (New York: Harcourt, Brace & World, 1956), p. 163.

4. Tom Wolfe, *Radical Chic & Mau-Mauing the Flak Catchers* (New York: Farrar, Straus and Giroux, 1970), p. 5.

5. Louis A. Coser and Irving Howe, eds. *The New Conservatives: A Critique from the Left* (New York: New American Library, 1976), p. 10.

6. Frederick von Hayek, *The Road to Serfdom*, 17th ed. (Chicago: University of Chicago Press, 1956). Milton and Rose Friedman, *Free to Choose* (New York: Harcourt, Brace, Jovanovich, 1980). Richard Weaver, *Ideas Have Consequences* (Chicago: University of Chicago Press, 1948). Allan Bloom, *The Closing of the American Mind* (New York: Simon & Schuster, 1987). Peter Viereck, *Conservatism Revisited* (New York: Greenwood Press, 1978).

7. Russell Kirk, *The Conservative Mind: From Burke to Eliot*, 7th ed. (Chicago: Regnery, 1986). Eric Voegelin, *The New Science of Politics* (Chicago: University of Chicago Press, 1952). William F. Buckley, Jr., *God and Man at Yale*, 2nd ed. (Chicago: Regnery, 1977). Gertrude Himmelfarb, *Lord Acton: A Study in Conscience and Politics* (Chicago: University of Chicago Press, 1952). Leo Strauss, *Natural Right and History* (Chicago: University of Chicago Press, 1953). John Hallowell, *The Moral Foundations of Democracy* (Chicago: University of Chicago Press, 1973). Robert Nisbet, *The Quest for Community* (New York: Oxford University Press, 1953). Clinton Rossiter, *Conservatism in America* (New York: Knopf, 1955).

8. Alexis de Tocqueville, *Democracy in America* (Garden City, N.Y.: Doubleday Anchor, 1969). Edmund Burke, "Reflections on the Revolution in France," in *Works* (Boston: Little, Brown, 1865).

9. Barry Goldwater, *The Conscience of a Conservative* (Shepardsville, Ky.: Victor, 1960).

10. William F. Buckley, *Up From Liberalism* (New York: Stein & Day, 1958). James J. Kilpatrick, *The Sovereign States* (Chicago: Regnery, 1957). M. Stanton Evans, *The Liberal Establishment* (New York: Devin-Adair, 1965).

11. Arthur M. Schlesinger, Jr., *The Cycles of American History* (Boston: Houghton Mifflin, 1986), pp. 26, 27. For a study of the role political cycles play in the election of presidents, see Stephen Skowronek, *The Politics Presidents Make* (London, England: The Belknap Press of Harvard University Press, 1993).

12. James Q. Wilson, *American Government*, 4th ed. (Lexington, Mass.: D. C. Heath, 1989), p. 154.

13. Russell Kirk, *The Conservative Mind*, 7th ed. (Chicago: Regnery, 1986).

14. Edmund Burke, "Religion and the State," in Robert Schuettinger, ed. *The Conservative Tradition in European Thought* (New York: Capricorn Books, 1971), pp. 55–57.

20 CHAPTER ONE

15. George Marsden, *Fundamentalism and American Culture* (New York: Oxford University Press, 1980).

16. Robert Wuthnow, *The Restructuring of American Religion* (Princeton, N.J.: Princeton University Press, 1988), p. 13.

17. James Q. Wilson, *American Government*, 4th. ed. (Lexington, Mass.: D. C. Heath, 1989), p. 105.

18. "The Counter-attack of God," *The Economist*, July 8, 1993, pp. 19–21.

19. Werner J. Dannhauser, "Religion and the Conservatives," *Commentary*, December 1985, pp. 51–55.

20. Garry Wills, *Reagan's America* (New York: Penguin/Doubleday, 1985), p. 456.

21. Richard A. Pride and J. David Woodard, *The Burden of Busing* (Knoxville, Tenn.: University of Tennessee Press, 1985).

22. "Neoconservative Guru to America's New Order," *Maclean's*, January 19, 1981.

23. Edward Banfield, *The Unheavenly City: The Nature and Foundation of Our Urban Crisis* (Boston: Little, Brown, 1970). Norman Podhoretz, *Breaking Ranks* (New York: Harper & Row, 1979).

24. Whittaker Chambers, *Witness* (Chicago: Regnery Press, 1952). James Burnham, *Containment or Liberation* (New York: John Day, 1953).

25. D. Grier Stephenson, Jr., et al., *American Government* (New York: Harper & Row, 1988), p. 199.

26. *New York Times*, July 16, 1980, p. 6.

27. Walter Dean Burnham, "The Reagan Heritage," in Gerald M. Pomper, ed., *The Election of 1988* (Chatham, N.J.: Chatham House Publishers, 1989), p. 10. Richard McKenzie, *What Went Right in the 1980s* (San Francisco: Pacific Research Institute for Public Policy, 1994.)

28. *New York Times*, July 21, 1989, p. 10.

29. John Kenneth White, *The New Politics of Old Values* (Hanover & London: University Press of New England, 1988), p. 50.

30. *Washington Post: Weekly Edition*, July 11–17, 1988, p. 13.

31. Newt Gingrich, *To Renew America* (New York: Harper Collins, 1995).

32. William J. Bennett, *The Book of Virtues* (New York: Simon and Schuster, 1993).

33. M. Stanton Evans, *The Theme is Freedom: Religion, Politics, and the American Tradition* (Washington, D.C.: Regnery Press, 1994).

34. *Wall Street Journal*, May 15, 1981, p. 34.

35. White, *The New Politics of Old Values*, pp. 37–55.

CHAPTER TWO

The Problem of Defining
Conservatism

*What is conservatism? Is it not adherence to the old and tried,
against the new and untried?*

ABRAHAM LINCOLN[1]

Apolitical culture is a patterned way of thinking about politics and government. The American political system is supported by a culture that fosters a sense of civic duty, takes pride in the nation's constitutional arrangements and provides support for the exercise of essential civil liberties. Although Jesse Jackson and Ronald Reagan, Ted Kennedy and William F. Buckley, Jr., Paul Simon and Jesse Helms differ on specific issues of public policy, they still have much in common. Even these political adversaries agree that the two-party system is important, that there should be free speech and the competition of ideas, and that one should respect the opinions of others. A political culture consists of the fundamental assumptions citizens have about how the political process should operate. It is the "rules of the political game" for the social order.

A political ideology differs from political culture by emphasizing what the political process should accomplish or do. How government and politics should function may find conservatives and liberals agreeing, but what government and politics should do customarily finds them differing. Their respective goals and desired results lead one to want to ban abortion, the other to support it; one to oppose passage of the Equal Rights Amendment, the other to desire its adoption; one to oppose new taxes, the other to support them. For political scientists, liberalism and conservatism are ideologies, meaning that they provide a guide for how the government should function. Not always are the differences between the two as crystal-clear as the examples above, but the tendency among ideologues is to disagree on major public policy questions.

In sum, political culture is the general agreement on the means to achieve political ends, while ideology is the reflection of differences on the ends to be achieved. Political culture is the common ground for conservatives and liberals while political ideology is most often their fighting ground: "The dimension of the division between liberalism and conservatism today refers to attitudes about government's role . . . in the protection of order and certain moral values and community standards."[2] To define political conservatism, we must examine it in context with liberalism. Both liberals and conservatives accept the existing political order. Both want to use established institutions of American government with their guaranteed procedures and principles, but they want to use them to achieve different results. One difference between liberals and conservatives is that each one places a different emphasis upon key points in the American political culture. American conservatives have looked to Tocqueville's *Democracy in America* and Russell Kirk's *The Roots of the American Order* as the best definitions of the original American political culture. These works stress the unique aspects of the American social order and the differences between the newly formed nation and its older ancestors in Europe.

For most of its history the United States of America has been an exception to the history and social fabric of Europe. It was founded in opposition to European ideals and traditions, and from the beginning the guiding rule of American foreign policy was to keep out of European affairs. Thomas Paine said that the Old World nations had their origin in conquest and tyranny, but the "Independence of America [was] accompanied by a Revolution in the principles and practices of Government."[3] To conservatives those standards of government involved agreement on certain ideals which defined the character of the new nation. To explain the American culture associated with how conservatism will be defined, we begin by examining elements of the "national character" of the country, as viewed by conservatives:

- Liberty—the importance of freedom to allow individuals to seek "life, liberty and the pursuit of happiness" with limited restraints.

- Property—granting individuals the right to own property, recognizing it is a primary means for individuals to find their place in society, and to determine what they want to do with their lives.

- Community—substantial deference to the role of the community in defining society's standards and providing stability and continuity from generation to generation.

- Theology—recognition of and respect for the important role religion plays in defining American values.

- Democracy—often called the "rule of law," meaning that governmental power must be exercised within constitutional limitations.

- Equality—of citizens before the law, allowing each American to compete for jobs, income, status and education on an equal basis with others.

- Opportunity—or "rugged individualism" referring to rewarding personal effort and achievement rather than a person's social class, family standing or some other arbitrary privilege that has not been personally earned.

- Duty—encouraging Americans to fulfill their civic duty to participate in politics and community affairs by voting and being tolerant of opposing views.

- Efficacy—the belief that each individual has the privilege of trying to influence the political system and American society.

According to conservatives, these nine beliefs blend together to form the unique "national character" of America. In such a system each trait is related, for example, with liberty necessitating property, and equality requiring opportunity. Conservatives give unique definitions to the terms in the list above. For example, equality is defined by them as opportunity to compete, not a guaranteed quota or insured result. Similarly, democracy is rule limited by the Constitution, it does not imply a license to political power for each disaffected group or interest. For conservatives the value of duty implies patriotism and allegiance to community; such loyalties dictate a rejection of government expansion.

Conservatism is about cultural traditions and values which defy simple definition. In America, the status quo which conservatism defends is a complex amalgamation of beliefs and values not easily summarized. A good way to begin the definition of conservatism is with an explanation of the cultural legacy so important to its premises.

European Roots of Conservatism

The vital ideas and faith within conservatism are best understood by examining the moral foundations of Western culture. Leo Strauss, a leading conservative scholar, argued that the soul of the historical West was rooted in an understanding of its intellectual tradition. For Strauss and numerous other conservatives, Western culture rested on the classical Greek and biblical heritages, what he called the "Great Tradition" of Western politics. The belief that classical political philosophy was being neglected and replaced by utopian ideologies like Marxism, fascism and socialism was the core of the crisis Strauss saw in Western thought.

For much of its history, the study of politics involved asking about the immutable principles of justice, history and natural rights for citizens. The new political science developed after World War II changed this focus. According to Strauss, who condemns political science for rejecting the traditional approach: "[For] them [modern political scientists], all human thought is historical and hence unable ever to grasp anything eternal."[4] Allan Bloom describes political science as a discipline that "resembles a rather haphazard bazaar shop kept by a mixed population."[5] On the one hand, Bloom contends that the discipline keeps contact with its past as the only social science that still has a significant branch in philosophy; on the other hand its modern pseudoscientific methods subvert the discussion of larger issues of democracy, law and justice.

The Greek tradition of political philosophy began with Socrates, who pursued knowledge of the whole, and at the same time sensed with wonder and piety the complexity of nature. The Greeks recognized the hierarchy of being in nature as pointing to a transcendent Truth or Good: "To know the Truth, to go out of the Platonic cave and to know fully the essence of the sun, would be inexpressibly exhilarating and would be the ultimate in attainment and satisfaction."[6] The logic of such a discovery would show that man was not self-produced, that there was such a thing as human knowledge and an unchangeable human nature. The best politics was that which recognized order in society, with the cornerstone of the state being the character of the individual citizen. In classical Greek thought neither institutions, nor science, nor environment could make men good; it was up to the individual to develop the intellectual and moral character necessary to improve the state.

The premise of traditional political philosophy was that men were by nature different and of unequal rank. You could have no virtue in a society until such differences were recognized. The classical philosophers knew the limitations of man. Their idealism was tempered by a realization that evil could not be eradicated—it could only be tempered with wisdom. The best political order entailed government by "good men," defined as ones "who are willing, and able, to prefer the common interest to their private interest and to the objects of their passions."[7]

The Judeo-Christian heritage was the second part of the "Great Tradition" of Western culture. Christianity teaches that there is a divine intent to history and a supreme God who holds subjects accountable for their behavior on earth. Man is not an accidental product of a blind evolutionary process; rather he is the capstone of creation. The Bible sets forth the demands of morality and religion in a way which stresses man's fulfillment in surrender to God's call. Obedience asks for a love of God with all one's heart, with all one's soul, and with all one's might before it is possible to see society as an assembly of brothers and sisters to be loved like oneself. In an insightful observation, Leo Strauss wrote, "One can create obstinacy by virtue of some great villainy, but one needs religion for creating hope."[8] The conservative belief is that only an appeal to transcendent virtues can make men wise.

Christianity gave a purpose and direction to millions of its followers since the first century. In contrast to the materialistic Greek concepts, man in the image of God gave a distinctively different humanness to society. Were it not for man's propensity to do evil, there would be no need for a state, but that same sinfulness meant that the political order had limits. The apostle Paul in Romans 13 instructed the Christians to be "subject to the governing authorities," which in his case were pagan Roman bureaucrats whom he called "ministers of God." But even the obedience injunction found a limitation in Peter's declaration in Acts 5:29 that "We must obey God rather than man." In any well-conceived community, matters such as marriage, vocation, and domestic life would properly fall under the jurisdiction of the church, not the state.

To know Western culture was to know the traditions of both Jerusalem and Athens. Augustine wrote, "We rate the Platonists above the rest of the philosophers."[9] Plato taught, as did the Bible, that heaven and earth were created by an invisible God who set in place the natural order of creation. Justice was compliance with this natural order, and it was man who adapted to the arrangement of nature, not vice versa. The common ground between Christians and Jews was the belief that the God of Abraham, Isaac, and Jacob revealed his character and nature in the Ten Commandments and that these rules were valid in all circumstances.

It was the Renaissance spirit which severed the classical tradition of Western political thought from its roots and asserted the role of man. Machiavelli broke with the classical tradition and denied that political power was a means in the service of higher ends such as justice, the good life, freedom, and service to God. Instead, Machiavelli assumes that power is an end in itself; he separates power from morality and sets up the state as an autonomous system of values independent of any other source. Consequently, Leo Strauss noted, "He [Machiavelli] is notorious as the classic of the evil way of political thinking and political acting."[10] By ignoring God, Machiavelli ascribed all religion to a human rather than a divine origin. To him political virtue was the pursuit of worldly power and honor. Gone were the classical values of self-denial and trust in God.

The practical implication of Machiavelli's work was to lower man to the level of the beasts. Before him, all political writing—from Plato and Aristotle through the Middle Ages to the Renaissance—had the goal of improving the ends of the state. After Machiavelli, political power was assumed to be an end in itself, and the higher values of justice, the good life, freedom and God were important only to the extent that they helped justify that end. In Machiavelli's *The Prince,* Strauss observed, "The characteristic feature of the work is precisely that it makes no distinction between prince and tyrant; it uses the term 'prince' to designate princes and tyrants alike."[11]

A remnant of the classical tradition survived in the Protestant Reformation and the traditions of the Catholic Church. They extolled the "Natural Law" which came from God and was not drawn up by man. It was handed down to us by Christianity, Roman law, and Teutonic culture and was knowable by revelation and "right reason." Edmund Burke wrote that we all come into this world "in subjection to one great, immutable, pre-existing law, a law . . . paramount to our feelings, by which we are connected in the eternal frame of reference."[12] The freedoms enjoyed by Americans and Europeans today blossomed gradually over the centuries for a people in tune with "the eternal frames of reference."

Of course, Protestants and Catholics could not agree on matters of the faith, and both were passionately religious. Protestants assailed the papacy for losing the original ideals of the Christian faith and for having adopted the worldly ambitions of lust, wealth, and power. Catholics, in turn, invoked the natural law tradition of their medieval past in an effort to remain the dominant force in European affairs. In the end, both the Renaissance and the Reformation were overshadowed by an emerging new faith in science, which threatened any belief in the supernatural. The modern ideologies of Marxism, utopian socialism, and secular humanism warred against the nature of things and attempted to superimpose a new design of solely human origin. In the end, both Catholics and Protestants agreed that natural law miraculously came from God and not from man.

The American Tradition of Conservatism

In the eighteenth century the Western world faced the twin phenomena of Scientific Rationalism and the Enlightenment. French writers of the period believed that human reason was the absolute standard by which political conduct and social institutions were to be measured. The French Revolution began with a call for the "rights of man." There was much talk about reason and the will of the people. Voltaire's admiration for English progress in science was such that "whenever he thought of God, [he] tended to think of Newton at the same time."[13] In the 1750s the intellectuals of the time were captured by the idealistic view of man which emboldened the French Enlightenment. The accent was on freedom of form and spirit, on feeling and originality, with a sympathy for primitive nature. Gone were such traditional religious doctrines as man born in sin facing judgment before an omnipotent God.

Modern American conservatism and liberalism trace their roots to the writings of this time. The Frenchman Jean Jacques Rousseau (1712–1778) and the Englishman Edmund Burke (1729–1797) presented differing conceptions of the nature of God, man, and the state. Rousseau believed that truth was derived from human reason, while Burke found inspiration from the tested traditions of nature and Holy Scripture. Burke approached the problems of society in the knowledge that "we owe an implicit reverence to all the institutions of our ancestors," and that "ideas of religion and government are closely connected." He railed at the reformers in France: "All your sophisters cannot produce anything better adapted to preserve a rational and manly freedom than the course that we have pursued."[14]

Conservatives rate Rousseau as the philosopher most responsible for the problems of modernity. He is said to have unleashed the romantic moral climate which so characterizes the West today. In his personal life Rousseau was vain and obscenely impious, declaring human passion as the center and measure of all things. In government he believed the state was so constituted that "man can be forced to be free." Through Rousseau's General Will there is the visage of the modern idol of collective man. Burke denied Rousseau's idea of "natural rights" based on a "state of nature." Laws and rights came from God, according to Burke, and were contained in the "natural law" tradition.

The Conservative Culture

The tension between Burke and Rousseau yesterday, and between liberals and conservatives today, is over the emphasis on certain cultural values at the expense of others. Leo Strauss gave a succinct definition of the new nation when he wrote that "The United States of America may be said to be the only country in the world which was founded in explicit opposition to Machiavellian principles."[15] Opposition to Machiavellian principles means that instead of crass self-interest and greed, the expressed principles of the American republic were a sense of community participation, an appreciation of natural rights, a respect for established religious values, and a degree of liberty unknown in Europe. Such are the values conservatives cherish.

As the nation developed from the truths in the Declaration of Independence, conservatives believe it took on a distinctive character which merits respect and protection. In Francis Wilson's *The Case for Conservatism* (1951), conservatism is defined as "a philosophy of social evolution, in which certain lasting values are defended within the framework of the tension of political conflict." This philosophy is "primarily a spirit animating political behavior . . . a way of life . . . a manner of judging life."[16] Wilson views conservatism as an attitude about government that is more than a mere political ideology guiding day-to-day political decisions.

Russell Kirk, who, like Wilson, does not believe that conservatism is an ideology, concludes: (1) that conservatism, unlike liberalism, offers no utopian agenda as the solution to society's problems; (2) that conservatism is more a state of mind about life than a program for action; and (3) that change should arise out of experience, history and tradition rather than being imposed upon society from some prescriptive rule book.[17] The last tenet, a traditionally accepted one of conservatism, holds that change—economic, political, religious, and social—should take place gradually and within the bounds of existing custom and local institutions rather than rapidly through expanding, centralized governmental bureaucracies. Like Wilson, Kirk believes conservatism is more an attitude toward life than a plan for political action.

While accepting much of what Wilson and Kirk have to say, Robert Nisbet disagrees with them about whether conservatism is an ideology. Nisbet defines an ideology as "any reasonably coherent body of moral, economic, social and cultural ideas that has a solid and well-known reference to politics and political power." Such a body of ideas serves as a "power base to make possible a victory for the body of ideas"; "remains alive for a considerable period of time"; "has major advocates and spokesmen"; and has "a respectable degree of institutionalization." Nisbet believes that conservatism is a viable political program that can be translated into specific policy proposals for consideration by voters.[18]

Willmoore Kendall critiques several definitions of conservatism emphasizing the uniqueness and specialness of the American experience. To Kendall, tradition by itself is not a sufficient guide for political action, especially if that tradition is rooted in relativism and positivism as it is in many European countries. These relative influences are found in contemporary society, even in the prescriptions of conservative thinkers. Kendall maintains that definitions of conservatism should be avoided until the criteria for judging the adequacy of such ideas can be specified. For him, government submits its ideas for scrutiny by the society as a whole and as a creature can never judge the truth in society.

Definition

Conservatives have been reluctant to define what they believe. The definitions by Nisbet, Kirk, Rossiter, and others have been subjected to unending scrutiny by peers, who find various flaws in need of correction. The definition of conservatism used here emphasizes the moral constitutional tradition of the West that produced a reasonable society able to judge the actions of its government. No characteristic of American conservatism is more prevalent than its preoccupation with the preservation of this unique cultural heritage.

Conservatism as it is defined here is both an attitude about life characterized by defending the status quo and a specific ideology based on the laws, customs and traditions that have proven useful in the past. Conservatives would agree that rapid change, even in the direction of a desirable or noble goal, is dangerous. They would avoid change that did not arise from the experience, history, or tradition of a society. Conservatives would defend the political, social and economic institutions from all but the most gradual and sure alteration. Finally, conservatives would agree that the experience of the United States in government is unique and serves as a beacon for emerging democracies around the world. *We define conservatism as a defense of the political, economic, religious, and social status quo from the forces of abrupt change, that is based on a belief that established customs, laws and traditions provide continuity and stability in the guidance of society.*

It is the conservative responsibility to keep cultural tradition intact by reasserting commitments to the moral tradition which gave it birth. Figure 2-1 presents a summary of conservative beliefs, as contrasted with liberal tendencies. The liberal tradition emphasizes human reason, the development of the individual free from the restraints of government, and governmental action in the redress of social and economic inequalities.

By contrast, conservatives tend to emphasize: (1) orthodox and traditional religious values; (2) less faith in the goodness, reason, and perfectability of mankind; (3) belief in less power for the centralized government; (4) more identification with state and local government in the federal system; (5) a nationalistic and patriotic spirit; (6) the duties of the individual more than his or her rights; (7) a trust in the free markets of capitalism; and (8) a desire that economic, political, religious, and social stability be maintained through gradual changes within existing institutions.

Conservatives have always believed that the political structure of a state, if it is to be stable, must reflect the traditions and customs of that society. In the past two decades America has been undergoing a political

FIGURE 2-1
Conservative and Liberal Beliefs:
Contrasting Emphases and Tendencies

Topic	Liberal	Conservative
1. Government		
Primary Focus	Individual	Community
Preferred Government	National	State and Local
Direction of Sentiment	Internationalist	Nationalist
Method of Government Influence	Direct	Indirect
Accountability of Government	To Man	To God
Rate/Type of Change	Faster/Utopian	Slower/Prescriptive
Relative Importance	Equality	Liberty
Justice Achieved By	Governmental Reform	Spiritual Regeneration
2. Economy		
Source of Authority	Central Government	Markets
Growth Sector	Public	Private
Government Function	Regulation	Competition
Tendency	Socialism	Capitalism
3. Cultural and Religious Values		
Ultimate Source of Knowledge	Reason	Nature/Bible
Biblical Interpretation	More Symbolic	More Literal
Moral Standards	Relative/Situational	Absolute/Orthodox
Relative Emphasis	Man	God
Moral Emphasis	Social	Personal
Relative Importance to Man	Rights	Responsibilities
Origin of Evil	Unjust Social Systems	Original Sin

crisis. Since the 1960s, the fear among conservatives has been that the United States is adopting values similar to those of secular Europe. They saw the siren song of socialism capture many intellectuals in the 1950s and 1960s, which led to an unhealthy experimentation with both the economy and the social fabric of the nation. The fear among conservatives is that metaphysical values (belief in God, respect for order and belief in community) have been eroded by the liberal faith in materialism and human reason.

At no place is this erosion more apparent than in universities and colleges. Most universities in the 1990s seek to promote pluralism and diversity by recruiting minorities for faculty positions and setting up separate courses for the purpose of denigrating alleged xenophobia, racism, and sexism in American history. Instead of inculcating the values of Western culture, the new university curriculum seeks to "empower" students to political action. Lost on the university campus is the belief that scholarship can move toward an ideal of truth. "Although the revolution first shook the humanities and the social sciences, its reverberations are now being felt in law schools, medical schools, and science departments, which long considered themselves largely exempt from campus agitation."[19]

The conservative view is that there are distinct limits to human reason in general and in the possibilities of governmental action in particular. The conservative believes that no one man or group of men has the capacity to foresee all the consequences of any single government policy. For this reason the conservative favors caution, humility and the broadest base of democratic support as the first requirement for sensible government. Order is better than social experimentation, and everyone has a stake in preserving order. In Figure 2-1 the conservative emphasis is on gradual change, obedience to God, personal responsibility, and community values.

Five Contemporary Types of Conservatism

After World War II conservatives offered their values as an alternative to the social agenda of reform liberals. But in the decades of the 1950s

TABLE 2-1
Representative Types of Conservatives as Defined by Conservative Scholars

English	Harbour	Lora	Nash	Rossiter
1. Instinctive	1. Authoritarian	1. Psychological	1. Libertarian	1. Temperamental
2. Economic	2. Economic	2. Possessive	2. Traditionalist	2. Possessive
3. Philosophical	3. Religious	3. Philosophical	3. Anticommunist	3. Practical
				4. Philosophical

See: Raymond English, "Conservatism: the Forbidden Faith," *American Scholar* 21 (Autumn 1952): pp. 393–412; William R. Harbour, *The Foundations of Conservative Thought* (1982), p. 103; Ronald Lora, *Conservative Minds in America* (1976), p. 3; George H. Nash, *The Conservative Intellectual Movement in America since 1945* (1976), pp. viii–ix; Clinton Rossiter, *Conservatism in America* (1962), pp. 6–11.

and 1960s, the nation was more interested in change than the preservation of traditional values. By the end of the 1970s the national mood was more somber, and conservative values seemed appropriate for the time.

Listed in Table 2-1 are five representative types of conservatism. Probably the most noticeable omissions from the lists are the movement neoconservatives and populist conservatives who will be discussed later. The emphasis of the table is on the various forms in which conservatism may be found.

Raymond English sees conservatives as clinging to the known and the accustomed, defending economic privilege, and adopting an attitude toward politics that stresses the value of tradition, habit, and authority. William R. Harbour pictures conservatives as longing for order in society, valuing the leadership of elites, desiring freedom for business and industry to function, and placing great importance on virtue and morality in private life. Ronald Lora views conservatives as wanting to preserve custom and opposing changes that would disrupt it. Lora also believes that conservatives understand virtue and will forego self-interest in the pursuit of philosophical convictions. The three types defined by George H. Nash include libertarians, traditionalists, and a new type, anticommunists. Libertarians defend free enterprise and oppose governmental interference in any market activity, while anticommunists believe in the importance of a strong national defense to contain foreign threats abroad. Finally, Clinton Rossiter distinguishes four types of conservatives: temperamental, possessive, practical, and philosophical. They, individually and collectively, oppose substantial change in society, seek to defend personal acquisitions, value community, and subscribe to principles designed to justify the established order.

These types show that one can be of a conservative temperament and not possess a philosophical or intellectual understanding of conservatism. In other words, it is possible to have the conservative "go-slow" state of mind, and at the same time favor an active role by the federal government in, say, the prosecution of southern school districts for a failure to desegregate public schools in the 1960s. Common to these types are a concern with property and the status quo on the individual level, an emphasis on community at the group level, and an intellectual defense of virtue on the societal level. Some types of conservatism are more concerned about preserving one's position in society, while other types emphasize an aggressive public stance toward life which is intellectual and philosophical.

This distinction, between "attitude-type" conservatives who have traits without necessarily thinking through the philosophy, and "action-type" conservatives who have a carefully constructed public philosophy, is in evidence in the political process. Politicians may adopt aspects of conservatism and then abandon the posture when a crisis or situation changes. For example, both Richard Nixon and Ronald Reagan built their careers in part on anticommunist conservatism, and both modified their position while holding the office of president. Nixon opened the door to mainland China, and Reagan concluded a missile treaty with the Soviet Union.

Conservatism and Liberalism Compared

American history shows that at various times and in diverse circum-stances political ideologies have meant different things to different peo-ple. Thomas Paine's writings emphasized the need to eliminate class distinctions and prevent development of an aristocracy. Alexander Ham-ilton, by contrast, advocated a society and government ruled principally by an elite class. These two positions, extreme even by the standards of their time, are examples of the divisions ideologies bring to politics. Liberals and conservatives differ among themselves in their attitude toward authority, their view of the economy and the role the United States should play in world politics. In Table 2-2 we present eight con-trasting tendencies of liberalism and conservatism.

The first tendency, stressing the authoritarian nature of ideologies, is seen in the conflict between Thomas Paine and Alexander Hamilton. Paine, with his emphasis on the elimination of rigid class lines, was a distinct contrast to Hamilton, who favored a leadership class. Both of these men, and their ideas, played an important part in American politi-cal, social and economic history; but each had a different view of how the society should be structured and who should be eligible to participate in political decisions.

Paine, for example, was an authoritarian in the sense that he wanted to use government power to eradicate class distinctions and to achieve egalitarianism. He did not believe in a leadership class like Hamilton

TABLE 2-2
Conservatism and Liberalism: Contrasting Dominant Tendencies

	Authoritarian	Economic	International	Political	Populist	Religious	Social
Liberalism	egalitarianism	socialism	idealism	equality	equity	relativism	change
Conservatism	elitism	capitalism	realism	liberty	morality	orthodoxy	order

did. Conservatives believe that in any society some people will be more dominant socially, economically and politically. Their leadership and influence give stability to society and ensure an orderly transfer of power and wealth. Authority rightly rests with them, and the conservative ethic is to recognize and reward achievement whenever it occurs in society. Elites are both inevitable and necessary, but not every conservative would wish to recognize elitism the way Hamilton desired.

Second, economic conservatism emphasizes private property and the profit motive as twin bases of the American economy designed to encourage individual initiative, while economic liberalism's emphasis on socialism has helped to bring into American life such ideas and practices as social security, Medicare and Medicaid. In practice many Americans, and many conservatives, support both the profit motive and social security.

Conservatives have always been defenders of the rights of property, recognizing that "property" includes more than material things. For example, the talent of an artist protected in a copyright or the academic freedom of a university professor is a property right. The exercise of an individual's right to improve himself economically is a basic conservative value. Capitalism is defended because it is the best system to allow individual expression, the accumulation of material goods, and the working of free markets.

Third, international conservatism stresses realism, pragmatism, and power politics in the conduct of American foreign policy, preferring to have a strong national defense, to develop new weapons systems, and to roll back the borders of communism. International liberalism, on the other hand, speaks more idealistically about American foreign policy in relation to foreign powers and the communist world, emphasizing good will and human rights. International liberalism has much more confidence in international organizations like the United Nations and is more likely to trust communist leaders in international agreements.

The realism of conservatism is based on a view of human nature that is suspicious of a person's promises and of a nation's treaties and agreements. In November 1985 the editors of the conservative journal *Commentary* invited more than thirty intellectuals to respond to questions about American developments since the end of World War II. The majority of the writers lamented the continued power and oppressive policies of the Soviet Union, but they maintained that the United States had remained powerful precisely because it was suspicious of moves the Soviets had made around the globe.[20]

Fourth, liberalism has historically emphasized the concept of equality, but not the absolute negation of liberty, and it has played a part in such movements as the abolitionist movement before the Civil War and the contemporary civil rights movement. Political conservatism with its emphasis on liberty has stressed the freedom of each citizen to pursue his ambition without undue restraint, especially from the government. Conservatives take special pride in the accomplishments and opportunities capitalism affords to its citizens.

Conservatism instinctively senses that the liberal passion for furthering equality can only be brought about by greater and greater uniformity. Centralized planning means a decrease in regional, neighborhood and individual autonomy, variety, and liberty. Part of the conservative allegiance is to known institutions which stand between the citizen and his government.

Fifth, populists, though historically considered liberal, have since the 1960s included a highly vocal conservative segment. Agrarian populists of the 1890s and 1920s emphasized redistribution of economic goods, setting forth a strong anti-business platform. Equity was the dominant theme of populist reformers. By contrast, conservative populists have emphasized a grass-roots agenda of traditional morality, pro-school prayer, anti-abortion, and anti-Equal Rights Amendment. Whether conservative or liberal, populists appeal to basic values held by common citizens.

Sixth, religious conservatism has a tradition beginning with the early settlers and continuing through the founders of most of the first colleges and universities, such as Harvard, Yale and Princeton. The first colleges were originally theologically conservative, but they gradually adopted liberal theological positions. Religious liberalism accommodated European values to the American experience.[22] It does not have as long a tradition in American history, but its roots go back to ideas like Thomas Jefferson's Deism. Today it continues with such groups as the National Council of Churches and Norman Lear's "People for the American Way."

The personal religious commitments of any particular liberal aside, it remains true that liberalism is less opposed to a secular society than is conservatism. Since the 1960s Catholics and Protestants have united to complain about the moral decline of the West.

Social conservatism, the seventh category in Table 2-2, is concerned with maintaining order and continuity in society, while social liberals are more interested in change to achieve certain desired ends. University of Chicago Professor Richard Weaver, a native of the South, wrote nostalgically about regional values and the threat to southern culture and tradition posed by social liberalism in his book *The Southern Tradition at Bay* (1968).[23] No region of the country is more supportive of social conservatism than the South. The ideas of person, position, and place have the greatest meaning in the South because of its unique history and social legacy. This type of conservatism is also found extensively in the vast rural, small-town, and agricultural regions of the nation. Social liberalism, by contrast, is of an urban sophistication and emphasizes change, especially to achieve major reforms. Social liberals have been in the vanguard of civil rights movements, organizations like the American Civil Liberties Union, and the labor movement.

For conservatives the primary need in any society is order. Without political stability nothing else—not justice, not equality, not liberty, and not prosperity—can be accomplished. Order is not an end in itself, rather it is a means by which one can bring disenfranchised groups into the society. No expansion of the benefits of a society is possible without political stability.

Although there are clear relationships among all eight conservative values in Table 2-2, there are also differences among those who adhere to them. For example, an economic conservative is not necessarily a religious conservative, nor is an economic liberal necessarily a religious liberal. Some liberals are very optimistic about human nature, and at the same time counsel a realistic foreign policy with adversaries. We see a strong relationship between the politics and theology of American politicians which we will discuss in Chapter Six.[24]

Neoconservatism

Neoconservatism and neoliberalism are products of the reaction in the 1960s to the excesses of liberalism. Though having much in common, they have moved in different directions politically. Many neoconservatives have adopted the Republican Party, while neoliberals ask for reforms within the Democratic Party. Neoconservatives support a strong national defense more than neoliberals do. Neoliberals are critical of large government bureaucracies and the historic ties Democrats have had to labor unions. They have revived an emphasis on the importance of community and the negative aspects of the welfare state. Neoliberal leader Charles Peters, editor of the magazine *Washington Monthly*, says that "Neoliberalism is first and foremost a movement of community. We believe in a society that shares its burdens and rewards. We reject the Me Decade and the proliferation of special interest groups."[21]

Peters argues that neoliberals want to free liberalism from automatically favoring big unions and big government against business and the military. He thinks the Democratic Party could gain by becoming critical of public education, the civil service, and labor unions, even though these groups have historically been staunch defenders of liberalism.

Neoliberal views show that conservative thought, with its distrust of large government programs and approval of community solutions, is having a dramatic impact on the political left. Neoliberalism and neoconservatism are both reactions to the social experimentation which characterized the 1960s, but neoliberalism is seeking to recapture those major blocks of voters lost to the Republican Party. White southerners and Catholics abandoned the Democratic Party in large numbers during the terms of the Reagan presidency. It is apparent that the Democratic Party cannot return to power unless it recovers these traditional constituencies.

Libertarianism

Libertarianism, sometimes considered a type of conservatism, believes in the autonomy of the individual and a minimal role for the government. The maximum reduction of social and government action is required so that the greatest possible room is left for each individual to act. Libertarians think that individuals should be free from governmental restraint in both economic and noneconomic areas. For example, libertarians would say that the government should not regulate abortion since that is a personal matter. The heart of contemporary libertarian belief is the primacy of the individual.

Although the Libertarian Party remains on the fringes of American politics, its ideas have stimulated much interest and admiration among traditional conservatives. Libertarians oppose the interference of government in the private lives of citizens, seek an unfettered free market, and oppose laws regulating the prices of consumer commodities. Libertarians favor nonintervention in the affairs of other nations, and call for a drastic reduction in the defense budget and defense policy.

Traditional American conservatism, modeled after Edmund Burke's philosophy and built on a substantial regard for religious values, would reject many libertarian proposals. Conservatism has great respect for community customs, morals, and the traditions that have guided public policies in the past. It holds that there are some religious and moral values that may be superior to individual rights and freedoms. Philosophical and religious conservatives attack contemporary libertarians as radicals who are unconcerned about preserving the historic values of a society. Libertarianism, the critics charge, is a form of rampant individualism which lacks a proper respect for custom and tradition. Still, most conservatives have great respect for the more modest libertarian belief in trying to restrain governmental activity in the economic realm.

The ideas of the libertarians have influenced both major parties. The Republican Party in 1980 took a much more aggressive stand against the social programs of the 1960s and 1970s partially as a result of libertarian influence. The programs to reduce income tax rates and deregulate some business and industry show a distinctly libertarian influence. The Democrats have become more critical of intervention in foreign affairs and supported broader freedom from government interference in so-called victimless crimes (prostitution, pornography, gambling) and the practice of abortion and gay rights also as a partial result of libertarian values.

Midwestern Conservatism

Midwestern conservatism has a long and distinguished tradition of service to the American experience. States like Ohio, Indiana, Illinois, Michigan, Iowa, Nebraska, and Kansas have regularly sent individuals to Congress who represented conservative, small-town values. Senators Robert A. Taft (R., Ohio) and Everett McKinley Dirksen (R., Ill.) along with former president Gerald Ford (R., Mich.) and current Senate leader Robert Dole (R., Kansas) are in this tradition.

They differ from other conservatives on at least two counts. First, they are less ideological, and more politically pragmatic and prone to compromise. Both Dirksen and Dole have been leaders in Congress, where their conservative ideology guides but does not dominate their political behavior. Second, they may accept or propose policies that would increase the size of government for pragmatic political, humanitarian or other reasons. In the late 1940s, for example, Senator Taft proposed a major public housing program; Senator Dirksen was the key legislative leader in gaining passage of the 1964 Civil Rights Act and the 1965 Voting Rights Act; although both measures were opposed by conservative Republican presidential candidate Barry Goldwater. Gerald Ford was opposed for the Republican presidential nomination in 1976 by Ronald Reagan, primarily because Ford's conservative ideology was much more pragmatic and less systematic than that of Reagan and his followers. Senator Robert Dole's pragmatic instincts have led him to compromise more frequently in ways that a more doctrinaire conservative would not. For example, in 1985 Dole angered many conservatives by forging a budget-cutting compromise which reduced many favorite weapons programs at the Pentagon.[22]

Conclusion

Conservatism is best defined by examining its various types and their differences with liberalism. To the extent that definitions overlap we find it important to note that both conservatism and liberalism hold certain values in common, such as agreement on the rules of the game in the political culture. However, liberals and conservatives disagree on which traits of the American character are most important and which ones should be nourished and protected by government. Conservatives place greater emphasis upon the roles of religion, individual duty, virtue, private property, community, and the rule of law.

We define conservatism as a defense of the political, economic, religious, and social status quo against the forces of abrupt change. Conservatives believe that established customs, laws, and traditions provide continuity and stability in guiding society. The conservative attraction to the past is rooted in a respect for institutions and a suspicion of modern political ideologies. Change must be accommodated to custom, history, and tradition—not imposed from some abstract blueprint or scheme. Conservative premises are traceable to the ancient traditions of both Athens and Jerusalem, as well as the modern tradition begun by Edmund Burke.

Conservatives differ among themselves as to whether their beliefs are an ideology, attitude, or state of mind. One thing is clear—many people are conservative without necessarily knowing it or having thought carefully about why. They are attitude-conservatives, accepting conservative premises, and can be contrasted with action-conservatives, who have a seriously prepared plan of political action. Of whatever stripe, and for whatever reason, conservatism has had a major impact on American society since 1980 as measured by electoral and political success. Liberals and neoliberals have been forced to adopt and shape conservative ideals to fit a new agenda.

Sometimes conservatism is referred to as communitarian individualism. Conservatives believe that the community serves as a healthy buffer between the onerous power of the government and the anarchical tendencies of rampant individualism. The community enables the individual to feel a part of one or more groups which transfer custom and tradition to him. It gives the individual not only a feeling of belonging, but also of being attached to the flow of history. In constrast, conservatives point out, socialists consider the state the principal reference point and the individual merely a tool for the ends of the state.

Though commonly considered conservative, libertarianism is actually opposed to the fundamental premises of conservatism. More typical of conservatism is the pragmatic midwestern variety that has incurred opposition from doctrinaire conservatism when it has either compromised with liberalism or espoused policies that would enlarge government or implement humanitarian objectives that might bring rapid change to the American social order. Religious, philosophical, and economic conservatives have become much more important since the 1940s, while anticommunist conservatives have decreased in importance.

Notes

1. Abraham Lincoln, Address, Cooper Union, New York, February 27, 1860.

2. James W. Ceaser, et al., *American Government* (New York: McGraw-Hill, 1984), p. 111.

3. Thomas Paine, "Thoughts on the Present State of American Affairs," in *Political Writings*, Bruce Huklide (ed.) (New York: Cambridge University Press, 1989), p. 29.

4. Leo Strauss, *Natural Right and History* (Chicago: University of Chicago Press, 1953), p. 12.

5. Allan Bloom, *The Closing of the American Mind* (New York: Simon and Schuster, 1987), p. 365.

6. John P. East, "Leo Strauss and American Conservatism," in *Modern Age*, Vol. XXI, Winter, 1977, pp. 2–19.

7. Leo Strauss, *What Is Political Philosophy?* (Glencoe, Ill.: Free Press, 1959), pp. 85–86.

8. Leo Strauss, *Thoughts on Machiavelli* (Seattle, Wash.: University of Washington Press, 1958), p. 150.

9. Augustine, *The City of God*, Henry Bettenson (Trans.). (Middlesex, England: Penguin Books, 1972) Book 8, Chapter 10.

10. Leo Strauss, *Thoughts on Machiavelli*, p. 10.

11. Leo Strauss, *What Is Political Philosophy?* (1959) p. 289.

12. Edmund Burke, "Reflections on the Revolution in France," in *Works* (Boston: Little, Brown, 1865).

13. Norman Hampson, *The Enlightenment* (New York: Penguin Books, 1968), p. 79.

14. Edmund Burke, "Reflections on the Revolution in France." Sebastian De Grazia, *Machiavelli in Hell* (Princeton, N.J.: Princeton University Press, 1989).

15. Leo Strauss, *Thoughts on Machiavelli*, p. 13.

16. Francis Wilson, *The Case for Conservatism* (Seattle, Wash.: University of Washington Press, 1958), p. 13.

17. Russell Kirk, *The Conservative Mind* (7th ed.; Chicago: Regnery Books, 1986), pp. 13–20.

18. Robert Nisbet, *Conservatism* (Minneapolis: University of Minnesota Press, 1986), pp. viii–20.

19. Dinesh D'Souza, "Illiberal Education," *The Atlantic*, v. 267; n. 3 (March 1991) p. 58.

20. "Symposium: How Has the United States Met Its Major Challenges Since 1945?" *Commentary* 80 (November 1985).

21. Charles Peters, *New Road for America: The Neoliberal Movement* (Lanham, Md.: Madison Books, 1985), p. 9.

22. Martin Marty says the crisis in Protestantism was due to four things: 1) the theory of evolution; 2) the denigration of the authority of the Bible; 3) the economic threat of socialism; and 4) urbanization in and immigration to the U.S. Martin E. Marty, *Pilgrims in Their Own Land* (New York: Viking Penguin Books, 1984), pp. 297–298.

23. Richard Weaver, *The Southern Tradition at Bay* (New Rochelle, N.Y.: Arlington House, 1968).

24. Charles W. Dunn, *American Political Theology* (New York: Praeger, 1984).

25. Hedrick Smith, *The Power Game* (New York: Random House, 1988), pp. 491–496.

CHAPTER THREE

The Ten Most Important Beliefs of Conservatism

To be a conservative in the "means" of communication is the road to effectiveness in modern life, in whatever direction one wishes to be effective.

E. D. HIRSCH, JR.[1]

The dictionary definition of culture, as the "ideas, customs, skills, and arts of a given people," has a particular affinity for conservatism. Conservatives have always believed that the political structure of a state, if it is to be stable, must reflect the traditions and customs of that society. "Do what you may," wrote Alexis de Tocqueville, "there is no true power among men except in the free union of their will; and patriotism and religion are the only two motives in the world that can long urge all the people toward the same end."[2] Conservatives believe that society is not a machine which can be tinkered with and altered at whim, rather it is a living organism nourished by the values of the culture.

The conservative fear is that the United States as a society is unaware of the past values which made it exceptional; as a result, it is in danger of adopting new ideas foreign to its history. The movements of Darwin, Marx, and Freud based on their ideas of evolution, economic determinism and the unconscious, and advances in modern science and technology have the potential of destroying modern man. In the minds of conservatives, the crisis of the hour in the United States is that the permanent metaphysical things of our culture (the belief in God and an understanding and shared sense of honor and duty) are gradually being replaced by the mindset of the twentieth century, which holds that such ideals are primitive figments of the imagination. In a book entitled *Out of My Life and Thought*, Albert Schweitzer wrote shortly before his death that two experiences had cast their shadows on his existence: the first was that the world was full of suffering, and the second was that he was "born at a time of the spiritual decline of humanity."[3] If Schweitzer is right, the conservative belief that there is a divine intent to history and that man has a duty to conform himself to God-given and immutable laws of morality no longer has meaning.

Of all the industrialized nations in the West, the United States has remained the one with the highest religious and moral commitment.[4] The European example dictated that as the United States became more secular, it would also become less religious; however, polls regularly find a stable core of Protestant, Catholic, and Jewish believers in the United States. Where moral values are concerned, the rule of thumb that "as Europe goes, so goes the United States" has been disproven. Europe modernized first and secularized first; the fear among conservatives is that America might follow its example and adopt values which deify politics and power, and denigrate piety and prayer.

The deterioration of cultural moorings is a special concern of E. D. Hirsch, Jr., whose book *Cultural Literacy* was a nationwide best-seller. Hirsch laments the loss of an American culture which fostered such unique values as "Yankee ingenuity," inventiveness, independent-mindedness, a connection to the frontier, and a beneficence to the world: "the American civil religion, as expressed in our national rites and symbols, is in fact a central source of coherence in American public culture, holding together various and even contradictory elements of its tradition."[5]

Hirsch discusses the importance of a "civil Bible" as an inherited set of religious sentiments honoring tolerance, equality, freedom, patriotism, duty, and cooperation in the society. The "civil Bible" of the American republic incorporated items like the Book of Genesis, the Declaration of Independence, the Gettysburg Address, certain articles from the *Federalist Papers*, Horace Mann's Twelfth Report to the Massachusetts Board of Education, and Martin Luther King's "I Have a Dream" speech. What these and other related documents have in common is a fundamental agreement on the principles of justice, freedom, and progress which make the American experiment unique. Many of these propositions are contradictory with respect to each other, but collectively they all have the effect of fostering a cultural heritage among the populace. They owe their origin and popularity to the religious heritage which gave birth to the republic.

The canons of conservatism are nothing more than the broad principles of society which are inherent in American culture. They are the standards embodied in the "civil Bible," the ideals of the past which make the society what it is at present. The definition of conservatism is the skeleton of the society; the canons are its flesh and blood. Once Winston Churchill was asked what made the British culture unique. He replied, "It is stirred on almost all occasions by sentiment and instinct, rather than by programmes or worldly calculation."[6] The canons of conservatism embody the instinct of which Churchill spoke; the impulse of a culture is the intangible values which motivate it to action.

The Soul of the Nation

In the 1980s an increase in the importance and use of the term "conservative" occurred. A National Opinion Research Center poll found that roughly 35 percent of the respondents said they were conservative compared with 24 percent who classified themselves as liberal.[7] President Reagan's economic policies, cutting taxes while decreasing federal spending and increasing defense spending, were characterized as conservative. Stands in other areas, like opposition to gun control and hostility to communism, also earned one the title of conservative.

At the same time there was a confusion in the meaning of the term. Conservatives argued against big government, and at the same time favored large government projects like the Star Wars program, more defense spending, and an expansion in biological warfare research. Conservatives were against the police state, yet were eager to extend powers to the FBI and the CIA. They were in favor of balanced budgets and fiscal responsibility, although the Reagan administration registered huge budget deficits. Conservatives claimed to be the prime defenders of Western civilization, while at the same time they presented no unified front on issues of biblical belief and opposition to abortion.

Not everyone labeled as conservative takes sides on every issue with those sharing the label. As Frank S. Meyer has written: "Within the consensus of American conservatism . . . there exist strains and tensions, the origins of which are both historical and intellectual."[8] What then are the "true conservative" beliefs, and how do they make the history of the United States unique? Are certain opinions on various issues actually related? Can one identify a true conservative by asking a series of questions?

If defining conservatism is difficult, stating its canons of belief is nearly impossible. Two verbatim descriptions of its tenets are given by Clinton Rossiter in *Conservatism in America* and by Russell Kirk in *The Conservative Mind*. Rossiter lists in one place twenty-one tenets of conservatism.[9] Russell Kirk includes six tenets that summarize many of Rossiter's qualities.[10] The ten canons of conservatism developed here are a synthesis of Kirk's and Rossiter's ideas along with those of a broad cross-section of other thinkers including Friedrich von Hayek, Richard Weaver, Peter Viereck, Eric Voegelin, William F. Buckley, Jr., Gertrude Himmelfarb, Leo Strauss, John Hallowell, Daniel Boorstin, and Robert Nisbet.[11] The ten canons or principles of belief to which conservatives generally subscribe are:

1. Continuity: Order and the Rate of Change
2. Authority: Power and the Limits of Government
3. Community: Decentralization of Social Institutions
4. Deity: Man and Morality
5. Duty: Responsibilities over Rights
6. Democracy: Limited Government and the Constitution
7. Property: The Role of Economics
8. Liberty: Equality's Other Brother
9. Meritocracy: The Leadership Class
10. Antipathy: The Anticommunist Impulse

These ten canons represent the best summary of what conservatives generally think are its most important principles. Together they form the unique American culture which conservatives seek to enrich and protect.

Continuity: Order and the Rate of Change

The most widely accepted conservative tenet is the belief in the importance of order in society. The conservative believes that respect for tradition is the first requirement for good government. The structure of society as a whole is said to contain the stability and wisdom of past generations—even the involvement of God in its development. Because the conservative treasures the maintenance of order in society so highly, he is opposed to broad or sweeping change, preferring instead slower change within existing institutions, sometimes called organic change.

Edmund Burke, who wrote extensively about the destruction of institutions and order in France during the French Revolution, developed the principles most often associated with modern conservatism. Burke saw the radicals of France, those who desired to totally remake the fabric of society based on their own reasoning, as the source of "sickness of morality and social decencies" as well as the cause of total disregard for all property rights in that country. He found human reason puny compared with the traditions established by providence: "We are afraid to put men to live and trade each on his own private stock of reason; because we suspect that this stock in each man is small, and that the individuals would do better to avail themselves of the general bank of capital of nations and ages."[12]

Clinton Rossiter affirms the indispensability and sanctity of inherited institutions, values, symbols, and rituals as central aspects of the stable society. He notes that the marks of the good society are order, unity, equity, stability, continuity, security, harmony, and the confinement of change. "The American," Rossiter observes, "*feels* more deeply than he *thinks* about political principles, and what he feels most deeply about them is that they are the gift of great men of old."[13] Russell Kirk mentions a profound distrust in the "sophisters, calculators, and economists" who would reconstruct society on abstract designs.[14]

Conservatives are not averse to change; they simply believe that it should be made in accordance with accepted principles in society. Peter Viereck, in his book *Conservatism Revisited,* quotes Edmund Burke as saying, "A state without some means of change . . . is without the means of its conservation."[15] Conservatives see change as necessary to preserve the order they love; it is the method and rate of change which makes it dangerous. The conservative values tradition, continuity, and order in society. These values must not be disregarded, however carefully reasoned or attractive an untested reform may be.

Authority: Power and the Limits of Government

Conservatives are sometimes attacked for the apparent contradiction between supporting increased government spending for defense and accusing the government of over-taxing and over-spending. But there is a coherent philosophy behind this policy, and it is closely tied to the conservative's passion for order. In the conservative philosophy, the state's primary function is to protect against foreign threats and to keep order at home.

M. Stanton Evans has written that "government is morally obligated to protect America's interests" in foreign affairs.[16] More strength and firmness in foreign policy is also stressed by many other conservative writers, ranging from neoconservative Irving Kristol to staunch anti-communist James Burnham.[17] The foundation of military strength is the belief that the American social order is unique and worthy of protection and respect.

The moral position of America means that it must necessarily act as umpire in a world which ignores international law. Military strength is the surest means of preventing conflict by restraining evil leaders who would otherwise exercise their option to destroy nations and violate international law. The realities of the twentieth century dictate that a strong defense is the best means of preventing international banditry. The 1991 war against Iraq is but the latest instance of American moral resolve in the face of international injustice.

Because the conservative values order so highly, it follows that the police power is necessary to maintain societal institutions. M. Stanton Evans indicts the U.S. government for its policy of stressing rehabilitation of criminals rather than their punishment. He concludes in *Clear and Present Dangers* that the "crime rate could be cut in half merely by requiring criminals already convicted to serve out their time."[18] The conservative sees the state as the most effective means of protecting against the selfish appetites of men, such aggression being manifest in both the aggression of foreign nations and the domestic disregard for civil authority.

At the same time, the conservative is skeptical of attempts by the state to use its power for large-scale social planning. The growth of socialism during this century, both in the United States and other countries, has fostered a reaction against state involvement in the economy and in society in general. Friedrich von Hayek stated in his landmark work, *The Road to Serfdom,* that the "central direction of all economic activity according to a single plan" brings "dictatorship" and "the suppression of freedom."[19] Alan Otten, Edward Banfield, and M. Stanton Evans all find that the liberal solutions to the problems of crime, poverty, economic growth, family, and domestic violence in society have failed.[20] Banfield and Evans even say that liberal reforms were the source of much unemployment; they explain the plight of the homeless and other serious problems as rooted in assumptions about man and society in the 1960s.[21]

The conservative distrust of centralized state power and planning is directly related to the conservative's desire for only slow, organic change. Russell Kirk puts it this way: "Change and reform are not always identical, and . . . innovation is a devouring flame of conflagration more often than it is the torch of progress."[22] Clinton Rossiter echoes that a basic belief of conservatism is "the desirability of diffusing and balancing power, social, economic, cultural and especially political . . . the indispensibility and sanctity of inherited institutions, values, symbols, and rituals, that is, tradition."[23]

Community: Decentralization of Social Institutions

The proper function of government, say conservatives, is not to concentrate power but to diffuse it to the institutions of organic society. Churches, trade unions, universities, newspapers, bar associations, farmers' unions, businessmen's clubs—in the conservative view, all have a special role standing between citizen and government. Institutions and regional associations serve as checks on the power of the central authority.

An important conservative idea which is linked to distrust of too much government power and a faith in traditional values is the belief in the necessity of strong social institutions—family (including extended family), church, neighborhood, and any other institution not controlled by the state. Robert Nisbet, a social psychologist who is a leading proponent of the importance of social institutions, warns of the "advancing power" of the state and the "moribundity of the social order." Nisbet says that if we are to have a "truly free and also stable society, there must be a revival of the prestige of the private as contrasted with the public."[24]

Nisbet notes two traditions in Western social and political thought: (1) the belief that the government has total control over all institutions, as expounded by Hobbes, Rousseau, Bentham and others; (2) the belief that there are clear distinctions between social institutions and the state, as expressed by Cicero, Aquinas, Bodin, Althusias, Burke, Tocqueville, and Proudon. He argues that the "cardinal proposition of the democratic dogma," as seen by Rousseau, was that "structures such as public schools" could do as well as families and kindred in raising and training children. Nisbet counters by asserting the conservative belief that the social institutions of the local community can better meet all the needs that government has taken upon itself. In other words, extended families do a better job handling welfare needs than state programs; and private schools perform better and with less expense than public schools.[25]

The stress on localism and neighborhood means the conservative places greater value on decentralized, area government as opposed to national bureaucracies. In the United States, World War II was a watershed after which the social and educational system gradually became much more centralized, asserting a significant influence in the local communities. With the New Deal came the large national welfare programs which were never reduced after the Depression. Conservatives are heartened by the recent emphasis on volunteerism as part of what they see as a trend toward a return to localism. Nisbet reiterates the conservative fondness for localism by stating that the "spirit of nationalism," unlike that of localism, has seldom "entered into great creative performance."[26]

Deity: Man and Morality

"Reverence for God and respect for history" is a significant element of the conservative tradition.[27] Russell Kirk, Frank S. Meyer, William Harbour, and Ronald Lora, as well as three other scholars, Robert Nisbet, Clinton Rossiter, and Frances Wilson, all list it as one of their tenets. The conservative generally has a strong belief in God and holds to traditional moral values as opposed to "subjectivism," also called "nominalism" or "relativism." C. S. Lewis describes subjectivism as the "whole attempt to jettison traditional values as something subjective and substitute a new scheme of values for them."[28] The main theme of Richard Weaver's *Ideas Have Consequences* is that "Western man" made an "evil decision" in following the "nominalism" of the twentieth century. Weaver writes, "Man has an irresistible desire to relate himself somehow to the totality . . . , and through religion [he] reveals his profoundest intuition regarding his origin, his mission on earth, and his future state."[29]

The conservative view of man is centered around the Biblical doctrine of "original sin"—the idea that man is morally flawed and imperfectible. It must be noted, however, that although some conservatives base this belief on the biblical account of the fall of man, such a belief is not a necessary condition for a conservative's distrust of human nature. A conservative may distrust human nature because he does not trust man's ability to hold to moral values or to govern without making serious mistakes.

Russell Kirk describes this central tenet as "belief in a transcendent order, or body of natural law, which rules society as well as conscience." He contends that political problems, at bottom, are religious and moral problems. True politics is the art of apprehending justice and applying it to the community of souls.[30]

Duty: Responsibilities over Rights

An important corollary to the conservative view of God and man is the belief in the preeminence of duties over rights. The conservative disagrees with French philosopher Jean Jacques Rousseau, who held that man was at his best in a state of nature, unbound by society. To the contrary, the conservative contends that man's nature must be restrained. Because man's selfish and evil appetites must be controlled, and because God has the final authority over man, men should place more emphasis on their duty to God and fellow man than on their own personal rights. As Edmund Burke stated in a speech on the floor of the House of Commons, man's rights "are indeed sacred things," but they must "exist only in obedience to God."[31]

Clinton Rossiter states that "rights are something to be earned rather than given. . . . The duties of man—service, effort, obedience, cultivation of virtue, and self-restraint—are the price of rights."[32] Conservatives believe in historic, not human rights and view men in the context of established communities more than as single alienated individuals. Man's natural condition was to be in community, according to Aristotle, and without that communal identity, man is lost.

The significance of this conservative tenet during and since the New Deal is extraordinary. Contemporary public policy initiatives emphasize rights, but there has been little, if any, corresponding accent on responsibilities. To conservatives, the liberal emphasis on rights encourages Americans to think more about what the government can do for them than about their responsibilities to do things for themselves. Conservatives believe they have frequently been put at a disadvantage in the debate on public policy issues emphasizing rights because it is politically difficult to oppose rights. In his 1961 inaugural address, President John F. Kennedy challenged the American people to "ask not what your country can do for you, but what you can do for your country." Today, the conservative wonders if John F. Kennedy or any president could make such a statement in an inaugural address since the American mind is so conditioned to emphasize rights over responsibilities.

The conservative emphasis on the responsibility of state and local government to solve their own problems rather than turning to the national government is, of course, challenged by the emphasis upon rights over responsibilities. Policies of the New Deal, Fair Deal, New Frontier, and Great Society caused state and local officials to look to Washington for solutions and money, instead of solving problems themselves without recourse to the largesse of the national government. Governmental policies designed to help local communities instead created a dependence on the federal government and contributed to the feeling that state and local governments were not responsible for solving their own problems. Politically, national politicians like the advantage they receive from giving out federal funds, and state and local officials enjoy the benefit of getting money for projects without raising taxes. Conservatives believe that these practices undermine not only individual responsibility, but also the corporate responsibilities of the local community.

Democracy: Limited Government and the Constitution

A focal point of American conservatism in particular is its view of the country's constitution. Because conservative and liberal views of the state are so different, their respective attitudes toward the Constitution and its interpretation are very different. Liberal scholars, such as Charles A. Beard and J. Allen Smith, indict the Founders for creating a document which protected their own material wealth and personal power.[33] Martin Diamond, an important conservative author, challenges the liberal point of view in his book *Our Democratic Republic* by arguing that the Founders proceeded on principles rather than a desire for material gain.[34] Forrest McDonald also attacked the "economic" interpretation of the Constitution put forward by Charles Beard and argued that the interplay of economics and politics created the unique American political system.[35]

The Constitution is attacked by liberal scholars, who desire more planning and change, while conservative scholars praise the wisdom of the Founders and advocate strict Constitutional interpretation. Conservatives argue that, where possible, the Constitution should be interpreted according to the "original intent" of the Founders unless and until the document has been amended. Not to do that, conservatives argue, is to allow the Constitution to be reshaped like putty by the moods and whims of the moment. If law changes with the circumstances of the time, it becomes uncertain and unstable. In such circumstances, Americans live under a government of men, not of laws.

It is not uncommon for conservatives and liberals to disagree on founding principles and the history of democracy and the Constitution. Such differences even extend to the description of the political system. Conservatives refer to the system as a constitutional democracy, to emphasize the constitutional limitations placed upon democracy by the Founders. Conservatives may also use the term "representative democracy" to emphasize that the Founders did not establish a direct democracy, but rather one that allows representatives to act on behalf of the people, a conservative tenet. Some conservatives say only that our inherited system is a federal republic. By whatever name, it is clear that all the definitions imply limits on the scope and role of government.

Property: The Role of Economics

The conservative view of the economy is traceable to John Locke, an eighteenth-century liberal who wrote in his "Second Treatise on Government" that the principal purpose of a people's government is "the mutual preservation of their lives, liberties, and estates, which I call by the general name, property."[36] The Lockean theory of property became a defense of capitalism, and a central premise of conservative thought.

Russell Kirk in *The Conservative Mind* says that "property and freedom are inseparably connected."[37] Property is more than material things; it is also the means whereby one develops his personality by changing the external surroundings. The conservative fears any attempt at economic leveling, the government's arbitrary taking and giving of property without regard to ownership in order to distribute more evenly a society's wealth. A distrust of wide-ranging government planning is closely related to the desire to protect the right of private property.

Along with the sanctity of private property, most conservatives adhere to the view that laissez-faire capitalism is the best economic system. Capitalism is built on the assumption of private property, and socialism on the principal of state intervention. To economic conservatives, government should interfere in the economy as little as possible, allowing the law of supply and demand to guide men in making profitable decisions. Manifestations of this philosophy include not only the efforts of former President Reagan to cut taxes, but also attempts to lessen government regulation of business.

Scholars such as Peter Viereck and Clinton Rossiter contend that private property and capitalism are very different.[38] Property gives man a place to stand, but no person can function in society and still be an extreme individualist. The just and stable economy "is a mixture of individual enterprise, group cooperation, and government regulation," according to Rossiter.[39]

Most conservatives endorse limited laissez-faire economics, but others advocate public housing and related social welfare projects. According to Rossiter, the final test of any government program is: "Does this law increase equality of opportunity?"[40] The common charge made against conservatives is that their belief in a laissez-faire capitalist system makes no provision for the genuinely needy who, through no fault of their own, cannot meet basic human needs. The conservative response is to stress private and community solutions to this problem on the assumption that increased governmental activity does more harm than good.

Liberty: Equality's Big Brother

Another key area of the conservative-liberal debate, which often centers on economic issues, concerns the balance between liberty and equality.

Despite the constant praise of both liberty and equality in our nation's tradition, the two concepts work against one another. Inequality seems a basic fact of nature, yet the vast differences between rich and poor demand some leveling. Making members of a society more equal in material wealth and political power involves some change in the order of things. To achieve equality, the state must take possessions, such as property and political influence, from some and give them to others. Leveling naturally infringes on the liberty of those from whom wealth or political power is taken; however, to allow some to acquire unrestricted wealth and political power creates inequality.

There is no easy solution to this dispute. Theoretically a society with total liberty has no equality; anarchy would be the result, as all members of society would have total freedom to do as they pleased. On the other hand, a society with total equality has no liberty and requires a totalitarian government to enforce common standards in all associations. Conservatism celebrates equality by holding that people are entitled by God and nature to be treated as a means and not an end. They are entitled to equality of opportunity and suffrage; beyond this the conservative is unwilling to go. In the conservative view, individuals have an infinite variety of talents and are entitled to find economic, political, and social rewards without fear of government license or redistribution.

Conservatism favors liberty in the equality-liberty equation, but it does not completely sacrifice equality on the altar of freedom. The conservative position in America holds that while liberty is relatively more important than equality, both must exist in a society if it is to become democratic. It is liberty that creates the wealth in the society, and the stability of a regime is ensured only in a context of economic growth. So liberty is equality's older brother in the sense that it creates the conditions for a discussion of redistribution.

There are three reasons why conservatives believe economic and political costs are low in a society where liberty is more important. First, government does not have to be enlarged to the extent of becoming oppressive as the enforcer of equality. As Harvey Mansfield points out: "A society of natural equals then needs government of unlimited scope, that is, an enormous inequality of political power, in order to protect its equality."[41] Second, when equality outstrips liberty in importance, people lose their incentive to excel. Third, material equality is not nearly as important as moral equality under God. Edmund Burke wrote that wealth is not the true source of happiness, and civil life establishes order for the sake of the poor as well as the rich.[42] Social stability can be difficult to achieve if the emphasis on equality undermines order in society.

In contemporary society, with the advent of the New Deal in the 1930s and the more recent civil rights and equal rights movement, equality has become sacrosanct and government has expanded accordingly. Until the 1980s conservatives often found themselves in the unenviable position of being perceived as opposing society's improvement. But a burdensome bureaucracy and expanding government power eventually led to a backlash. The conservative emphasis on liberty found a receptive audience when the economy began to collapse under the weight of government regulation and interest group demands.

The most dramatic example of this backlash was the controversy over the Equal Rights Amendment (ERA), a proposal which would have extended a wide range of rights to women. In 1972 Congress passed the amendment by a wide margin and sent it to the states for consideration. Within the first year, the legislatures in twenty-two states ratified the ERA by overwhelming votes. By 1974–75, the ERA encountered unexpectedly stiff opposition from conservatives. Thirty-five states ratified the amendment by 1978, three short of the necessary three-fourths needed, but four states rescinded their earlier ratification. By 1982, the Equal Rights Amendment was dead. In the end, the ERA was an issue that symbolized the conflict over a broad range of cultural values in the United States. Conservatives succeeded by raising the spectre of women being drafted for combat duty and disallowing provisions which at the time protected women in the workplace. In sum, the equality provisions of the amendment were antithetical to the liberty women currently enjoyed in society.

Meritocracy: The Leadership Class

A belief in the importance of an aristocratic class is an idea that has long been a firm belief of conservatives. In its American application, this belief was changed in important ways. When Edmund Burke defended the aristocratic class, he defended a specific group of titled nobles in England; however, America was founded as a society opposed to titles of nobility. Peter Viereck notes that in the United States conservatives such as John Adams spoke of a "natural aristocracy," which anyone could join by virtue of merit and ability.[43]

Despite the difference between the American and English aristocracies, the basic reason for the conservatives' regard for an aristocratic class in both contexts is the same: an elite class provides order. Kirk notes that the conservative believes that "civilized society requires orders and classes."[44] The American aristocratic class includes, among others, those officials elected in our republican democracy to represent the people, thus protecting against a tyranny of the majority, which conservatives fear. Viereck stresses noblesse oblige rather than the elite class. He emphasizes the importance of service by the meritocracy of society. To Viereck, aristocracy is important only in the sense of the "aristocratic heritage."[45]

Antipathy: The Anticommunist Impulse

Because conservatives believe American values are unique and deserving of respect, anticommunism has played a major role in the growth of the movement and has become a very recognizable part of the conservative philosophy. George H. Nash, in *The Conservative Intellectual Movement in America,* identifies the anticommunists as one of the three major groups which brought about the revival of conservatism since 1945.[46] Nash's list of key anticommunist thinkers includes Whittaker Chambers, James Burnham, and Frank Meyer, who once embraced communism in the 1930s and turned against it in the 1940s and 1950s. Meyer's experience was not unusual among other anticommunists of the time who earlier flirted with communism only to find it destructive of the rights of the individual and damaging to the interests of the local community.[47]

As a belief, anticommunism includes virtually every canon of conservatism. Those who hold particularly to the importance of maintaining a strong national defense against foreign invasion and preserving the internal domestic order saw communism as a threat from external hostile Soviet actions and from communist sympathizers internally. Communism is the ultimate manifestation of the conservative fear of a powerful central government which squashes freedom to impose its plans. Communism is also, to paraphrase Whittaker Chambers, the alternate faith to a belief in God.[48] Conservatives are appalled at the total obliteration of traditional values in the face of "godless communism." The historical record of the systematic starvation of the peasants in Stalin's Russia and the oppression of the population by a totalitarian political system which denied the transcendent haunts conservative fears about socialism in the West.

The mainline conservative attitude toward communism is strong distrust. Most conservatives are opposed to the type of demagoguery represented by Senator Joseph McCarthy and the conspiracy theories of the John Birch Society whose president, Robert Welch, even accused President Eisenhower of being in league with the Soviet Union.[49] The balanced conservative point of view is that while overreaction to communism in the form of demagoguery and conspiracy theories is unwise, a vigilant attitude toward communism must be maintained.

The evidence undergirding the conservative attitude includes not only the lack of liberty in communist countries, but also the list of human rights atrocities committed in surrogate countries like Czechoslovakia, Hungary, and Afghanistan. The squalid prisons in Cuba described by Armando Valladares in his book *Against All Hope,* and the hopelessness of the slave labor camps documented by Alexander Solzhenitsyn in *The Gulag Archipelago: 1918–1956,* are the true reality of communism. The chief crime of communism is not that it takes away property, but that it removes freedom upon which property is based.

Conclusion

During his terms as president, Ronald Reagan made it a habit to invite special guests to sit in the visitor's balcony during his State of the Union messages to Congress. In an address in his first term he hailed Lenny Skutnik, who had earlier rescued several drowning passengers from an airplane that had crashed in the Potomac River. Two years later he lauded Sergeant Stephen Trujillo, an Army medic who risked his life saving the wounded in Grenada. The president used this nationally televised speech to recognize a Vietnamese refugee who graduated with honors from West Point, a Harlem resident who cared for drug-addicted infants, and a high school student whose science experiment was carried aboard the ill-fated Challenger shuttle. The subjects of these introductions were frequently criticized by the press as a diversion from the real issues facing the nation, but the critics failed to realize the crucial role symbolic values play in governing.

The stories of these individuals were an embodiment of a common theme: "For [Americans] faith, work, family, neighborhood, freedom, and peace are not just words; they're expressions of what America means, definitions of what makes us a good and loving people."[50] In short, America is a special place. Critics of Reagan's speeches to Congress and his presidency failed to realize that most Americans want to believe that their nation is both good and unique. Conservatism appeals to this heartfelt desire. It is fundamentally an attitude toward man and society that examines the issues of life through principle.

The ten canons described here are really ten principles that conservatives use to guide their personal lives and to work within communities. Conservatism embodies a deep respect for the lessons of history and an abiding regard for the work of deity within that record. It is ultimately a statement of personal faith that emphasizes the responsibility of man to his Maker and also to his fellow man. Conservatism teaches mankind to look first at what one can do to solve one's own problems rather than seeking solutions from another source.

Person, position, and place are important hallmarks of the conservative faith. Recognition of who one is in a society and one's responsibilities to that society, respect for one's own position as well as for the positions of others in society, and reverence for place or sense of local community are important to the conservative in creating and sustaining social harmony and stability. The conservative views success as achieving what one can within the confines of one's abilities, rather than attaining something that one either has not worked for or does not have the ability to earn. Contemporary conservatives believe that the state must promote virtue and social responsibility and take appropriate measures to improve the moral climate of society.

Notes

1. E. D. Hirsch, Jr., *Cultural Literacy* (Boston: Houghton Mifflin, 1987), pp. 21–22.
2. Alexis de Tocqueville, *Democracy in America* (New York: Knopf, 1945), p. 97.

3. Albert Schweitzer, *Out of My Life and Thought: An Autobiography*. C. T. Campion (trans.) (New York: Henry Holt, 1933), p. 219.

4. Robert Wuthnow, *The Restructuring of American Religion* (Princeton, N.J.: Princeton University Press, 1988), p. 17. Wuthnow finds that in the postwar years, "polls revealed that 94 percent of the [American] public believed in God, a substantially larger share than in England, Holland, Sweden, Denmark, or France." Wuthnow also finds a decline in regular church attendance (people who said they had been to a religious service within the past week) in the U.S. from a high of 49 percent in 1958 to a level 40 percent in the 1980s (p. 159).

5. E. D. Hirsch, Jr., *Cultural Literacy*, p. 99.

6. The clearest expression of this impulse is found in William Manchester, *The Last Lion: Winston Spencer Churchill* (Boston: Little, Brown, 1983), pp. 3–18.

7. D. Grier Stephenson, Robert J. Bresler, Robert J. Friedrich and Jospehy J. Karlesky, *American Government* (New York: Harper & Row, 1988), p. 200.

8. Frank S. Meyer, *The Conservative Mainstream* (New Rochelle, N.Y.: Arlington House, 1969), p. 16.

9. Clinton Rossiter, *Conservatism in America* (New York: Vintage Books, 1962), pp. 64–66.

10. Russell Kirk, *The Conservative Mind* (7th ed.; Chicago: Regnery, 1986), pp. 8–9.

11. Friedrich A. von Hayek, *The Road to Serfdom* (Chicago: University of Chicago Press, 1944). Richard Weaver, *Ideas Have Consequences* (Chicago: University Press, 1948). Peter Viereck, *Conservatism* (Westport, Conn.: Greenwood Press, 1978). Eric Voegelin, *Order and History,* (5 Vols.; Baton Rouge, La.: Louisiana State University Press, 1956). William F. Buckley, Jr., *Up From Liberalism* (New York: Stein and Day, 1959). Gertrude Himmelfarb, *The Idea of Poverty* (New York: Knopf, 1984). Leo Strauss, *Natural Right and History* (Chicago: University of Chicago Press, 1965). John Hallowell, *The Moral Foundations of Democracy* (Chicago: University of Chicago Press, 1973). Daniel Boorstin, *The Genius of American Politics* (Chicago: University of Chicago Press, 1979). Robert Nisbet, *The Quest for Community* (New York: Oxford University Press, 1953).

12. Russell Kirk, *The Conservative Mind* (Chicago: Regnery, 1953), pp. 36–37.

13. Clinton Rossiter, *Conservatism in America,* p. 74.

14. Russell Kirk, *The Conservative Mind* (7th ed., Chicago: Regnery, 1986).

15. Peter R. Viereck, *Conservatism Revisited* (New York: Collier Books, 1962), p. 24.

16. M. Stanton Evans, *Clear and Present Dangers* (New York: Harcourt, Brace, Jovanovich, 1975), pp. 301–302.

17. Irving Kristol, *Reflections of a Neoconservative* (New York: Basic Books, 1983), pp. 228–273. George H. Nash, *The Conservative Intellectual Movement in America Since 1945* (New York: Basic Books, 1976), pp. 91–95.

18. M. Stanton Evans, *Clear and Present Dangers,* p. 330.

19. Quoted in: George H. Nash, *The Conservative Intellectual Movement in America,* p. 5.

20. Edward Banfield, *The Unheavenly City* (Boston: Little, Brown, 1970). M. Stanton Evans, *The Liberal Establishment* (New York: Devin-Adair, 1965).

21. George H. Nash, *The Conservative Intellectual Movement in America,* pp. 326–328. Edward Banfield, *The Unheavenly City* (Boston: Little, Brown, 1971).

22. Russell Kirk, *The Conservative Mind*, p. 8.

23. Clinton Rossiter, *Conservatism in America* (New York: Knopf, 1955), pp. 64–66.

24. Robert Nisbet as quoted in Russell Kirk (ed.), *The Portable Conservative Reader* (New York: Viking-Penguin, 1982), p. 645.

25. Robert Nisbet, *The Quest for Community*.

26. Nisbet quoted in Kirk (ed.), *The Portable Conservative Reader*, pp. 660–685.

27. Clinton Rossiter, *Conservatism in America*, p. 45.

28. C. S. Lewis, "The Poison of Subjectivism," in Kirk (ed.), *The Portable Conservative Reader*, p. 512.

29. Richard Weaver, *Life Without Prejudice and Other Essays* (Chicago: University of Chicago Press, 1965), p. 45. George Nash, *The Conservative Intellectual Movement in America*, pp. 38–39.

30. Russell Kirk, *The Conservative Mind*, p. 8.

31. Edmund Burke quoted in Kirk, *The Conservative Mind*, p. 43.

32. Clinton Rossiter, *Conservatism Revisited*, p. 64.

33. In Martin Diamond, *The Founding of the Democratic Republic* (Itasca, Ill.: F. E. Peacock, 1981), p. 47.

34. Martin Diamond, *The Founding of the Democratic Republic*, pp. 49, 63.

35. Forrest McDonald, *A Constitutional History of the United States* (New York: Franklin Watts, 1982). Forrest McDonald, *Novus Ordo Seclorum: The Intellectual Origins of the Constitution* (Lawrence, Kan.: University of Kansas Press, 1985).

36. William Ebenstein, *Great Political Thinkers: Plato to the Present* (4th ed.; New York: Holt, Rinehart & Winston, 1969), p. 407.

37. Russell Kirk, *The Conservative Mind*, pp. 7–8.

38. Peter Viereck, *Conservatism Revisited*, p. 39. Clinton Rossiter, *Conservatism in America*, pp. 38–49.

39. Clinton Rossiter, *Conservatism in America* (2nd ed.; Cambridge, Mass.: Harvard University Press, 1982), p. 238.

40. Clinton Rossiter, *Conservatism Revisited*, p. 191.

41. Harvey C. Mansfield, *The Spirit of Liberalism* (Cambridge, Mass.: Harvard University Press, 1978), p. 39.

42. Russell Kirk, *The Conservative Mind*, p. 16.

43. Peter Viereck, *Conservatism* (Westport, Conn.: Greenwood Press, 1978), p. 89.

44. Russell Kirk, *The Conservative Mind*, pp. 7–8.

45. Peter Viereck, *Conservatism Revisited*, p. 38.

46. Peter Viereck, *Conservatism Revisited*, p. 38.

47. Frank S. Meyer, *The Conservative Mainstream* (New Rochelle, N.Y.: Arlington House, 1969).

48. George H. Nash, *The Conservative Intellectual Movement in America*, pp. 84–123.

49. George H. Nash, *The Conservative Intellectual Movement in America*, pp. 91–95.

50. John Kenneth White, *The New Politics of Old Values* (Hanover, N.H.: University Press of New England, 1988), p. 61.

CHAPTER FOUR

The Classical Roots of Conservative Thought

*. . . [T]here is no doubt that conservatism as a modern
movement is a response to the excesses of rationalistic zeal let
loose by eighteenth-century radicals such as Jean Jacques
Rousseau (1712–1778). Indeed, the word "conservative"
was coined from the French word* conservateur, *a name given
to certain French writers who wished to return to the conditions
existing prior to the rise of Napoleon I (1769–1821) and the
French Revolution.*

JAY A. SIGLER[1]

All political action is guided by some thought of better or worse.
Political things are by their nature subject to approval and disapproval, to choice and rejection, to praise and blame. In democracies,
government power is retained only after the people approve of the
choices their leaders make. Politicians balance their decisions between
the extremes of preservation and change: "When desiring to preserve,
we wish to prevent a change to the worse; when desiring to change, we
wish to bring about something better."[2] Judgments about the rate and
type of change do not exist in a vacuum, they rest on some conception
of what should be, of what is best for society.

The foundation of conservatism is the belief that the good society has
a reverence for proven values which guide the integration of new ideas
through time-tested institutions. Tradition is nothing more than the
concrete experience of this truth which is carried in common by the
society. Knowledge of the past is the spiritual substance of shared living
that makes society distinctively human. The fundamental values of conservatism, the premises of resistance to change and protection of past
values, are best understood today as a reaction to the idealism of the

Renaissance, the flawed vision of the Enlightenment which culminated in the French Revolution, and the mistaken promises of modern utopian ideologies.

The points of reaction which sparked the development of modern conservative thought were diverse. Movements like the Renaissance and the Enlightenment were complex social phenomena, but they still evinced a distinct theme and view of man and the state which influenced subsequent political thought. The French Revolution, the Protestant Reformation, and the decline of the Roman Catholic Church's authority in society had a similar impact on social relations and politics. No one of these events standing alone could explain the emergence of modern conservatism, but together they led to an articulate conservative reaction to the changes being wrought in society by these movements, events, ideologies, and personalities.

It was Protagoras who said, "Man is the measure of all things, of what is that it is and of what is not that it is not."[3] In all the movements to which conservatism reacted, there was a preoccupation with man—his mind, his reason, and his ability to solve his own problems. Conservatism, with its religious roots (especially in the Roman Catholic Church) and its classical ties (to the writings of Plato and Aristotle, with their emphasis on balance and order in society) looked less to mankind and more to deity, less to reason and revolution and more to principles and traditions. In this chapter these foundations of conservatism are examined and explained.

Classical Political Thought

In the twentieth century, states are so large, so remote, and so impersonal that they cannot fill the place in modern life that the city filled in the life of ancient Greece. Four centuries before Christ, the art, religion, ethics, economics, and politics of a citizen were set by the city in which he lived. The life of a city was a social experience; its constitution, as Aristotle said of Athens, was a "mode of life" rather than a legal structure. Consequently, the guiding ideal of classical political thought was the harmony of life held in common in the community. The "polis" was a divine association, where order ruled over chaos and where the ways of the gods, the ways of nature, and the ways of man came to close approximation.

In Greece, the city was a place where its inhabitants were to live in agreement, with as many citizens as possible taking an active part in a common life. In ancient Athens offices were rotated to give more citizens a share in the government. On the basis of figures given by Aristotle in his *Constitution of Athens,* it is estimated that in any year as many as one citizen in six might have had some share in the civil government, even though it might have amounted to no more than jury service. Even if he held no office, a citizen could still meet in a general assembly to discuss city business at least ten times a year.

Classical political philosophy was characterized by its ideals, which were directly related to political life. Looking at political life from the perspective of an enlightened citizen or statesman in ancient Athens meant that one day's political discussions might be the next day's government policy. Discussion of laws naturally involved agreement as to what was best for the society. Good rulers were those who placed this common interest above their private interest; good decisions for the polity were those most in accordance with the requirements of human excellence: "Since political controversies are concerned with 'good things' and 'just things,' classical political philosophy was naturally guided by considerations of 'goodness' and 'justice.' "[4]

The distinct question which guided the Platonic dialogues was "What is virtue?" The ideas of harmony and proportionality as applied to the ethics of life were a critical concern of classical political philosophy. The fundamental thought in the Greek idea of the state was the harmony of a life shared in common by all its members. Life was conceived as an activity directed toward some goal, but in order to pursue a specific goal, a society had to be constituted in accordance with that goal. Classical philosophy was guided by the question of the best regime, even though that ideal might never be reached.

An example of this philosophy is Plato's most famous book, the *Republic,* written in his mature manhood, probably within a decade of the opening of his school in the fourth century B.C. The book emphasizes that knowledge is virtue, a proposition which implies that there is an objective good to be known and that it can in fact be known by rational or logical investigation rather than by intuition, guesswork, or luck. Government, to be just, must be based on this abstract good, which could only be realized by leaders who were properly educated: "Plato's theory is therefore divisible into two main parts or theses: first, that government ought to be an art depending on exact knowledge and, second, that society is a mutual satisfaction of needs by persons whose capacities supplement each other."[5]

The ideals of the *Republic* were never realized; today it is regarded as the greatest of utopias. Still, its romantic ideas of free intelligence guided by custom and the voice of reason remain as a legacy centuries after Plato elaborated them. The book's voice is that of the scholar, whose faith in structured activity society would do well to rely upon. Classical philosophy strives for knowledge of the whole, the totality of the parts, even though such knowledge may ultimately elude us.

Modern Political Thought

Modern political thought, by contrast, rejects the classical schemes as unrealizable and unrealistic. The founder of modern political philosophy was Machiavelli (1469–1527), who objected to the classical approach to politics which emphasized an unrealized utopia. The description of the ideal regime did not interest Machiavelli because its realization was improbable; instead he took as his standard the objectives actually pursued by existing societies. His lowering of the requirements of conduct meant that virtue could no longer define the good society; rather, the state must have as its objectives the lesser ideals of prosperity, glory, empire, and freedom from foreign domination.

By Machiavelli's time the classical tradition had undergone profound changes; the contemplative life had found its home in monestaries. Moral virtue in the sixteenth century meant Christian charity. Machiavelli had no sense of religion as a deep personal experience; he saw it only as an instrument of political domination. He held the church particularly responsible for the current state of affairs: it was too weak to unite Italy and too strong to prevent anyone else from doing so. Ultimate thoughts about the good were useless—what counted were ends and means, power and its exercise: "The consuming problem of the sixteenth century was whether the state is to be regarded as a moral organism or simply as a power bloc."[6] The great exponents of the ethical state stood in the classical tradition; Machiavelli was positioned in the amoral camp.

The Renaissance

Today we remember the Renaissance as a time of artistic and creative greatness. The revival of commerce and urban life produced in Italy a galaxy of brilliant city-states which contrived to balance political power among themselves and endow their particular communities with the greatest of artistic achievements. The Renaissance "ideal was the exploration of all learning and all skills. . . . The universal man, the 'uomo universale,' essayed to excel in sport, art, literature, exploration or war."[7] It is common to say that the Renaissance represented a rebirth in learning, but it is more accurate to say that it embodied a rebirth of an idea about man.

A change in thinking took place; medieval Christian notions that man was a flawed and sinful creature in God's universe were replaced by an understanding that man himself was the center of all things. One commentator has written of Leonardo da Vinci, who is commonly regarded as a prototype of the Renaissance man, that "throughout the thousands of pages he covered with notes and ideas, God is seldom mentioned, but nature appears innumerable times. . . . For [him] there was no authority higher than that of the eye, which he characterized as the 'window of the soul.' "[8] The abilities of Da Vinci and Michelangelo were models as to what man is capable of being and doing. The change in attitudes about the nature and purposes of man are clearly seen in the art of the time.

In 1501, the government of Florence invited sculptors to submit their designs for using a 17-foot block of Carrara marble that had lain in the cathedral courtyard for seventy years. An earlier sculptor had begun work on the marble but had given up, and subsequent artists judged the marble to have been gouged so deeply as to be ruined. The winning design was submitted by Michelangelo, who carved on the flawed marble for three years until he completed his masterpiece, "David." Asked how he found the solution to the ruined marble, Michelangelo said simply that he had seen the figure imprisoned and set it free. Such was the Renaissance vision.

The view Michelangelo had of David is a prototype of the Renaissance ideal for man. One scholar comments, "[the statue] towers above us as revelation of a transferred humanity. . . . It is characteristic that such a figure should appear dreamlike."[9] In the perfect body of David, the undercutting of the hair, and the strong anatomical features lie the message that man has unlimited abilities. The ultimate hope of the Renaissance was that all men would realize and attain a perfection never before known.

Not surprisingly, Machiavelli longed for a political David, a strong and powerful leader who would return Italy to greatness. He assumed that power was an end in itself, and he confined his inquiries to the means best suited to acquire, retain, and expand power. Caesar Borgia, who assassinated his older brother and the husband of his sister, was held up "as an example to be imitated by all who by fortune and with the arms of others have risen to power. . . . One can find no better example than the actions of this man."[10] Machiavelli, more than any other political thinker, defined the philosophy of the modern nation-state by idealizing the power of its rulers. In this view, the organized force and supreme authority of the state obligate and regulate other institutions in society.

The Reformation

The sixteenth century witnessed two great revolutions in thinking. The Renaissance flourished in the city-states of southern Europe, while the Reformation was characteristic of nation-states in northern Europe. Although the original ideas of the Reformation were religious, religion was readily used as a cloak for less lofty aspirations: "Nowhere was the issue purely religious; in all countries it was mixed with political, dynastic, economic and diplomatic considerations."[11]

In many ways the Reformation was a reaction against the secular church and humanism of the Renaissance. Renaissance idealism was based on a revival of Greek and Latin models of man and human learning. Aristotle had been canonized when his philosophy was grafted onto Christian theology by Thomas Aquinas in the Middle Ages. The Church's approval had been extended in a general way to cover Aristotle's scientific as well as his philosophical ideas. Protestant reformers, from Luther onwards, stressed the supreme authority of scripture and the fallacy of human reason. "The Reformation [took] the form of a revolt against the Roman Church, accused of having departed from the true faith as revealed in the Bible."[12]

Martin Luther was born in 1483 and lived until 1546. As a young priest he was shocked by the immorality in the church of his time. His proffered remedy was "Sola Scriptura," a return to the Bible and a rejection of the humanist tradition in the secular church. In a letter to a friend written in May 1517 Luther wrote, "Aristotle is going downhill and perhaps he will go all the way down to hell."[13] A few months after writing this, on October 31, 1517, Luther nailed to the door of the Wittenburg Church the "Ninety-Five Theses," which ended with a bold declaration, "I am neither so rash as to wish that my sole opinion should be preferred to that of all other men, nor so senseless as to be willing that the word of God should be made to give place to fables, devised by human reason."[14]

The Reformation was a reaction to the fables, humanism, heresy, and perversions that human reason had added to alter the pristine faith of the early church. It was a specific rejection of the Renaissance, with its idealism and hopes for "uomo universale." To the reformers, the religion of the Renaissance was little more than pantheism, a belief that God is not a personality but a force or manifestation that is behind all religions. The vision of the reformers was that man was fallen, finite and frail; they were not romantic about man. Each Reformation country showed the practice of checks and balances in its government constitution to guard against the accumulation of power by rulers.

The Catholic fight against Protestantism encouraged a corresponding reform movement within the Roman Catholic Church, the Counter-Reformation. In 1534, Ignatius Loyola founded his Society of Jesus, the Jesuit order, for the propagation and defense of the faith. Whereas Luther discovered the Epistle of Romans and subjected his self-will to the grace of God, Ignatius concentrated on the suffering Christ and obedience to the representatives of the Church. The Jesuits took the lead in refuting Protestant theologians and stimulating changes in the Catholic Church. "The history of the Counter-Reformation is in part the history of the triumph of the conservative and the militant over the conciliatory and the liberal."[15] The Council of Trent, which began its deliberation in 1545, affirmed the traditions of the Catholic Church and at the same time legislated new rules cleansing the Church of past excesses.

For Roman Catholics particularly, the Reformation is seen as a chal-

lenge to conservatism because it severed ties to a continuous line of
authority, spiritual and temporal, over several centuries. At cross purposes were two diametrically opposed doctrines, the Protestant's doctrine of the authoritative Bible and the Catholic's belief in the
authoritative Church. While both Roman Catholicism and Protestantism have produced many conservative scholars, their view of the Reformation differs. Contemporary conservative Russell Kirk, a Catholic by
conversion, puts the issue this way:

> Obedience, submission to God, is the secret of justice in society and tran-
> quility in life, quite as much as it is indispensable to eternal salvation. To
> redeem Americans from sectarianism is the task of the intelligent social
> reformer as well as the duty of the priest; for free political institutions can
> be secure only when the people are imbued with religious veneration.
> Democracy, more than any other form of government, rests upon the
> postulate of a moral law, ordained by an authority superior to human
> wisdom. . . .
>
> Under Protestantism, the sect governs religion, rather than submitting
> to governance; the congregations bully their ministers and insist upon
> palatable sermons, flattering to their vanity; Protestantism cannot sustain
> popular liberty because it is itself subject to popular control, and must
> follow in all things the popular will, passion, interest, prejudice, or caprice.
> The modern spirit, of which Protestantism is one expression, detests the
> idea of loyalty, upon which the whole hierarchy of this world and the
> next is founded. . . .[16]

Historically, Protestants would vehemently dispute Kirk's view of the
matter. For them, the Protestant Reformation was conservative in that
it reconnected Christianity to its historic past, one that was nearly lost
through the corruption of doctrine and practices of the Roman Catholic
Church. Protestants believe that the Roman Catholic Church had
warped the foundations and traditions of the church. They endeavored
to return the church to its scriptural roots: "One could say that the
Renaissance centered in autonomous man, while the Reformation centered in the infinite-personal God who had spoken in the Bible."[17]

To the Protestant the Bible is the ultimate authority; to the Roman
Catholic the church is the ultimate authority. The Roman Catholic conservative believes that the church is the repository of the continuity of
the ages, and her traditions are, therefore, authoritative. The Protestant

conservative argues to the contrary that the Bible is the touchstone of truth and that all human action must be measured against it. Whenever traditions violate Scripture, Protestants hold that those practices must give way to biblical truth. Kirk's argument that Protestantism is subject to popular control is met with the Protestant retort that the failure of Roman Catholicism to subject itself to the truth of the Bible led to the corruption of doctrine and practices, which were the cause of the Reformation in the first place.

The Protestant view is that the Reformation was genuinely conservative in that it reconnected Christianity to its true foundations and correct traditions. To the Protestant, the Bible provides a standard of certainty by which to judge faith and practice. The Roman Catholic Church, by contrast, offers no certainty since its standards are liable to change from generation to generation. As one Protestant writer has said, "The Bible gives a different way to come to God from that teaching which had grown up in the church through the previous centuries. . . . The individual person, they taught, could come to God directly 'by faith' through the finished work of Christ."[18]

Loyalty, the other issue raised by Kirk, also arouses a Protestant response. Kirk's standard of loyalty is measured by loyalty to the Roman Catholic Church and her traditions. Protestants, by contrast, have historically measured loyalty by one's willingness to believe in and to practice the teachings of the Bible as understood in common versions of the original translations. It was this type of loyalty which caused the Puritans to embark on a journey to the New World in the first place, and it was a similar allegiance that moved others to challenge church practices with the question, "Is it biblical?"

While Roman Catholics and Protestants have these fundamental differences, there is still much that unites them. Both reject the Renaissance humanism and idealism of that era, and both shame the corruption which led to the original schism between Catholic and Protestant. The measuring rod of conservatism might differ between the two, but they are in agreement that later currents of opinion are blasphemous to the respective conservative traditions which both seek to protect.

The Enlightenment

"Rich and weighty as were the legacies bequeathed to us by ancient Greece and Rome, the Middle Ages, the Renaissance, and the Reformation," writes Paul Hazard in *European Thought in the 18th Century*, "it is the Enlightenment of which we are the direct and lineal descendants."[19] The legacy of the French Enlightenment was a belief in the universal regeneration of mankind, who, when remade by reason, would become beautiful new creatures, happy and thoroughly secular in their thinking. In such a vision man and society were perfectible. The romantic ideal of the new political community would be one where all previous religions would be replaced by a new civic religion, that of rationalistic humanism in which the civic bonds themselves would constitute a kind of sacred association.

Today most college courses on the Enlightenment examine in detail the writings of French personalities like Rousseau, Voltaire, and Diderot. Very little attention is given to the Anglo-Scottish Enlightenment, and writers like Locke, Hume, and Adam Smith. Yet it is the Anglo-Scottish Enlightenment which most directly influenced the American experience. The traditions of the latter movement aimed "at gradual improvement of the human condition—a process, moreover, in which each individual bears his share of responsibility for a successful outcome, rather than salvation being provided 'from above' by a ruling party or class."[20] Although the American Revolution was inspired by a casual mixing of the two Enlightenments, it was the Anglo-Scottish tradition that was decisive in the end. Instead of a reign of terror, the American Revolution ended in the Constitutional Convention. Instead of fratricidal warfare among revolutionaries arguing over utopian expectations, the American Founders compromised on a limited government with divided power.

The French Enlightenment was fueled by the vision of two men: Voltaire (1694–1778), who sketched out four periods of history culminating with the France of his time as the apex; and Jean Jacques Rousseau (1712–1778), who saw the primitive as innocent, and autonomous freedom as realizable. Voltaire made freedom of speech his crusade, but he had little interest in politics and no interest in the masses, whom he regarded as cruel and stupid. Rousseau's freedom was a release from God, culture, authority, and any kind of restraint—his pride was in the "noble savage." Social conventions were the "chains" of his famous dictum in *The Social Contract*: "Man is born free and everywhere he is in chains." Deity, history and community—the nametags of conservatism—were anathema to Rousseau. In the period of the French Revolution, his ideas gave birth to the laws which made divorce as easy as marriage, abolished the distinction between legitimate and illegitimate children, gave France a new calendar with ten days in each week, and established a new state religion based on reason.[21]

The Anglo-Scottish Enlightenment had more modest ambitions. Instead of a new state religion, it aimed at the formation of religious toleration. Even though many of the Anglo-Scottish Enlightenment thinkers were religious skeptics, or at most deists, they recognized that organized religion was a necessary part of community life which inculcated moral habits and obviated the need for government instruction. The envisioned society of Anglo-Scottish temperance was ruled by a limited government, one restrained in power and authority. The success of the English-speaking Enlightenment was that it did not destroy the old order but created a new and viable one out of existing institutions: "The Anglo-Scottish Enlightenment was no less rationalist than the French, but it found its appropriate expression in a calm historical sociology rather than in a fervent political messianism."[22]

French Revolution

The French revolutionaries wanted to produce a new man through education, persuasion, and, if required, force and terror. To achieve this goal with these means, they were willing to destroy all social and governmental institutions. The history of France at this time is replete with accounts of revolutionary tribunals dispensing revolutionary justice, a reign of terror, and bloodthirsty proclamations by mobs before guillotines. As it turned out, the French revolutionaries were more interested in power than freedom. Rousseau's writings were the feast of the revolutionaries, who pillaged France's guilds, monasteries, and economy in the name of citizenship. The new sentimentality denied morality and national boundaries. Rousseau wrote, "Today there are no Frenchmen, Germans, Spaniards, or even Englishmen; there are only Europeans. . . . They are at home wherever there is money to steal or women to seduce."[23]

The French mutiny savagely attacked the patriarchal family, declaring marriage a civil contract and abolishing the traditionally accepted laws of paternal authority, primogeniture, and entail. By 1794 the number of divorces exceeded the number of marriages. Property, a key embodiment of human liberty and freedom for the conservative, was severely restricted by destroying the relationships between property and community groups, such as family, church, guild, and monastery. The aim of the revolution was to refashion a people—to destroy their past, alter their habits, and purify their desires. Why was the French Revolution like this? "It was perhaps Romanticism," writes Simon Schama in his book on the period, "its fondness for the vertiginous and the macabre; its concept of political energy as, above all, electrical; its obsession with the heart; its preference for passion over reason, for virtue over peace, that supplied the crucial ingredient in the mentality of the revolutionary elite: its association of liberty with wildness."[24] The result of this social experimentation was a bloodbath and rapid breakdown of authority culminating in the authoritarian rule of Napoleon Bonaparte.

It was this spectacle which caused Edmund Burke to take up his pen and state the general principle of English constitutionalism which he had previously accepted as a part of the natural order of things. For Burke, and generations of conservatives after him, civilization was the possession not of individuals, but of communities. To conservatives, the civic culture is all of man's inherited spiritual possessions; its art, moral ideas, science, and learning are not something to be ransacked by revolutionaries in the name of change. The revolution was in Burke's own words, both "sublime and terrible." "In England we have not yet been completely embowelled of our natural entrails; we still feel within us, and we cherish and cultivate, those inbred sentiments which are the faithful guardians, the active monitors of our duty."[25]

Utopian Ideologies

The French Revolution expanded the political and intellectual divisions in Europe. In the nineteenth century, democracy seemed inevitable, even in politically backward states with long-standing dynasties like Russia and Germany. The political virtues of self-government were accorded lip service by autocrats, and gradual experiments in democracy were tried. However, the twentieth century gave rise to violent revolution and the authoritarian excesses of fascism, Nazism, and communism.

Dictatorships in the twentieth century are of three types: (1) the autocratic military ruler; (2) a single individual in a ruling group; and (3) a "kind of dictatorship [which] seeks to refashion human society in terms of some ideology or doctrine."[26] The practice of terror, propaganda and rulership by a single political party has characterized dictatorships in the twentieth century of both the Right and Left, by the fascists, Nazis, and communists. The social and technological changes of modern times, especially the expansion of radio and television, have had the effect of making authoritarian states more powerful.

The rise of totalitarianism in the twentieth century has provoked the surviving democracies to examine their foundations. Conservatives have benefited from such scrutiny since their ideals explain past social achievements. The primary reason many conservatives oppose having conservatism labeled an ideology is that the term—especially in the twentieth century—is associated with utopian ideas like communism and socialism. The goal of an ideology is to remake society and humans in the image of some ideal. Conservatism, on the other hand, teaches that we should understand society through experience and learning. Society's behavior should be determined by links to the past, not by the imposition of an abstract dogma. Action is the motif of the ideologue, reflection is the manner of the conservative.

While the conservative cherishes diversity, the ideologue prizes uniformity. The ideologue views men as instruments to be manipulated in the interest of obtaining a uniformity of practice. By contrast, conservatives value variety, complexity, subtlety, and nuance. Community, the benchmark of human organization for the conservative, is the embodiment of those values. The individual learns standards of acceptable behavior more through community institutions like the family, church, neighborhood, and voluntary associations, than through laws and standards imposed by government.

The neoconservative movement of the 1980s was triggered by a disillusion with utopian promises and experiments. The experiences of permissiveness, poverty, crime, inflation, and moral disarray that came to be associated with liberalism's social and economic agenda since the 1930s led to an increasing ambivalence about the role of government in the life of its citizens. The feeling among neoconservatives was that Washington had tried for too long to do too much and, for the most part, had done it badly. The adversarial stance toward general culture which characterized radical thought in the 1960s led to a reaction by those who wished to protect and defend the fundamental values of the free society.

Conclusion

Without the challenges posed by the Renaissance, the Enlightenment, the French Revolution, and utopian ideologies, there would be no articulate modern conservatism. The uniform characteristic of all these movements is a faith in human reason and capacities. In conservative eyes, the ideal of human association liberated from custom has seldom brought freedom, and never spawned lasting social improvement. Reaction, then, is a characteristic of modern conservatism. As society began to adopt the idealism of the Renaissance and incorporate the beliefs of the Enlightenment, conservatives elaborated the virtues of a well-ordered past.

The French Revolution was especially important in the development of conservative thought. It was Edmund Burke who saw the need to react to the challenges to order and authority in evidence in the Jacobin excesses. After Burke, much conservative writing has been in response to threats undermining the values of community and society.

The clearest definition of the premises necessary for a stable society are found in the writings of classical philosophy. In all classical political thought is a concern with the good state, justice, and the improvement of the citizenry. Modern political thought, by contrast, is mainly interested in the accumulation and exercise of power.

The roots of conservative thought follow both Roman Catholicism, with its unifying thread of church tradition and classical values, and Protestantism, with its emphasis upon the importance of biblical authority. Conservative scholars like Frances Wilson, Russell Kirk, Frank Meyer, and Willmoore Kendall were all Roman Catholics. In recent decades, the Catholic Church's hierarchy in the United States has found itself at odds with more traditional authorities in Rome and their followers in the United States. The ink was hardly dry on the American Roman Catholic Bishop's statement on the economy before conservative American Catholics rebutted it. Conservative Catholic orders of priests and nuns have been able to attract the young more than the liberal orders. The liberal Jesuits, for example, have suffered enormous losses from their ranks, while the conservative Opus Dei and Legionnaires of Christ have enjoyed extraordinary growth.

In Protestantism, reaction has also been at work. In all major denominations conservatives have responded to the dominant liberal theology by forging a counter-revolution to reestablish traditional practices. Mainline Protestant churches that emphasize material and social issues, ordain women to the priesthood and the pastorate, and no longer hold the Bible as the authoritative Word of God, have seen their memberships dwindle. *Time* magazine reports that "a preoccupation with political and social issues at the expense of good old-fashioned faith has alienated many [mainline] members."[27] The fastest growing churches in recent years have been those offering certainty of doctrine and practice. Such congregations are less likely to address economic, political, and social issues except when they feel forced to react to liberal positions on homosexuality, the role of women in society, the prohibition of school prayer, and other innovations that they believe undermine the historically accepted customs and practices of the faith.

Kierkegaard wrote, "Everything that passes for politics today will be unmasked as religion tomorrow."[28] If the saying is accurate it may portend an alliance between Protestants and Catholics in the future. Conservative Catholics and Protestants alike decry the decadence of society, the deterioration of the public schools, the loss of respect for authority, and the dependence upon government rather than personal initiative. They see these trends as the logical and awful fulfillment of the self-centered pride flowing from the movements of the Renaissance and the Enlightenment and the confidence in the modern political utopias. Such viewpoints spawned conservative Catholic groups like the Eagle Forum, and conservative Protestant groups like Concerned Women of America.

Both conservative Catholics and conservative Protestants are reacting to changes that threaten values which they believe important. In most instances, they are reacting to the same things in the political realm. Abortion, for instance, has resulted in limited efforts by conservative Catholics and Protestants to join together in opposition to threatening moral changes. However, lingering differences about ultimate authority make their cooperation effective only on specific issues.

Reaction is the foundation of modern conservatism. Neoconservatism is the most recent manifestation of a movement which reappraises American culture after finding fault with the social experiments of the 1960s. Typically, conservative movements begin in reaction to hostile movements, ideas, and events. The fires of its contemporary resurgence are fueled by threats to the accepted customs and traditions of a society posed by past flirtations with experimentation.

Notes

1. Jay A. Sigler (ed.), *The Conservative Tradition in American Thought* (New York: G. P. Putnam's Sons, 1969), p. 2.

2. Leo Strauss, *What Is Political Philosophy?* (Chicago: University of Chicago Press, 1959), p. 10.

3. George H. Sabine and Thomas L. Thorson, *A History of Political Theory* (4th ed.; Hinsdale, Ill.: Dryden Press, 1973), p. 40.

4. Leo Strauss, *What Is Political Philosophy?*, p. 89.

5. George H. Sabine and Thomas L. Thorson, *A History of Political Theory*, p. 54.

6. Roland H. Bainton, *The Reformation of the Sixteenth Century* (Boston: Beacon Press, 1952), p. 231.

7. Roland H. Bainton, *The Reformation of the Sixteenth Century*, p. 16.

8. Frederick Hartt, *Art: A History of Painting, Sculpture, Architecture* (New York: Prentice-Hall, 1976), pp. 117–118.

9. Frederick Hartt, *Art: A History of Painting, Sculpture, Architecture*, p. 125.

10. William Ebenstein, *Great Political Thinkers* (4th ed.; New York: Holt, Rinehart and Winston, 1969), p. 287.

11. William Ebenstein, *Great Political Thinkers*, p. 304.

12. Norman Hampson, *The Enlightenment* (New York: Penguin Books, 1981), p. 16.

13. Owen Chadwick, *The Reformation* (New York: Penguin Books, 1964), p. 46.

14. Jacob Bronowski and Bruce Mazlish, *The Western Intellectual Tradition* (New York: Harper & Row, 1960), p. 82.

15. Owen Chadwick, *The Reformation*, p. 267.

16. Russell Kirk, *The Conservative Mind* (7th ed.; Chicago: Regnery Books, 1986), pp. 246–247.

17. Francis A. Schaeffer, *How Should We Then Live?* (Old Tappan, N.J.: Fleming H. Revell, 1976), p. 84.

18. Francis A. Schaeffer, *How Should We Then Live?*, p. 87.

19. Paul Hazard, *European Thought in the 18th Century* (Cleveland, Ohio: World Publishers, 1963), p. xvii.

20. Irving Kristol, *Reflections of a Neoconservative* (New York: Basic Books, 1983), pp. 139–176.

21. Simon Schama, *Citizens: A Chronicle of the French Revolution* (New York: Knopf, 1989), pp. 770–771, 776–781.

22. Irving Kristol, *Reflections on a Neoconservative*, p. 151.

23. George H. Sabine and Thomas L. Thorson, *A History of Political Theory*, p. 545.

24. Simon Schama, *Citizens*, pp. 860–861.

25. William Ebenstein, *Great Political Thinkers*, p. 498.

26. Leslie Lipson, *The Great Issues of Politics* (6th ed.; Englewood Cliffs, N.J.: Prentice-Hall, 1981), pp. 201–202.

27. *Time*, "Those Mainline Blues," May 22, 1989, pp. 94–95.

28. Cited in Irving Kristol, *Reflections of a Neoconservative*, p. vi.

CHAPTER FIVE

The Historical Development of American Conservatism

The future, as always, is veiled from our vision. But for the moment the conservative intellectual movement in America, born in the wilderness a generation ago, has undeniably achieved an unprecedented level of influence and importance . . . to understand this intellectual movement and its aspirations, one must understand history.

GEORGE H. NASH[1]

"The United States," writes Seymour Martin Lipset, "may properly claim the title of the first new nation." This designation means that it was the first country to successfully develop an industrial economy with an integrated social structure and a stable democratic polity without disintegrating in the process.[2] But the nation did not spring from virgin soil without a value system rooted in years of toil and experience. There is a type of spiritual history, what Eric Voegelin calls "paradigmatic" history, which traces the intellectual and cultural development of a nation.[3] Every person loves something, and these attachments structure existence in some way. To understand America is first to comprehend the values which guided the formation of its institutions in the early republic. Conservatives focus on a set of values which defined the "good life" in America at the time of its founding. The American economy owed its success to hard, continuous work, frugality, self-disciplined living, and individual initiative. Such values came from across the Atlantic, from notions of individual honesty that grew out of the Reformation and would later be known as the Protestant work ethic. More immediately, the political system owed its genesis to the English Revolution of 1640 and the subsequent transfer of power to Parliament institutionalized by the Glorious Revolution of 1688. In England, parliamentary democracy replaced royal absolutism, commercial and industrial wealth replaced land as the base of economic influence, and the middle class stamped society with its outlook and morality where once the aristocracy had ruled. The pattern of a peaceful, restructured society was set a hundred years before the American Revolution.

The absence of a monarchy and an aristocracy made the American belief in equality and opportunity crucial. The revolutionary leaders in America quickly turned the experiment into a stable order. Such was not the case in France, whose revolution began two years after the Constitution of the United States was framed. The Jacobin ideas of liberty, fraternity, and equality were completely at odds with the limited revolutionary notions in England and the United States.

Edmund Burke wrote that while there were structural reasons for the French Revolution, such injustices could never justify the complete dismemberment of society. It was custom, tradition, and membership in society, far more than reason, that gave quality to human nature. Burke wrote that the deep-seated historical forces at work in France were less important in explaining the excesses of the Revolution than the false doctrines of philosophers captivated by an Enlightenment optimism and a fanatical atheism. Although designated as the founder of American conservatism, Edmund Burke's title is somewhat misleading. The French Revolution was the foil of other prominent writers who surfaced simultaneously with Burke.[4] While their ideas differed in some ways, such widespread and similar responses give evidence that basic conservative ideas and values were in evidence before Burke so skillfully articulated and defended them. Burke spoke out forcefully against the collapse of the moral and social order in France, and identified the principles causing the societal breakdown: (1) faith in a priori change and human reason, and (2) a lack of respect for traditional values and property rights.

Unlike the limited American Revolution, the French experience was a destructive and chaotic break between past and present. Custom, history and tradition were eclipsed in France, where they had been exalted in America. The American Revolution was a limited one, aimed at allowing Americans the benefits derived from the experiences of the English. The Constitution was seen as an extension of the ideas of the Magna Carta and the English Bill of Rights. The policies of King George were criticized because they stood in the path of this legacy which was reserved for free men.

The development of the "Rights of Englishmen" from the Magna Carta, the Petition of Rights, and the Bill of Rights were sacred to the American colonists. Much of the colonial resistance took the form of arguing that these rights of fundamental law, which were largely due process rights, were being denied to them as colonists. The ordering documents of the colonies—for example, the Massachusetts Body of Liberties—reflected a concern to establish these rights. The popularity of Coke's *Institutes* and later Blackstone's *Commentaries* was a manifestation of concern that these due process rights be preserved. All this made the American Revolution quite tame; it was a conservative (even reactionary) revolution.

In this chapter, the evolution of American conservatism is traced from the founding ideas of Edmund Burke to the recent prescriptions of Ronald Reagan and George Bush. American conservatism has passed through three distinct periods in the past two hundred years. These are, first, from colonial times to the Civil War; second, from the Civil War to the New Deal; and third, from the New Deal to the present. The theme which unites all these periods is best articulated by George H. Nash, author of the landmark work on the conservative intellectual movement since World War II:

> If there is a single philosophical premise that distinguishes recent American conservatism, it is the conviction that "ideas have consequences." We live in a decade in which, for the first time in generations, the ideas of self-identified conservatives seem ascendant—an era in which the arguments of "academic scribblers" of the Right are being translated, however imperfectly, into public policy.[5]

For conservatives, form precedes content—ideas are the determinants of culture. To understand a nation is to ask questions about its standards and values. Our purpose here is not to argue whether America is conservative or liberal in its heritage, but rather to describe and analyze the flow of American conservative thought during its life as a nation.

The Early Era: Colonial Times to the Civil War

This era is broken down into a discussion of several themes and time periods. We identify the intellectual personalities and varieties of conservative thought in the periods of (1) the colonial and founding period; (2) the Federalists versus Republicans period; and (3) the pre-Civil War period, including the writings of John Randolph and John Calhoun. Conservative thinkers will be discussed individually and in the context of historical thought.

The Colonial and Founding Period

At the time of the American Revolution about three-quarters of the North American colonists were of Puritan extraction.[6] Puritans might have attended a Congregationalist, Presbyterian, Anabaptist, or even Anglican church, but what united them all was the belief that the official church of England was not a true Christian church and needed cleansing from its elaborate ceremonies and forms. Clinton Rossiter, in *Conservatism in America*, describes this sense of shared values among the colonists as a common belief in "original sin" and an obligation to law and duty. Such was the assembly of "visible saints" who gathered in John Winthrop's "Shining City" of Massachusetts to deliberate matters of state. Winthrop described them in his journal as a people who "in all differences and agitations . . . continued in brotherly love."[7]

Puritanism was the dominant political and intellectual force in the new nation through the seventeenth and eighteenth centuries. John Winthrop, John Davenport, John Cotton, Nathaniel Ward, John Eliot, William Stoughton, Samuel Willard, and all the Mathers stamped the nation with a set of conservative values which emphasized respect for the established order, leadership by the favored few, the importance of community, and a preference for gradual change.[8] The Puritans also gave the nation institutions like a written constitution, regular elections, and the secret ballot, and principles like the work ethic, the federalist principle, and the separation of church and state. In sum, the national institutions and values were influenced by Calvinism more than Deism, by the Reformation more than the Enlightenment, and by the revolution in England more than the revolution in France.

The Puritans traced their roots not to England, but to Moses. Old Testament Israel was the source of inspiration for the "New Jerusalem" in Massachusetts. Russell Kirk writes that in such a heritage, the Christian faith is the principle of modern civilization: its theological and moral doctrines inform us "of the nature of God and man . . . , human dignity and the rights and duties of human persons."[9] Although in colonial times there were no arguments over the benefits of capitalism as opposed to socialism, or the importance of a strong national defense, or any clear expression of what would later be called a conservative philosophy, the influence of the Bible was everywhere apparent. Conservative values about the nature of man and the limits of government characterized political debate in the colonies from the time of their settlement to the American Revolution.

The founding of the American republic presents a rare opportunity to observe the authors of a constitution grappling with the fundamental problems of forming a new government. Their activity took place after a "reluctant revolution," to use the words of Irving Kristol, which protected the social institutions of society. Unlike the French Revolution, the leaders of the American Revolution lived out their lives in peace after it was over.[10] Peter Viereck says the American Revolution "reflected England's heritage of 1688," noting that Edmund Burke "favored their revolution as defending the traditional rights of freeborn Englishmen against new-fangled royal usurpations."[11]

The victory of conservative principles in forming the government is borne out by the fashionable criticisms the framers of the Constitution have received from revisionist historians. Charles A. Beard called the framers "hardfisted conservatives" who attempted to "hamstring the masses."[11] Others criticized them for having an "eighteenth century" view of man as depraved, and for trying to frustrate the will of the majority. Clearly, the Founders created a constitutional democracy dominated by "republican tendencies." A full-fledged democracy would have relied on majority votes, given stronger power to the national government to act on behalf of all the people, and provided for a unified executive to speak on behalf of the nation. But the resulting constitutional republic established a limited government, restrained by the elements of checks and balances among the branches of the national government, a division of power between the national and state authorities, and a requirement of extraordinary majorities to amend the Constitution or to override a veto. The result was a system which restrained action, allowing for gradual change.

The work of the Founders is in large measure due to what Russell G. Fryer calls the "consensual character of the ideological legacy of the Revolutionary Constitutional period." Fryer finds three distinctive tra-

ditions in the political thought and history of the time which contributed to this underlying value consensus. These were the ideas of "natural
law, natural rights and limited government," which "united the Founders on the key issues of popular sovereignty and the virtues of limited
government."[13] In large part, these ideas were contained in the common
law tradition in evidence in virtually every colonial ordering document.

The men themselves shared common values; they "were men of the
English and Scottish Enlightenment, not the French . . . [who] were
closer to Hobbes than Rousseau." The Founders were well-educated
men for their time whose "discourse was history . . . with no more than
five exceptions (and perhaps no more than three) they were orthodox
members of one of the established Christian communions."[14] In sum,
the delegates to the Constitutional Convention had substantial political
experience as well as business and property holdings, and they were
determined to draft a document which reflected the English common
law tradition of limited government with a protection for individuals.
The real constitution in America was not the paper document, but the
whole constellation of customs and traditions that had formed in the two
centuries of the colonial settlement and revolutionary experience.

Three personalities, John Dickinson, James Madison, and John Taylor,
are exemplary of conservative attitudes during the founding period. John
Dickinson (1732–1808), a Philadelphia lawyer who participated in most
of the important events of the time, wrote *Letters From a Farmer in Pennsylvania*. In his treatise, Dickinson said, "Experience must be our only
guide . . . reason may mislead us." His conservative views held that the
objective of government must be to free men so that they can choose
their own ends, rather than allowing government to select ends for the
populace.[15] James Madison (1751–1836) is often placed outside the conservative tradition by writers. But Madison's conservative instincts are
best illustrated in his strong preference for the separation and balancing
of powers. He is the author of a renowned statement on the subject: "In
framing a government which is to be administered by men over men,
the great difficulty lies in this: you must first enable the government to
control the governed; and in the next place oblige it to control itself."[16]
Madison's acceptance of the Bill of Rights was born out of the necessity
to compromise with the Anti-Federalists, not out of a conscious desire
to plant the doctrine of "natural rights" in the document. John Taylor
of Carolina (1753–1824) was a fierce Anti-Federalist who typified the

conservative southern planter. Taylor viewed the Constitution as an instrument to protect state power from domination by a central government. Ideas of hierarchy, community, custom, and religion pervade Taylor's writing. Taylor believed that administration of law, not the imposition of an abstract vision of social justice, is the chief obligation of government.[17]

The Federalists versus Republicans Period

The initial controversy under the Constitution resulted in the formation of the first American political parties. Thomas Jefferson and James Madison formed the Democratic-Republicans in the 1790s to oppose Alexander Hamilton and John Adams, whose party was known as the Federalists. The quarrel between these parties encompassed a great variety of issues, but it began with opposition to the financial policies developed by Hamilton and heated reactions to the events surrounding the French Revolution. The conservative-liberal debate is characterized by Russell Kirk: "The Republicans, Jefferson and Madison chief among them . . . came to sympathize with French equalitarian theories. Their opponents, the Federalists, appealed to the lessons of history, the legacy of British liberties, and the guarantees of prescriptive constitutions."[18]

The conservative ideas came to be identified with the Federalist Party. John Adams (1735–1826), the nation's second president and author of *Defense of Constitutions,* was the most significant of the Federalists. Russell Kirk identifies Adams as the "founder of true conservatism in America."[19] Ronald Lora qualifies the Adams legacy by saying that Adams only agreed with Edmund Burke on two issues—the importance of property and human inequality. Adams was not as firm a supporter of aristocracy as Burke; he favored a conventional balance between aristocracy and democracy. But in his stands on property, constitutions, and the dangers of the French Revolution, Adams was a true conservative.

Alexander Hamilton (1757–1804) was a contemporary of Adams and an activist in the Federalist Party. Hamilton's views on religion and order are strikingly similar to those of Burke. Hamilton declared: "The attempt by the rulers of a nation to destroy all religious opinion, and to pervert a whole nation to atheism, is a phenomenon of profligacy reserved to consummate the infamy of the unprincipled reformers of France." He tied this disregard for religion to the breakdown of French family ties and all order in that country, manifested in easy divorce, children testifying against their parents, and the frequent prescription of murder.[20]

Hamiltonian conservatism deserves special attention, however, in that it differs in several key ways from traditional conservatism (i.e., that which was expressed by Burke and conforms to the basic views already discussed). Hamilton announced at a New York Convention in 1788, "But there is another object, equally important (as liberty), and which our enthusiasm rendered us (at the formation of our 'confederation') little capable of regarding . . . I mean a principle of strength and stability in the organization of our government, and of vigor in its operation."[21] He was, of course, referring to a strong presidency (actually a monarchy) and a strong central government. Hamilton's economic ideas were also very different from traditional conservative beliefs in that he wanted strong government direction of the economy. Kirk calls Hamilton's economic ideas those of mercantilism, a tenet of which was revealed in this statement by the first Secretary of the Treasury in the new United States, "to preserve the balance of trade in favor of a nation ought to be a leading aim of its policy."[22]

Why did Hamilton have such different views on the power of the state and economic policy? While he held to many traditional conservative beliefs, such as a desire for slow, organic change, the importance of religion in social life, and a distrust of man's abilities to plan, his reasoning branched off in a different direction from traditional conservatism. Kirk's analysis of Hamilton is that "he believed that salvation from the consequence of leveling ideas lay in establishing invincible national authority. . . . [It] seems hardly to have occurred to Hamilton's mind that a consolidated nation might also be a leveling nation, though he had the example of Jacobin France before him; and he does not appear to have reflected upon the possibility that force in government may be applied to other purposes than the maintenance of a conservative order."[23]

Hamilton's brand of conservatism may be properly labeled authoritarian conservatism. While the origin of authoritarian conservatism is generally traced to Joseph de Maistre (1753–1821), authoritarian thought existed before Maistre much as traditional conservative beliefs existed before Burke. It was Maistre, however, who expressed authoritarian conservatism most clearly in response to the ideas of the Enlightenment

and the French Revolution. Maistre favored a strong central government so firmly that he even declared the public executioner the very
cornerstone of proper governmental power over the people: "All gran-
deur, all power, subordination rests on the executioner; he is the horror
and the bond of human association."[24] Peter Viereck describes the authoritarian conservative as a "reactionary 'Ottantotist,' " referring to one
who wants to go backward to better days in the past. Viereck considers
authoritarian conservatives extreme in their emphasis upon authority as
contrasted with the traditional or Burkean conservatives' emphasis upon
liberties.[25] The primacy of political authority and the desire to move
backward in time are at the heart of the difference between authoritarian
and traditional conservatism.

These differences are apparent when the conservatism of Hamilton is
contrasted with that of Adams. Adams wanted to protect against "tyranny," whatever its cause, whether from monarch or democracy (the
majority infringing upon minority rights).[26] Hamilton, by contrast, did
not trust the people and desired a limited monarchy, a titled aristocracy,
and government direction of the economy. He wanted to go back to the
central authority of England. Fisher Ames, another Federalist leader,
went so far in his indictment of democracy to say, "Our disease is democracy. It is not the skin that festers—our very bones are carrions, and
their marrow blackens with gangrene. What rogues shall be first, is of
no moment—our republicanism must die and I'm sorry for it."[27]

Ames believed that the "democracy" of the French Revolution was
an ideological threat to the ordered liberty in the United States. He
believed that only an aristocracy of talent could sustain the ideals set
forth in the Constitution. Though not well known today as a conservative leader, Fisher Ames was the leader of the Federalists in the first four
sessions of Congress and was instrumental in shaping the language of the
First Amendment. His writings resonate with great feeling about the
principles of conservatism.[28]

The Pre-Civil War Period

The election of Andrew Jackson to the presidency in 1828 marked
the first major decline in conservative influence in American politics.
While the previous contests between Federalists and Republicans witnessed the election of men with liberal views, such as Thomas Jefferson,

the period was marked by a consensus on basic ideas. Jefferson himself saw the danger in "frequent and untried change," and believed in the importance of a natural aristocracy aware of the bad side of human nature.[29] Jacksonian democracy, by contrast, came to symbolize the growing sway of social and political equality in the United States. Jackson was from Tennessee (all previous presidents of the United States had been from Virginia or Massachusetts), and brought with him all the passions and impulses of frontier individualism. Gone were the aristocratic habits and traditions of the east; in their place were those of planters, farmers, mechanics, and laborers.

This change of emphasis was not merely due to Jackson. His predecessor, John Quincy Adams, whose conservative credentials were impeccable, had come to believe that man could be improved by the workings of democracy. Jackson's party built victory from the bottom up rather than, as during the nation's founding period, from the top down. Jackson vetoed acts of Congress and declared himself a "Tribune of the People" whose responsibilities were superior to those of Congress.[30] The popular mood undermined conservative values of elite rule and traditional values.

Still, there were important conservative thinkers during this decline of conservative thought. John Randolph (1773–1833) was one of the more important voices opposing the new egalitarianism. He thought Jackson's election meant that "the country is ruined past redemption . . . it is ruined in the spirit and character of the people."[31] While Randolph's words sound antidemocratic in retrospect, it was tyranny and government "innovation" which he feared more than the policies of the new administration.[32] In a speech to the Virginia Constitutional Convention (1829–1830), Randolph spoke out against this tyranny, which he called "King Numbers." He felt that the Virginia Constitution did not need to be changed, particularly in the direction of expanding the electorate and majority rule. He stated that were he a young man who would have to live under the Constitution for a long time, he "would not live under King Numbers."[33]

In his same speech at the Virginia Constitutional Convention, Randolph spoke out against governmental social programs. His argument was that such programs benefited their administrators more than the poor, and he said that he had several friends who had "amassed opulent fortunes: as administrators." Randolph spoke out against the prevailing idea that "all things must be done for them [the people] by the govern-ment."[34] The need for Randolph to take such stands against majoritarian power and increased government shows the clear decline of conservative influence in government.

It is fashionable among historians to indict John C. Calhoun (1782–1851) and his "doctrine of nullification" (which held that states could ignore or nullify an act of the central government) as a contributing factor to the breakdown of order before the Civil War. But Calhoun knew that true nationalism sprang from a love of one's own region. Calhoun wanted to preserve the southern heritage, but he feared the expansion of central government as a threat to all areas of the nation. Both Peter Viereck and Russell Kirk attribute great importance to Cal-houn in the development of American conservatism.[35]

Calhoun stood firmly in favor of checks on majorities and the idea of "concurrent majorities," as set up by the Constitution, to protect against the majoritarian tyranny that Randolph, Adams, and others had feared. He recognized the fallacy that rule by simple majority was rule by the people, and believed that the important question was how to "vest the powers of the Government in the whole—the entire people—to make it in truth and reality the Government of the people instead of Govern-ment of a dominant over a subject part." His own answer was that this could be accomplished "by judicious and wise division and organization of the Government and community . . . and the concurrence of all as the voice of the whole."[36] Calhoun stood for the republican restraints of the Constitution upon democracy as established by the Founders at a time when majority rule enjoyed strong support. He saw that tyranny of the majority could be just as iniquitous as tyranny of the minority.

The Civil War created a discrepancy apparent to Calhoun and other thinkers already discussed. Southern society was a stronghold of the con-servative values of the importance of family and community, distrust of rapid change, and the importance of religious beliefs. Yet the South disrupted the national order by removing itself from the national gov-ernment's authority in order to support the institution of slavery. This discrepancy causes some confusion about the conservative versus liberal leadership of that era. Although President Abraham Lincoln expanded presidential power (generally considered a liberal act), such an expansion was used to preserve the Union, an objective consistent with conservative traditions. Once a stronger national power was in place, the nature of the Union was permanently changed.

Conservative Literature and Jurists

Some of the major conservative thinkers of this era were writers, rather than politicians or political philosophers. Orestes Brownson (1803–1876) personally symbolized the paradox of the Civil War. He supported the Union, but preferred southern society to the "gospel of material success" and "radical notions of human progress" prevalent in the North. He identified the Civil War as a struggle between "just authority and anarchic impulses," not a battle of "democratic ideologues" against a "conservative society."[37]

Brownson's religious past included association with Congregationalism, Presbyterianism, Universalism, socialism, atheism, and Unitarianism, and culminated in Roman Catholicism. The logic of his seemingly convoluted path was a desire to locate religious authority with absolutes that required obedience. For Brownson, the belief in such absolutes was the foundation for a stable society. Should the nation obey the moral authority of the Roman Catholic Church, he believed, it would be free to pursue the common good rather than be divided by the fickleness of public opinion and the caprice of individual judgment. Brownson became not only the leading cultural defender of Roman Catholicism in America during the 1800s, he also foreshadowed what would happen in the 1900s. Many prominent American conservatives since 1945 have been Roman Catholics or converts to Roman Catholicism. They have in common the conservative emphasis on religious order and social stability.

Nathaniel Hawthorne (1804–1864) shared Brownson's skepticism about the claims of progress. According to Russell Kirk, Hawthorne "dwells almost wholly upon sin, its reality, nature, and consequences; the contemplation of sin is his obsession, his vocation, almost his life. Here he becomes a major preceptor of conservatives." Hawthorne distrusted man's nature and believed in the importance of traditional values. He stood out against the transcendentalist view of the essential goodness of man, and he looked with affection on the past, with its conserving and molding forces. To Kirk, Hawthorne's writings develop a close relationship between the spiritual and the material:

Whenever man tries to ignore sin . . . progress material and spiritual collapses, and the reality of evil is impressed upon men's minds by terror and suffering. Only one species of reform really is worth attempting: reform of conscience.[38]

James Fenimore Cooper (1789–1851) was another writer who championed the freedom and dignity of democracy while at the same time warning that abstract ideals of equality and liberty were not attainable. In *The American Democrat,* Cooper emphasizes the guiding role culture and continuity play in society, and the corresponding weaknesses of public opinion as a means to control government excesses. Property rights, another conservative tenet, were very important to Cooper. He believed that a democracy could only flourish if its leaders were gentlemen; such designations were defined not primarily by wealth but by public spiritedness and prudence.

The two leading jurists of the era, James Kent (1763–1847) and Joseph Story (1779–1845), were conservatives whose influence extended through a generation of lawyers. Kent strongly defended such conservative legal tenets as common law, with its emphasis on precedents:

The reports of judicial decisions contain the most certain evidence, and the most authoritative and precise application of the rules of common law. . . . The evils resulting from an indigestible heap of laws, and legal authorities, are great and manifest. They destroy the certainty of the law, and promote litigation, delay and subtilty. . . . It would therefore be extremely inconvenient to the public, if precedents were not duly regarded and pretty implicitly followed. It is by the notoriety and stability of such rules, that professional men can give safe advice to those who consult them.[39]

Also holding strongly to the common law tradition was Justice Joseph Story, an Associate Justice of the Supreme Court from 1811 to 1845. Story wrote the textbook of the day for America's legal profession, *Commentaries on the Constitution.* Common law, to Story, "comprehends natural theology, moral philosophy, and political philosophy . . . man's duties to God, to himself, to other men, and as a member of political society." Story rejected John Locke's theory of natural rights, a principal basis for claims by liberals for changes in the law.[40]

Conclusion: Colonial Times to the Civil War

It is clear from this discussion of early American conservatism that there are different types of conservatism. Religious conservatism was especially prevalent in the colonial period among the Puritans. Political conservatism made important contributions to the Constitutional Convention and was in evidence in the general culture. Authoritarian conservatism manifested itself in the ideas of Alexander Hamilton, while social conservatism was characteristic of the American South. Of course, the traditional conservatism of Edmund Burke contained the tenets of religious, political and social conservatism in evidence elsewhere.

The line of demarcation between conservatism and liberal thought is not always clear. For example, Thomas Jefferson held to some important conservative tenets even though he is considered a founder of liberal American thought. Similarly, James Madison has been labeled as a liberal, but careful analysis of his views reflects a significant strain of thought consistent with political conservatism, especially as it relates to ideas of republican government which restrict rapid change. Likewise, differences among conservatives are sometimes unclear. John Adams is considered the direct heir to Burkean conservatism, although, with respect to the importance of the aristocracy, Adams was in disagreement with Burke. Alexander Hamilton's authoritarian conservatism included a solid foundation in traditional conservatism's religious, political and social values. The conservative position on the Civil War was divided between southern conservatives who supported the South and northern conservatives who saw the responsibility of preserving the Union.

It is clear from this discussion that conservatism is more than political writings or stands on issues of public policy. The constellation of culture involves all the ideas, habits, values, prejudices and institutions which make up a society. The ideas of conservatism pervade much of literature. Works by Hawthorne, Cooper, Brownson, and many others emphasized the values of community, the legacy of the past and the individual's circumstances before God as important determinants of life. Conservatism had a significant impact on American law through the influence of conservative jurists like Kent and Story. In their view, law had a religious and moral foundation which should conform to the heritage of custom and tradition embodied in common law. Christian religious values are central to the definition of conservatism. Roman Catholic converts have been prominent among spokesmen for the movement as have conservative Protestants who stand in the tradition of the Puritans. Southern conservatism found expression in the writings of Taylor, Randolph and Calhoun.

Conservatism suffered a reversal during the Jacksonian era as the importance of public opinion, an expanded electorate, and social equality grew. The decline in traditional attitudes was so severe that some conservatives lamented the very passing of conservatism as a belief system. At the end of the Civil War, southern conservatives believed their conservative crusade for state and community rights was at an end.

The Middle Era: The Civil War to the New Deal

The Civil War left a searing scar on the political system. Those who supported the Union became, for generations, Republicans; those who supported the Confederacy, or who had opposed the war, became Democrats. Conservatives in both parties came to see the constant growth of the central government as a threat to the whole society. Millions of Europeans emigrated to the United States between 1880 and World War I, bringing with them different ideas such as Darwinism and Marxism, and a variety of religious and political convictions. Catholics from Poland, Italy, and Ireland, and Jews from Russia and Eastern Europe sought a new start on American shores. Their differing religious and social values were not easily accepted by established groups in American society.

Liberalism, as a doctrine emphasizing the full development of the individual free from the restraints of government, religion, and social conventions, became a dominant force for action during these decades. The labor movement, advocates of the "Social Gospel," muckrakers, and progressive intellectuals all campaigned for social restructuring during this time. Mainline Protestant denominations, colleges, universities, and seminaries began to turn to the liberal theologies popular in Europe, while politically liberal presidents like Theodore Roosevelt and Woodrow Wilson made a major impact on American government and society.[41]

With change came an expansion in government power; this prompted a strong reaction in the writings of various conservatives. Russell Kirk said that he saw during this era "how easily an abstraction like capitalism might succumb to another abstraction called Communism."[42] The conservative temper of the times was one of reaction against the tide of alien ideas which threatened American institutions. After 1900, opposition to socialism became a benchmark belief among conservatives. Conservatives do not like the abstract political and social philosophies of either the left or the right. In this section we examine the thinkers who stood against the support for expanded government. These writers are classified as follows: (1) critics of democracy; (2) New Humanists; (3) critics of progress; (4) Libertarians; and (5) miscellaneous critics.

Critics of Democracy

Both Henry Adams (1838–1918) and Brooks Adams (1848–1927) saw a danger in placing too much faith in the judgment of the common man. In this belief they echoed their ancestor, John Quincy Adams, whose suspicions of democracy were fueled by the admission of new states on the frontier. Henry Adams wrote in *The Degradation of the Democratic Dogma* (1920) that "at this particular juncture of human affairs the tendency is very strong throughout the world to deify the democratic dogma, and to look to democracy to accomplish pretty promptly some approach to a millennium among men."[43] His book *Democracy* (1908) is described by Russell Kirk as showing a "contempt for democratic corruption."[44]

Brooks Adams's sense of fear of the overconfidence in democracy came from his conservative view of man. He stated that the country was in a "social war" because it "tried to ignore certain fundamental facts which are stronger than democratic theories." The nation should not expect too much from democracy because "the strongest of human passions are fear and greed."[45] Some conservatives have discounted the Adams brothers because they grew virtually reactionary in their pessimism about the world, in contrast to the guarded optimism and joy of accomplishment which characterizes traditional conservatism. Ronald Lora writes that Brooks Adams eventually came to believe the world was in complete chaos, while Henry Adams, based on his work of applying scientific ideas to philosophy, concluded that the world would end in inertia due to the Second Law of Thermodynamics.[46]

The increased confidence in democracy and in expanding the role of government (possibly leading to socialism) was also the concern of E. L.

Godkin (1831–1902). Godkin was the editor of *The Nation,* which is one of today's most liberal magazines but at that time was a fountainhead of conservative capitalistic notions. Godkin believed that the basic problem of socialism was its failure to consider costs. Improvements in society were laudable, but the question was who would pay for them. He compared socialism to a man who decides to move from his "small flat to a house on Fifth Avenue, for the good of the family; but, he had received no raise in his income."[47] Godkin was uneasy about the degradation of democracy and condemned "yellow journalism," which he believed fueled the flames of mass sentiment and undermined considered judgment.

The New Humanists

Two very important conservative writers of the middle era were Irving Babbitt (1865–1933) and Paul Elmer More (1867–1937). They called their beliefs "humanist," but it was not the humanism of liberalism and the *Humanist Manifesto,* which both vigorously opposed. As Babbitt describes it, "The humanist exercises the will to refrain, but the end he has in view is not the renunciation of the expansive desires but the subduing of them to the law of measure." He saw humanist belief as a third possible attitude toward life between a "pure traditionalist" religious view and that of a "mere modernist" like Rousseau. While Babbitt praised the virtues of religion, he saw humanist virtues as similar but "more accessible" than those of "the saint."[48] Babbitt's idea of humanism was not to deny the claims of religion in its own sphere; what he disputed was the necessity of deriving the norms of justice solely from revelation.[49]

Babbitt's beliefs were those of the traditional conservative in almost every area. He blamed Rousseau for the myth that man is good, a myth which conservatives agree has had serious consequences in the modern world. Babbitt also associated Rousseau with the utilitarian "glorification of man's increasing control over the forces of nature under the name of progress."[50] He praised Edmund Burke's "realism" and "humility" (in submission to God), as opposed to Rousseau's nominalism and pride.[51] He also emphasized the importance of duties that come with rights, as opposed to natural rights.[52]

Perhaps Irving Babbitt's greatest interest was in the area of education.

He said the educational system was heavily influenced by Rousseau, whose book *Emile* argues for the natural development of a child without societal barriers. As a result, the educational system viewed anything that set "bounds" as "prejudiced." Babbitt argued that what was needed was more, not less, discipline in schooling. He urged a "classical education" to teach people to live by standards, and he praised the order of classicism as opposed to romanticism.[53] Though a scholar and a Harvard professor, Babbitt scorned the ivory tower and the intellectual treason of professors who were lured by the muses of ideology away from the precincts of reality.[54]

Paul Elmer More, like Irving Babbitt, was an advocate of "classical education."[55] More had a conservative view of man and warned of those who would change the institutions of government to "adapt them to the nature of man as he should be" and "relax the rigor of the law, in pity for the degree of injustice inherent in earthly life."[56] He stood against the mood of economic equality of the time. In an essay dealing with the United Mine Workers' strike against John D. Rockefeller, he was angered that while the rights of the mine workers were voiced by journalists everywhere, Rockefeller's personal rights and property rights were voiced by no one.[57] More feared the results of insecure property, and said that it was "safer . . . to err on the side of natural inequality than on the side of ideal justice."[58]

In the eyes of Francis G. Wilson and Russell Kirk, More should be considered "the greatest of our intellectual conservatives" and the "greatest of American Critics." More's humanism gradually evolved until he converted to Christianity and became an orthodox Anglican. As an editor, an historian and a literary critic, he argued democracy, to be successful, had to be leavened with aristocracy; that private property is essential to national stability; and that our understanding of God and man depends upon our knowledge of the Incarnation.[59]

Critics of Progress

The Progressive Movement began in America during the 1890s and continued until World War I. Most historians agree that it was a movement of the urban middle-class to curb the worst excesses of industrialism, achieve humanitarian reforms, and democratize politics. But not everyone agreed with the critique of American society in evidence among the progressives. George Santayana (1863–1952) said that the "ideal liberal" would say progress is "continued change for the better" in "whatever direction" a man wants to go. He notes, however, that the liberal would be displeased if people did not go toward "vast numbers, material complexity, moral uniformity, and economic interdependence" and he himself tried to turn them in that direction.[60] Santayana contended that the liberal becomes the reformer who believes he knows what is best and right and allows no other authority to challenge him. The paradox of contemporary liberalism, as foreseen by Santayana, is that it professes a faith in a "Will" which cannot allow any other source of authority, but at the same time denies the legitimacy of traditional institutions and beliefs in society. That is, the liberal is content with pluralism so long as it does not challenge what he believes is best and right. In the liberal scheme, the institutions of society are usually the culprits inhibiting the just society.

Santayana, a Harvard University professor of philosophy, said that a knowledge of the past, the arts, and human limitations were essential to produce proper individualism. The individualism of mass society, he argued, is a false individualism based only upon economic incentives. Despite Santayana's critique of liberalism, he stood against many traditional values associated with conservatism. He criticized conservatives for "quashing free love" under limits of "vows" or "age" or "sex." He was also an atheist in religious belief.[61]

The Progressive Movement was urban and middle-class; the traditions and values of rural and small-town America were scorned as backward and antidemocratic. In the middle of all this "progress" a number of southerners vigorously defended their region. These included the self-styled "Agrarians," among them Allen Tate, Robert Penn Warren, and John Crowe Ransom. The Agrarians, several of whom taught at Vanderbilt University, denounced the corrosive effects of technology and modernism on the South. In *I'll Take My Stand* (1930) they asked their fellow southerners to take pride in the past and reject the onslaught of industrialism. The wellsprings of culture they argued, were local, and they resented "culture poured in from the top."[62]

The Libertarians

Both Albert J. Nock (1870–1945) and H. L. Mencken (1880–1956) contributed to conservative thought in America. Mencken had what

Ronald Lora calls a conservative "view of history." He did not trust man in "engineering a society compatible with human welfare."[63] Mencken was critical of small-town values, and his philosophical base was more libertarian than conservative. Likewise Nock feared the threat of the state to the exercise of liberty. His book, *Our Enemy the State,* was a biting critique of the growth of government. "If we look beneath the surface of our public affairs," he maintained, "we can discern one fundamental fact, namely: a great redistribution of power between society and the State."[64] Nock was an individualist who rejected any right of government to direct human affairs.

While Nock and Mencken held conservative views about government power, being wary of state planning, and desiring laissez-faire economics, they clearly differed from traditional conservatism on important basic beliefs. Nock opposed the traditional conservative desire for order and held views of individual rights at odds with conservative views about responsibility to society. Mencken hated small-town, rural America, and once declared that the farmer did not belong to the human race and the South was ruled by "Baptist and Methodist barbarism."[65]

What explains the glaring differences in the thought of these two men from that of traditional conservatism? Authoritarian conservatism begins with basic conservative beliefs—order, distrust of change, belief in traditional values—and branches in the direction of favoring state power to protect these beliefs. Libertarianism has an entirely different set of core beliefs which are based upon nineteenth-century liberalism. Those beliefs subordinate the order of a community to the desire for individuality and stress personal rights over personal responsibilities. Libertarians move away from state power to secure maximum liberty for the individual. Authoritarian conservatives are like traditional conservatives in their belief in established values, while libertarians are like traditional conservatives in their desire for limited government. Traditional conservatives and libertarians, however, differ in the degree of their belief in limited government. Libertarians are extreme in their opposition to state power while traditional conservatives are more moderate in their opposition. Traditional conservatives are much more likely to accept some state power than are libertarians.

Russell Kirk, in an article entitled "Libertarians: Chirping Sectaries," identifies practical areas where the libertarians' basic beliefs are opposed by traditional conservatives. He notes that libertarians want to reduce the power of the state in all areas, including defense and police power.[66] Because of their belief in "moral freedom" for the individual, libertarians see no problem with abortion. A true libertarian is not genuinely a conservative, as Kirk writes, although some conservatives may use the name libertarian without full knowledge of its meaning. Indeed, libertarians see man as basically good—he needs to be free to achieve his goodness—which is a belief of Rousseau and completely contrary to traditional conservative canons.[67]

Miscellaneous Conservative Critics

The profound accomplishments of Western civilization are the theme of Agnes Repplier (1855–1950). Few writers could match her insight into the nature of the differences between liberalism and conservatism. A writer and critic over several decades, Repplier observed, "The sanguine assurance that men and nations can be legislated into goodness, that pressure from without is equivalent to moral change from within, needs a strong backing of inexperience."[68] Repplier was not impressed with the hopes of the new century and saw the promises of socialism as empty.

William Graham Sumner (1840–1910) was a contributor to the conservative cause who defied easy classification. Sumner was a disciple of Charles Darwin and Herbert Spencer. Spencer had introduced the concept of evolution into political and social speculations, and held that the same basic law of growth and evolution pervaded the physical, animal and human worlds. For him, the state should not promote religion, regulate trade and commerce, encourage colonization, aid the poor, or enforce sanitary conditions. Sumner defended the free market from the perspective of individual liberty. He opposed interference by the government in the economy. He liked neither the welfare state nor the elitist state controlled by large corporations.[69]

Conclusion: The Middle Era

The Progressive Movement, with its emphasis on governmental reform and pluralism, represents a nadir for conservative thought. Particularly in the early years of the century, urbanization and immigration issues minimized the appeal of conservative solutions. Yet, there were some noteworthy changes occurred in this time period that are still being felt today.

First, the era produced two new types of conservatives, the humanists, who accepted imperfect ideals, and the libertarians, who embraced individualism. Second, the rise of libertarian thought increased the tension between traditional conservatives and libertarians. Third, the era produced some first-rate, if lonely, voices in defense of conservatism. More, Godkin, Mencken and Babbitt were able to command the attention of intellectuals and elites interested in different solutions to American problems. Fourth, much of the writing of the era was a reaction to the ascendance of liberalism and progressive ideas. The Adams brothers and Godkin, to take just two examples, were clearly writing as critics of the new values in society—especially the value of accepting government solutions to social problems.

The Modern Era: The New Deal to the Present

Industrialization following the Civil War brought a major change in American conservatism. Conservatives embraced laissez-faire economics, believing that an economic system that operated free of government control was the only suitable alternative for America. In short, conservatism became the ideology of the nation's business class, and its views were dominant during the 1920s. But the Great Depression of the 1930s ended America's romance with conservatism. It brought about the election of Franklin Roosevelt and the beginning of the New Deal with its numerous state welfare programs.

Conservative values became inappropriate as the support for government intervention in society increased through the New Deal, Fair Deal, New Frontier and Great Society. As the national government began to intervene in many areas previously left to local communities and as liberalism became an accepted part of American life, conservatives responded with ideas critical of government policies. Gradually, as cracks appeared in the liberal assumptions guiding government expansion, conservative writers gained a wider and, by 1980, very substantial audience. The principal voices came from five types of conservatives: (1) traditionalists; (2) economic conservatives; (3) anticommunist conservatives; (4) neoconservatives; and (5) classical conservatives.

Traditional Conservatives

The best known and most influential of the traditionalists are Russell Kirk and Peter Viereck, who pioneered the reemergence of traditional conservative thought. Kirk is one of the most, if not the most, prolific writers of the modern era. Much of the knowledge of conservative thought is traceable to his pen. He is the author of some twenty books, several edited journals, and numerous journal articles. Traditional conservatism as defined by Kirk blends economic, political, religious, and social conservatism.

George H. Nash says of Kirk's *The Conservative Mind* that "here, at long last, was a geneology of good men and valuable thoughts."[70] The importance of Kirk's book cannot be overestimated; it is now in its seventh edition and has served as a guide for numerous conservative writers and commentators. One of the main tasks facing conservatism's adherents during the decline of conservative thought was to demonstrate a viable tradition in American political history as an alternative vision to ascendant liberal ideas. Kirk did this in a convincing way.[71]

Russell Kirk is a true traditional conservative. He traces the roots of conservative thought to Edmund Burke and generally agrees with Burke on the fundamentals of conservatism. Included among his tenets are opposition to political centralization, the belief that divine intent rules society, a distrust of change, and the defense of private property.[72]

Peter Viereck, although not agreeing with Kirk on all points, must generally be classified as a traditionalist as well. His desire for traditional values, emphasis on the need for education to "limit the instincts of behavior," and strong anticommunist stand mark him with the traditionalist label.[73] Viereck's *Conservatism Revisited* (1949) was one of the two or three most important conservative books that sparked renewed interest in conservatism.

Where some conservatives part company with Viereck is in his attitude toward liberalism. While some conservatives would view liberal thought as dangerously near communism, Viereck believes that conservatives and liberals should unite, despite their important differences, against radicalism—defined as communism and fascism.[74] Mutual self-protection and a common agreement on the principles and procedures of American government prompt this proffered alliance.

Viereck also leans toward the liberal view of government social action and speaks harshly of laissez-faire economics. He contends there is "no substantial moral objection" to being against laissez-faire economics; he believes that human compassion is a higher goal than the preference of more to less. The problem, as Viereck sees it, comes when "reforms cross a line beyond which welfare laws are inflated into the welfare superstate."[75] His acceptance of aspects of the welfare state has resulted in criticism of Viereck by some conservatives, but his ideas have had an important impact on postwar conservatism. A contemporary writer who shares Viereck's ideas about the welfare state is George F. Will. In *State-craft as Soulcraft*, Will argues that a certain amount of welfare is necessary for creating and maintaining social harmony and social stability.[76]

Perhaps Viereck's critique of modern conservatism is his most interesting contribution, or at least the one that sparks the most resistance. In an additional section of the 1962 edition of *Conservatism Revisited*, he claims that the major problem of the contemporary conservative movement is a "rootless nostalgia for roots," and a "dream of aristocratic, agrarian restoration." Modern conservatives, he argues, have "stereotyped" rather than "organically grown" values.[77] He also blasts "Old Guard Republicans" as well as Russell Kirk and Barry Goldwater. Viereck is angered by conservatives who make people "feel ashamed of generous social impulses"; he is critical of Kirk for failing to oppose McCarthyism and judges Goldwater as an "enemy of social reform."[78]

The *National Review,* founded by William F. Buckley, Jr., has published articles over the years by almost every leading conservative regardless of type, including some with libertarian economic tendencies, such as Frank Meyer and Frank Chodorov. While Buckley may be more properly classified as a traditional conservative, his magazine has served the interests of trying to unite traditional, economic (including libertarian), and anticommunist conservatives. Frank Meyer probably became the leading proponent of such an alliance when he published his book *The Conservative Mainstream* in 1969.

As for Buckley himself, he has written on an array of conservative subjects that cross the traditionalist, economic, and anticommunist tendencies. For example, upon graduation from Yale he wrote *God and Man at Yale: The Superstitutions of Academic Freedom* (1951). He said the "philosophy of free enterprise, private property, and limited government" was "dying at Yale, and without a fight." Buckley also lamented the loss of Yale's original concern with religious beliefs, as evidenced by the book's title. This, his first book, set the stage for most of his long list of books on conservatism.[79]

Buckley has become a fixture on television and the American cultural landscape through his articles in the *National Review* and his weekly television show "Firing Line." His greatest service to conservatism has been orchestrating a number of brilliant but diverse minds into a coherent chorus of political ideas: "Through the force of his personality and his ability to find a workable center, Buckley helped to hold the movement together and weld it into a formidable influence in the national debate."[80]

Economic Conservatives

Since publication of Friedrich A. von Hayek's *The Road to Serfdom* (1944), economic conservatives have also had internal disagreements. Although published in Great Britain, Hayek's book received little attention because the "question of freedom versus planning" was already resolved there. But in the United States, it sparked great interest since enthusiasm for government intervention in the economy was the central issue of political discourse. His thesis that "planning leads to dictatorship" stirred much interest and aroused considerable support in the United States.[81]

Hayek is one of a host of economists associated with the "Austrian School" of economic thought. Proponents of this school of thought usually cite Ludwig von Mises (1881–1973) as a prophetic figure in their thinking. The Austrians hold that the economy is not a machine with predictable moving parts, but a host of individuals making choices in markets of uncertainty. They critique Keynesian economics by arguing that no centralized government bureaucracy can have sufficient knowledge to regulate the economy. Mises was also a firm proponent of the gold standard and a stable money supply.

Whether or not Hayek was a libertarian, like many in the Austrian School, is still debated, but the movement his writing helped start could not avoid the debate about how far the conservative economic position should be taken. The more moderate conservative economic position is illustrated in the writings of such individuals as Milton Friedman and George Gilder.[82] Unlike the more radical libertarians, Friedman and Gilder do not advocate the general cessation of government involvement in the economy. Rather, their arguments concern the types of programs and policies that should be maintained. Friedman and the Chicago School of economists are monetarists in economic policy. While they oppose many government programs, their opposition is not necessarily to government programs per se.

The libertarian movement owes some postwar respectability to Murray Rothbard, who criticized traditional conservatives for their moderate stands on communism. Rothbard advocated radical libertarian positions like private police departments and a private national defense as well as legalization of marijuana and abolition of victimless crimes. Rothbard took the position that "the United States was solely at fault in the Cold War, and Russia was the aggrieved party."[83]

Anticommunist Conservatives

Anticommunist conservatism deserves mention here because of the significant role it played in the revival of conservative thought in the early 1980s. Many of the anticommunist conservatives had actually been communists or communist-sympathizers, but turned from communism when it produced the terror of Joseph Stalin instead of a more perfect society. For example, James Burnham broke with the Trotskyites and wrote *The Struggle for the World* (1954), *The Coming Defeat of Communism* (1950), and *Containment or Liberation* (1953).

One of the most important anticommunist conservatives was Whittaker Chambers, who was an editor with *Time* magazine. Chambers had dropped out of Columbia University before graduating to become a radical, sometimes romantic social reformer. He joined the Communist Party and became an underground agent. When news of the Stalin purges surfaced, Chambers turned into a government witness to name communist spies. His testimony that State Department official Alger Hiss was a communist helped lead to the conviction of Hiss and the polarization of the nation as to the extent of communist involvement in American affairs. President Truman and Secretary of State Dean Acheson supported Hiss, while an array of conservatives supported Chambers. Chambers's book *Witness* (1952) became the principal rallying cry of anticommunist conservatives. Peter Viereck also contributed to the anticommunist literature with his *Shame and Glory of Intellectuals* (1953), which indicted prominent thinkers for recognizing the Nazi danger but ignoring the communist threat.

The Senate committee hearings chaired by Joseph McCarthy greatly affected conservatism, in some ways polarizing the movement with reference to different values. William F. Buckley, Jr. and L. Brent Bozell supported McCarthy in *McCarthy and His Enemies* (1954), but Peter Viereck said McCarthy aided communism by the manner of his attacks. William A. Rusher said the liberals used McCarthy as the target of a counterattack for the Hiss case, but Will Herberg asserted that McCarthy's actions were those of "irresponsible mass-democracy."[84] Despite McCarthy and the division he caused, most conservatives generally united in their opposition to communism and its associated forms of socialist policy.

Neoconservatism

The basic characteristic of those who brand themselves as neoconservatives is their earlier belief in liberal policies and even their support for communism. Daniel Patrick Moynihan, a neoconservative, stated in a speech before the national board of Americans for Democratic Action in 1967 that "Liberals must see more clearly that their essential interest is in the stability of the social order" and must "divest themselves of the notion that the nation . . . can be run from agencies in Washington."[85] Other neoconservatives include Daniel Bell, Nathan Glazer, James Q. Wilson, and Edward Banfield. Perhaps the best-known neoconservative is Irving Kristol, who, with Daniel Bell, founded the highly regarded neoconservative journal, *The Public Interest*.

Russell Kirk considers neoconservatives to be conservatives, but many neoconservatives reject the label. While they have traditional conservative values, some neoconservatives still have old liberal ties. Irving Kristol, to take the best-known example, supports censorship to maintain the quality of life in society.[86] He praises the laissez-faire idea of the *Wealth of Nations* because with the necessity of property ownership, "liberty [is] practically inevitable."[87] Kristol also criticizes the State Department for not placing a primary importance upon protecting the national interest and speaks against the way the United States has allowed itself to be "blackmailed" by other countries.[88] The neoconservatives have given a distinct and important critique of American intellectual and social life.

Classical Conservatives

Although they hold many of the same beliefs as traditional conservatives, classical conservatives look to a different tradition as the fountainhead of Western culture. Leo Strauss (1899–1973) was the best-known proponent of classical conservatism, finding the values for culture in the writings of Plato and Aristotle. At the University of Chicago Strauss taught many students the classical or Straussian form of conservatism.

Strauss's affection for classical Greek political philosophy was the distinctive characteristic of his work. The writings of the ancients always sought to discover the right way of life. The search for the good or best society based on individual character, "on merit, on human excellence, on 'virtue' " was the most laudable aspect of Plato's writing.[89] Unlike the modern philosophies of Marxism and even liberalism, classical philosophy never accepted that evil could be eradicated from the face of the earth, so its mood was one of an acceptance of reality as it presented itself.

Eric Voegelin (1901–1985) was another significant figure who found serious problems with the way politics was being studied at the end of the twentieth century. In his classic work *The New Science of Policies,* Voegelin showed the inadequacy of the positivist doctrines of the discipline.[90] He presented an alternative view of the study of politics in his multivolume work *Order and History.*[91]

Voegelin develops a theory of man as transcendental, that is, man's humanity is defined by a love of and loyalty to transcendental values. For Voegelin, man's fundamental existence may be known from within. Any attempt to confine knowledge to an externalizing perspective—to step outside existence and contemplate it with neutrality as modern political science attempts—falsifies both knowledge and the reality known. Man is inevitably a limited knower and he can never know things with certainty; his only confidence comes from faith—the trust that reality as a whole is transcendentally ordered. Voegelin's constant appeal is to experience, because human experience is the only sure reality.

In Voegelin's writings human beings constantly long for what they cannot have, something beyond the finite: "This is the experience that

Voegelin calls the tension of existence, a state of tending or longing toward what lies beyond all the imperfections of limited existence, beyond knowledge of particulars toward the true as such, beyond particular enjoyments toward the good as such."[92] Man's desire for certainty is understandable, but his attraction to utopias which offer certainty or even a calculable probability of certainty is dangerous. In Voegelin's thought, faith, hope, and love are as basic to knowing as reason. The search for knowledge is really an enrichment of the soul as it surrenders and gives itself to the love of God.

The major importance of Voegelin's contribution is his articulation of theoretical principles and his framework for studying politics. In many ways he defies political classification. Still, his attraction to order, transcendence, and the limits of man make him a fundamental conservative scholar.

Conclusion: The Modern Era

In a book-length bibliography of American conservative thought, Gregory Wolfe lists fifty conservatives of the modern era.[93] While certainly not an exhaustive list, Wolfe's is an instructive list. Content analysis of Wolfe's very brief biographical statements about the fifty conservatives yields the following conclusions.

First, traditional conservatives constitute by far the largest bloc with twenty-eight proponents. Economic conservatives constitute the next largest bloc with ten. Anticommunist conservatives are next with six. Neoconservatives and classical conservatives number three each. Of these fifty, almost all have either an academic or a journalistic background. Within their academic backgrounds, the disciplines represented are economics, English, history, philosophy, political science, and sociology. Twelve members of the list are former communists, socialists, or strong sympathizers with a leftist cause.

The ideas of tradition and continuity as well as religious authority are important to all these writers. Scattered among the list are a significant number of Roman Catholics: Orestes Brownson, who was a prominent conservative in the years before the Civil War, and more recent thinkers like Russell Kirk, Frank Meyer, and Willmoore Kendall. There are also a number of prominent Jews associated with conservatism, especially among the neoconservatives, with Irving Kristol, Nathan Glazer and

Norman Podhoretz being perhaps the best-known examples. Three individuals on the list represent the southern tradition. Generally omitted from Wolfe's biographical summaries are persons of the evangelical or conservative Protestant background. This is understandable, since only in recent years has much effort been made to articulate a conservative political position among this group of Protestants.

Second, of the five groups of conservatives we have discussed in the modern era, three represent new additions to the evolution of conservative thought. They are the anticommunist, classical, and neoconservative categories. Such additions reflect the fact that conservatism is not a stagnant body of beliefs, divorced from culture and the infusion of new blood. The triumph of conservative politicians in the 1980s shows that the past remains a vibrant guide to the future.

Third, conservatism, like most movements, produces tensions. In the modern era, there have been several important clashes: (1) whether libertarianism or some part of it may rightfully be considered as a legitimate part of the American conservative tradition; (2) whether Senator Mc-Carthy's tactics should be defended by the conservative movement; (3) whether neoconservatism should be incorporated into the conservative tradition; and (4) whether some portion of the welfare state should be justified on the grounds that it enhances social harmony and societal stability even though it also increases the role of government in society.

Fourth, within the modern conservative tradition, it is probably safe to say that the anticommunist element is no longer as strong as it once was, and that the evangelical and conservative Protestant component is not as strong as it will become. In recent years, there has emerged a populist conservatism of Protestants and Catholics united in their views of morality, school prayer, and abortion. The more radical libertarian mode of conservatism has moved outside the mainstream of conservatism, while the more moderate libertarians have remained within it.

Conservatism began outside the mainstream of American thought during the modern era. While it very successfully penetrated public consciousness in the political realm, it still remains outside the mainstream of academic and scholarly thought. Conservatism has developed its own publishing houses, magazines, and scholarly journals to compensate for being left out of mainstream publications. Gregory Wolfe lists sixty conservative journals and periodicals, most of which have come into existence during the modern era.[94]

Conclusion

Conservatism played a major role during the founding period of the country. The Federalist emphasis on the sanctity of private property and distrust of unchecked popular rule gave rise to the two-party system. With the expansion of the frontier and the admission of new states to the union, strong democratic and populist forces resulted in an expanding electorate which, in turn, led to a retreat from conservative ideals.

The Civil War divorced southern traditionalists from the mainstream of American intellectual life, but the industrial revolution gave rise to the popularity of conservative ideas like laissez-faire economics, individualism, and social Darwinism. Conservatives identified with the government role to promote a healthy economic environment for market exchanges during the time of westward expansion. Urban immigration gave rise to a growing liberal movement of social and economic reform known as progressivism. Progressives supported government programs to ease the problems of industrialization, while conservatives favored a restricted role for government.

Progressives achieved their major successes in the early part of the twentieth century. Laissez-faire economics was again dominant during the 1920s, but the Great Depression ended the dominance of conservatism. Roosevelt's New Deal took the concerns of populists and progressives a step further than they had ever imagined. In the postwar era conservatism was characterized more by its anticommunist rhetoric than its economic agenda. The rampant inflation of the 1970s led to a distrust of established liberal solutions. Ronald Reagan was the first genuinely conservative president since the 1920s.

The conservatism of the recent era is no longer suspicious of the masses. It accepts some government role in the economy as inevitable, but it still stresses private solutions and a strong defense policy. Conservatives believe there should be reduced government spending on social programs, revamped tax policies to encourage economic growth, and limited action by government to redress racial and gender inequalities. The stress of conservatism is the creation, not redistribution, of wealth.

Notes

1. George H. Nash, *The Conservative Intellectual Movement in America Since 1945* (New York: Basic Books, 1976), p. xi.

2. Seymour Martin Lipset, *The First New Nation* (Garden City, N.Y.: Doubleday, 1963), p. 17.

3. Eric Voegelin, *From Enlightenment to Revolution* (Durham, N.C.: Duke University Press, 1975), pp. 9–11.

4. Robert Nisbet, "Foreword" to Jack Libely (ed.), *The Works of Joseph De Maistre* (New York: Schocken Books, 1971), p. xiii.

5. George H. Nash, "Introduction" to John P. East, *The American Conservative Movement* (Chicago: Regnery Books, 1986), p. 9.

6. Benjamin Hart, *Faith and Freedom* (Dallas, Tex.: Lewis & Stanley, 1988), p. 83.

7. John Winthrop, *History of New England, 1630–1649.* James Savage (ed.) (2 Vols.; Boston: Little, Brown, 1853) p. 252, Vol. 1.

8. Clinton Rossiter, *Conservatism in America*, pp. 102–103.

9. Russell Kirk, "Cultural Debris," in Kirk (ed.), *The Portable Conservative Reader*, p. 707.

10. Irving Kristol, *Reflections of a Neoconservative* (New York: Basic Books, 1983), p. 85.

11. Peter R. Viereck, *Conservatism* (Westport, Conn.: Greenwood Press, 1978), p. 87.

12. Martin Diamond, *The Founding of the American Republic* (Itasca, Ill.: Peacock Publishers, 1981), pp. 47–48.

13. Russell G. Fryer, *Recent Conservative Political Thought* (Washington, D.C.: University Press of America, 1979), pp. 1–2.

14. M. E. Bradford, *A Worthy Company* (Marlborough, N.H.: Plymouth Rock Foundation, 1982), pp. viii–ix.

15. M. E. Bradford, *Better Guide Than Reason* (LaSalle, Ill.: Sherwood Sugden, 1979), p. 93. M. E. Bradford, *The Political Writings of John Dickinson* (New York: DaCapo, 1970).

16. Clinton Rossiter (ed.), *The Federalist Papers* (New York: New American Library, 1961), p. 322.

17. Russell Kirk, *The Conservative Mind*, pp. 94–112. M. E. Bradford, "Introduction" to *Arator: Being a Series of Agricultural Essays* (Indianapolis, Ind.: Liberty Classics, 1977). M. E. Bradford, *Construction Construed, and Constitutions Vindicated* (New York: DaCapo, 1970). M. E. Bradford, *New Views of the Constitution of the United States* (New York: DaCapo, 1971).

18. Russell Kirk, *The Conservative Mind*, p. 63.

19. Russell Kirk, *The Conservative Mind*, p. 62.

20. Alexander Hamilton, "The Spectacle of Revolutionary France," in Russell Kirk (ed.), *The Portable Conservative Reader*, p. 79.

21. Russell Kirk, *The Conservative Mind*, p. 66.

22. Russell Kirk, *The Conservative Mind*, p. 68.

23. Russell Kirk, *The Conservative Mind*, p. 66.

24. Robert Nisbet, *Conservatism* (Minneapolis, Minn.: University of Minnesota Press, 1986), pp. 41–42.

25. Peter Viereck, *Conservatism*, p. 11.

26. Peter Viereck, *Conservatism,* p. 93.

27. Fisher Ames in Russell Kirk, *The Conservative Mind,* p. 73.

28. William B. Allen, "Introduction" to *Works of Fisher Ames* (Indianapolis, Ind.: Liberty Classics, 1983). Winfred E. A. Bernhard, *Fisher Ames: Federalist Statesman* (Chapel Hill, N.C.: University of North Carolina Press, 1965).

29. Clinton Rossiter, *Conservatism in America,* p. 88.

30. James Q. Wilson, *American Government* (Lexington, Mass.: D.C. Heath, 1989), p. 325.

31. Brooks Adams, "Introductory Note" to Henry Adams, *Degradation of the Democratic Dogma* (New York: Macmillan, 1919), pp. v–vi.

32. H. H. Garland, *Life of John Randolph, II.* pp. 317–318 in Arthur M. Schlesinger, *The Age of Jackson* (Boston: Little, Brown, 1950), p. 7.

33. Russell Kirk (ed.), *The Portable Conservative Reader,* p. 131.

34. John Randolph, "King Numbers," in Russell Kirk (ed.), *The Portable Conservative Reader,* p. 154.

35. Peter Viereck, *Conservatism,* p. 38. John C. Calhoun, "On the Veto Power," in Russell Kirk (ed.), *The Portable Conservative Reader,* pp. 163–164.

36. Russell Kirk (ed.), *The Portable Conservative Reader,* p. xxvi.

37. Orestes A. Brownson, "Liberalism and Progress," in Russell Kirk (ed.), *The Portable Conservative Reader,* p. 268. Orestes A. Brownson, *The American Republic* (New Haven, Conn.: College and University Press, 1972). Thomas R. Ryan, *Orestes A. Brownson* (Huntington, Ind.: Our Sunday Visitor, 1976).

38. Russell Kirk, *The Conservative Mind,* p. 254.

39. James Kent, *Commentaries on American Law,* Vol. 1, (New York: Clayton and Van Norden, 1836), pp. 473–75.

40. James McClellan, *Joseph Story and the American Constitution* (Norman, Okla.: University of Oklahoma Press, 1971), pp. 66, 67.

41. George Marsden, *Fundamentalism and American Culture* (New York: Oxford University Press, 1980), pp. 141–195.

42. Russell Kirk (ed.), *The Portable Conservative Reader,* p. 245.

43. Henry Adams, *The Degredation of the Democratic Dogma,* p. 5.

44. Russell Kirk (ed.), *The Portable Conservative Reader,* p. 323.

45. Russell Kirk (ed.), *The Portable Conservative Reader,* p. 340.

46. Ronald Lora, *Conservative Minds in America* (Cambridge, Mass.: Harvard University Press, 1982), pp. 62–64.

47. E. L. Godkin, "Who Will Pay the Bills of Socialism," in Russell Kirk (ed.), *The Portable Conservative Reader,* pp. 326–334.

48. Irving Babbitt, "What I Believe," in *Irving Babbitt: Representative Writings,* George A. Panichas (ed.) (Lincoln, Neb.: University of Nebraska Press, 1981), pp. 12–13. Ronald Lora, *Conservative Minds in America,* pp. 70–75.

49. Claes G. Ryn, "The Humanism of Irving Babbitt Revisited," *Modern Age,* (Summer, 1977), pp. 251–262.

50. Irving Babbitt, "What I Believe," p. 13.

51. Irving Babbitt, "What I Believe," pp. 5–6.

52. Irving Babbitt, "Burke and the Moral Imagination," in Russell Kirk (ed.), *The Portable Conservative Reader,* p. 464.

53. Irving Babbitt, "What I Believe," pp. 14–16.

54. Ronald Lora, *Conservative Minds in America,* pp. 75, 80. George A. Panichas and Claes G. Ryn (eds.), *Irving Babbitt in Time* (Washington, D.C.: Catholic University Press, 1986). J. David Hoeveler, *The New Humanism: A Critique of Modern America, 1900–1940* (Charlottesville, Va.: University of Virginia Press, 1977).

55. Ronald Lora, *Conservative Minds in America,* pp. 75, 80.

56. Francis G. Wilson, *The Case for Conservatism* (Seattle, Wash.: University of Washington Press, 1951), p. 74.

57. Paul Elmer More, "Property and Law," in Russell Kirk (ed.), *The Portable Conservative Reader,* p. 437.

58. Paul Elmer More, "Property and Law," pp. 450–451, 445. Bryon C. Lambert, "Paul Elmer More and the Redemption of History," *Modern Age* (Summer, 1969), pp. 277–288.

59. Russell Kirk, *The Conservative Mind,* pp.432–443. J. David Hoeveler, *The New Humanism: A Critique of Modern America, 1900–1940* (Charlottesville, Va.: University of Virginia, 1977).

60. George Santayana, "The Irony of Liberalism," in Russell Kirk (ed.), *The Portable Conservative Reader,* pp. 469–470.

61. George Santayana, "The Irony of Liberalism," p. 470. Thomas J. Munson, S.J., *The Essential Wisdom of George Santayana* (New York: Columbia University Press, 1962), pp. 90–100.

62. Andrew Lytle, "They Took Their Stand: The Agrarian View After Fifty Years," *Modern Age,* (Spring, 1980), pp. 346–352.

63. Ronald Lora, *Conservative Minds in America,* pp. 88–89.

64. Albert Jay Nock, *Our Enemy the State* (New York: Arno Press, 1972), p. 3.

65. David R. Contosta and Robert Muccigrosso, *America in the Twentieth Century* (New York: Harper & Row, 1988), p. 140.

66. Russell Kirk, "Libertarians: Chirping Sectaries," *The Heritage Lectures: Proclaiming a Patrimony* (Washington, D.C.: The Heritage Foundation, 1982), pp. 5, 32.

67. Russell Kirk, "Libertarians," pp. 8, 30–33.

68. Agnes Repplier, *Times and Tendencies* (Freeport, N.Y.: Books for Libraries Press, 1971), p. 57.

69. George H. Nash, *The Conservative Intellectual Movement in America,* pp. viii–ix.

70. George H. Nash, *The Conservative Intellectual Movement in America,* p. 59.

71. George H. Nash, *The Conservative Intellectual Movement in America,* p. xiv.

72. Russell Kirk, *The Conservative Mind,* pp. 6–8. Russell Kirk (ed.), *The Portable Conservative Reader,* p. xxviii.

73. Peter R. Viereck, *Conservatism Revisited,* p. 35.

74. Peter R. Viereck, *Conservatism Revisited,* p. 23.

75. Peter R. Viereck, *Conservatism Revisited,* p. 39.

76. George F. Will, *Statecraft as Soulcraft* (New York: Simon & Schuster, 1983), pp. 122–139.

77. Peter R. Viereck, *Conservatism Revisited*, pp. 125–128.

78. Peter R. Viereck, *Conservatism Revisited*, pp. 140–147.

79. William F. Buckley, Jr., *God and Man at Yale* (2nd ed.; Chicago: Regnery Gateway, 1977). pp. xiv, 113.

80. Gregory Wolfe, *Right Minds* (Chicago: Regnery Books, 1987), p. 147.

81. George H. Nash, *The Conservative Intellectual Movement in America*, pp. 5–9. Friedrich A. von Hayek, *The Road to Serfdom* (Chicago: University of Chicago Press, 1956).

82. Milton Friedman, *Capitalism and Freedom* (Chicago: University of Chicago Press, 1962). George Gilder, *Wealth and Poverty* (New York: Basic Books, 1981).

83. George H. Nash, *The Conservative Intellectual Movement in America*, p. 316. Murray Rothbard, *America's Great Depression* (New York: New York University Press, 1975).

84. George H. Nash, *The Conservative Intellectual Movement in America*, pp. 109–118.

85. George H. Nash, *The Conservative Intellectual Movement in America*, pp. 320–321.

86. Irving Kristol, *Reflections of a Neoconservative* (New York: Basic Books, 1983), pp. 43–51.

87. Irving Kristol, *Reflections of a Neoconservative*, p. 165.

88. Irving Kristol, *Reflections of a Neoconservative*, pp. 228–229, 256.

89. Leo Strauss, *What is Political Philosophy* (Glencoe, Ill.: Free Press, 1959), pp. 85–86.

90. Eric Voegelin, *The New Science of Politics* (Chicago: University of Chicago Press, 1952).

91. Eric Voegelin, *Order and History* (5 Vols.; Baton Rouge, La.: Louisiana State University Press, 1956–1971).

92. Eugene Webb, *Eric Voegelin* (Seattle, Wash.: University of Washington Press, 1981), pp. 268–273.

93. Gregory Wolfe, *Right Minds: A Sourcebook of American Conservative Thought* (Chicago: Regnery Gateway, 1987), pp. 145–184.

94. Gregory Wolfe, *Right Minds*, pp. 187–233.

CHAPTER SIX

The Competing Conservative Traditions in America

All at once, nothing seemed certain in the movements of the spheres. . . . At the beginning of the 1920s the belief began to circulate, for the first time at a popular level, that there were no longer any absolutes: of time and space, of good and evil, of knowledge, above all of value.

PAUL JOHNSON[1]

The beginning of twentieth-century thinking, according to Paul Johnson in his book *Modern Times*, is found in the phrase "everything is relative and there are no absolutes." Albert Einstein's principle of relativity held that "the totality of physical phenomena is of such a character that it gives no basis for the introduction of the concept of 'absolute motion'; or, shorter but less precise: There is no absolute motion."[2] From Einstein's premise it was argued that good and evil, right and wrong, and traditional notions of moral behavior were as relative and subject to interpretation as the expanse of the physical universe. While Einstein himself believed passionately in absolute right and wrong and detested the moral relativism attributed to his theory, the legacy of his scientific research was that values should change to fit cultural conventions.[3]

Soon the ideals of relativity became a part of everyday life. Popularizers mistakenly took the "relativity" of space, time and length in the natural realm, for "relativism" in moral law. The nineteenth century witnessed the climax of the Judeo-Christian philosophy of personal responsibility—that each individual was accountable for their actions. In the twentieth century the individual conscience was seared; existential angst and personal despair characterized thinking and the state began to swallow up the independence of the person.

The earlier confidence in man vanished on twentieth-century battle-fields. Barbara Tuchman, in her book *The Guns of August*, describes a poet in Belgium who, before 1914, was a dedicated socialist and human-itarian, one whose artistic work aimed at erasing national differences in Europe. After witnessing the carnage of war in his native land, he pref-aced his next volume of verse with these words: "He who writes this book in which hate is not hidden was formerly a pacifist . . . for him no disillusionment was ever greater or more sudden . . . he dedicates these pages with emotion, to the man he used to be."[4] The poignant testi-mony of this poet captures the mood of an entire generation, who wit-nessed conferences on universal disarmament only to later see nations mobilize more than 58 million troops for battle. Twentieth-century hopelessness could be dedicated—like the verse of the Belgian poet—to the ideals that used to be.[5]

With the emergence of mass destruction, the role of politics and be-havior by the state expanded, and a corresponding faith in the individual diminished. In the twentieth century the following beliefs gained much currency: (1) that man evolved from animals through natural processes; (2) that there is no God; (3) that governmental authority may impose its will on the individual; and (4) that there is no absolute right and wrong. Alexander Solzhenitsyn in his Harvard University commencement ad-dress said, "The West kept advancing socially in accordance with its proclaimed intentions. And all of a sudden it found itself in its present state of weakness." The past was ignored, and the mention of absolute values stamped one as uninformed about the modern situation. Solzhen-itsyn attributed the new thinking to the liberal ethic, with its faith in reason and change. He indicted it for undermining proven traditional values in three significant ways.

First, an excess of freedom that has led to human decadence and irre-sponsibility, including pornography and violence, is undermining such institutions as the family, home, school, neighborhood, and community upon which a democratic society depends for stability. Second, Solzhen-itsyn argued, the demise of American democracy has occurred gradually; reformers and government officials erroneously think that reforming economic, political, and social systems and government policies will stem the tide of decay. Third, the early democracies, such as America, were based upon a religious value—man's accountability and responsi-bility to God—which has been largely forgotten in recent years.[6]

The unbounded demands of welfare-state liberalism led to a freedom from the restraints of community, a hallmark of conservative society and the glue that held associations together through family, neighborhood, and church. Western culture began with the idea that each individual in the society would limit his own behavior through the understood conventions and restraints of community. The law alone did not restrain people; rather, membership in society meant that all understood what could and could not be done. But with the loss of a serious moral basis for society, the emphasis shifted to a preoccupation with rights and a diminution of responsibilities.[7]

Against the thinking of the new age, conservatives call for an intimate knowledge of the past. The tradition of conservatism is a reminder that the roots of a society nourish its vision of the future. No nation can retain a sense of direction or know how far along the road it has traveled without remembering where it has been. The conflict in the West today is between the traditional Judeo-Christian heritage and the secular power of the new faith in science and materialism, between a belief in God and one in man. The schism today is between two irreconcilable conceptions of man as a creature made in the image of his Creator or an independent personality trapped in time and space; between unity and reason in the cosmos and chaos ruled by chance; and between a government ruled by established values or one in a constant state of revision to fit changing times.

No better example of the clash between liberal idealism and the conservative tradition is to be found than in the abortion debate, which galvanized the nation in the decade of the 1980s. Liberals maintained that the freedom and right of the mother to choose whether or not to have an abortion is fundamental. Reason, advances in medical science, and the prospect of utopian family planning underlie their case for individual choice. Conservatives, rooted in the religious traditions of the past, decry what they consider to be the casual approach to sexuality and the disregard for human life implicit in the abortion decision. The limits of social planning and the acceptance of a divine order to things are the basis of their arguments against abortion. All the utopian ideals and real world difficulties of modern liberalism are in evidence in the abortion discussion. For conservatives, an increase in child abuse, a deterioration in family stability, and the spread of disease are the legacy of the new sexual license, a calamity created in the name of improving family relations.

In this chapter we review the evidence for the conservative commitment to absolutes in the midst of relative thinking. The religious, political, and economic traditions of conservatism are examined. Common to all of these traditions is a commitment to truths about man's condition and nature, be it the picture of man as revealed in Scriptures or the desire of man for material gain as seen in classical economic texts.

The Conservative Political Tradition

Christian ideas about man, society, and divine intent are basic for conservative thought. Conservatives believe, with the Founders, that government is at best a necessary evil—and one necessarily restrained by the Constitution. But the view of minimal state interference presupposes that men are self-controlling, moral beings. In the twentieth century self-restraint has been in short supply. In its sixtieth anniversary issue, the editors of *Time* magazine characterized the years since its founding in 1923 in terms of one value, freedom: "America was not merely free; it was freed, unshackled . . . to be free was to be modern; to be modern was to take chances . . . behind most of these events lay the assumption, almost a moral imperative, that what was not free ought to be free, that limits were intrinsically evil."[8]

Accompanying this experimentation was a great politicization of thinking. Higher truths and traditional authorities over men decreased in importance, and in their place political questions were increasingly resolved by governmental bodies. Today, Americans are inundated by politics; hardly a news item appears that is not subject to government inquiry. When every problem becomes political, the state is the only body available to find solutions. Conservatives always point out that America was founded on a desire to limit centralized political power. The colonists fought for their independence from onerous taxes and government interference under the banner "Don't Tread on Me." In their view, politics was a problem, not a solution.

There is a direct parentage between the American religious tradition and the conservative political legacy. First, a biblical view of the nature of man helped determine the type of government the Founders established, one limited by the checks and balances of power among the several branches of government and one that protected the individual from the capricious exercise of governmental power through the Bill of Rights. Their distrust of man's nature led to the creation of a government in which the people directly elected only the members of the House of Representatives, with the Senate, the courts, and the president being indirectly selected by other bodies. Summarizing this relationship between a conservative religious tradition and the functioning of American government, Alexis de Tocqueville said:

> The greatest part of British America was peopled by men, who having shaken off the authority of the Pope, acknowledged no other religious supremacy. They brought with them into the New World a form of Christianity which I cannot better describe than by styling it a democratic and republican religion.[9]

The strong emphasis on "the Fall of man" underscored the fact that every person was indeed a sinner, and that checks and balances were needed to restrain those in power.

Second, laws and legal precedents were required to be in accordance with the rules given in Scriptures. In the Declaration of Independence, the phrase "the laws of nature" was not a reference to the universe but to the divine law of God. In eighteenth-century England and America, this phrase enjoyed a clear and consistent meaning. It referred to the majesty and will of God as revealed in the natural order of creation. Even John Locke, often cited by liberals as a key philosopher for the American experience, declared in his *Second Treatise on Government*: "Thus the law of nature stands as an eternal rule of all men, legislators as well as others. The rules that they make for other men's actions, must . . . be conformable to the law of nature, i.e., to the will of God. . . ."[10] In 1695, Locke wrote in his treatise *The Reasonableness of Christianity as Defined in The Scriptures* that "As Christians we have Jesus the Messiah for our king, and are under the law revealed by Him in the Gospel."[11]

William Blackstone, author of *Commentaries on the Laws of England*, which was the single most popular influence on the foundation of the American legal system and required reading by all students of the law throughout much of American history, said: "As man depends absolutely upon his Maker for everything, it is necessary that he should at all points conform to his Maker's will." Blackstone carefully differentiated natural law from the law of nature by stating, "The revealed law is of infinitely more authority than what we generally call the natural law. Because one is the law of nature, expressly declared to be by God himself; the other is only what, by the assistance of human reason, we imagine to be that law."[12]

In writing the Declaration of Independence, Jefferson and others formulated their case on truths which were unchanging and immutable because they came from the Creator himself: "We hold these truths to be self-evident, that all men are created equal, that they are endowed by their Creator with certain inalienable rights. . . ." Man's rights do not come from man, but from God, and they are unchangeable. Man does not depend upon government for the statement of rights, but for securing them. The purpose of government, from a conservative point of view, is to protect God's ordained rights. This is reflected in the Declaration's statement, "That to secure these rights governments are instituted among men. . . ." The rights of man are primary, and the governments instituted to secure those rights are secondary.

Third, the idea of covenant, borrowed from the conservative religious tradition, figured prominently in the role of written laws and agreements binding men together in solemn assembly. The Mayflower Compact, for example, reads: "We . . . do by Presents, solemnly and mutually in the Presence of God and one another, covenant and combine ourselves together into a civil Body Politick." Governments were to embody the concept of a people covenanting under God to establish a government answerable to God and His law. Political scientist Daniel Elazar has concluded that:

> The constitutions of the American states in the founding era were perhaps the greatest products of the American covenant tradition. . . . The creation of new states, even new towns, across the United States throughout the 19th century reflected the covenanting impulse.
>
> For Americans, covenant provided a means for a free people to form political communities without sacrificing their essential freedom and without making energetic government possible.[13]

In the Judeo-Christian tradition a constitution was a solemn agreement between parties, a reflection of the divine covenant God made with his people throughout history.

Fourth, the Constitution created a form of government that moderates the rate of change. The conservative believes that meaningful change is only possible within the bounds of existing institutions. Edmund Burke wrote, "A state without the means of some change is without the means of its conservation."[14] Change is necessary to conserve the essence of society's traditions and foundations, but rapid change or change which occurs outside of established institutions threatens stability and the continuity of tradition.

The fact that change is not easy under the provisions of the American Constitution is one of the reasons liberals are frustrated by it. Rexford Guy Tugwell, a New Deal economist and presidential adviser, once said, "The intention of the eighteenth- and nineteenth-century law was to install and protect the principle of conflict."[15] Tugwell suggested in the 1930s that large-scale business enterprises be federally incorporated and directed by a tripartite body of business, labor, and consumers. He would later say of the delays in achieving his economic reform that "Organization for these purposes was very inefficient because they were not acknowledged intentions. Much of the lagging reluctance was owed to the constantly reiterated intention that what was being done was in pursuit of the aims of the Constitution."[16]

For economic, political, and social change to be made within the boundaries of the Constitution, numerous hurdles must be cleared. The decision-making rules in the document protect minorities at many points by creating a complicated set of restraints on quick action by the majority. For example, a minority of one-third plus one can prevent an amendment from being proposed in either house of the Congress and a minority of one-fourth plus one can prevent the necessary three-fourths of the states from ratifying a constitutional amendment. Only one of four units of the national government—House, Senate, Supreme Court, and President—was a popularly elected body or person in the original draft of the Constitution. Even now, with direct popular election of both the House and Senate, the doctrine of separation of powers effectively precludes quick action on most legislation.

The doctrine of division of powers and its complex allocation of powers between the national and state governments allows for the national government to exercise some powers exclusively, the states to retain some exclusively, and both to retain some commonly. Throughout American political history, a heated debate has occurred between nationalists and states rightists about the boundary line between the respective powers of the national and state governments.

Collectively, these constitutional doctrines and concepts of government lead to two central conclusions about economic, political, and social change: (1) complexity and diversity in the decision-making process make it difficult to achieve change quickly; and (2) a multiplicity of decision-makers at the national and state levels of government, including local government, diminish opportunities for hurried change. Historically, incrementalism or gradualism is the pattern of American economic, political, and social change.

The political landscape is littered with the debris of popular crusades that were unable to complete the obstacle course of power in the American political system. The Equal Rights Amendment was quickly proposed by overwhelming majorities in both houses of Congress and appeared to be heading for quick ratification by three-fourths of the state legislatures, but it was stymied by one-fourth of the state legislatures, which failed to ratify. President Franklin D. Roosevelt chafed under the checks the Supreme Court placed on the centerpieces of his New Deal programs. President Ronald Reagan proposed legislation and constitutional amendments that never saw the light of day because of the numerous congressional checks that preclude hasty action. Ironically, his conservative social and economic agenda had to be filtered through a conservative system of restraint and entrenched interests that led to defeat at many points along the way.

Change under a system of divided government is difficult to achieve. During his tenure in Washington, Rexford G. Tugwell helped devise an indirect way of speeding up the process; his proposal allowed for constitutional reinterpretation without amending the Constitution. Conservatives opposed such revisions, holding that it is incumbent upon the Supreme Court to determine the original intent of the Founders with regard to an issue. Failure to do so means that there is no constitution in the true sense, since new meanings are constantly being poured into the mold of old words, creating new powers and new rights. Sam Ervin, former senator from North Carolina, once said, "Everyone will concede that the Constitution is written in words. If these words have no fixed meaning, they make the Constitution conform to Mark Twain's description of the dictionary . . . 'a wonderful vocabulary, but no plot.' "[17]

The major change in redefining the meaning of the Constitution began during the New Deal. Justice Felix Frankfurter, for example, said that words in the Constitution are "so restricted by their intrinsic meaning or by their history or by tradition or by prior decisions that they leave the individual justice free, if indeed they do not compel him, to gather meaning not from reading the Constitution but from reading life."[18] Justice Oliver Wendell Holmes said much the same thing: "When we are dealing with words that also are a constituent act, like the Constitution of the United States, we must realize that they have called into life a being the development of which could not have been foreseen by the most gifted of begetters."[19] This reasoning led to substantial changes in constitutional interpretation, altering or revising the national government to foster more rapid economic, political, and social change.

Gradually the terms in the Constitution assumed a relative meaning characteristic of twentieth-century thought. In 1936, the Supreme Court declared that the "general welfare" clause of Article I, Section 8 permitted Congress to appropriate funds for just about any purpose it chose without regard to limitations on Congress found in the Constitution.[20] In 1937, "interstate commerce" in Article I, Section 8 was redefined as anything that substantially affects the flow of interstate business, regardless of whether it crosses state lines.[21] In 1942, the Court held that the national government could regulate a product even if the producer did not intend to sell it, because the product could still affect interstate commerce.[22] More recently, the clauses of the 14th Amendment guaranteeing "equal protection of the laws" and "due process of law" have been used to establish national regulation in matters dealing with education and criminal law. For over one hundred seventy-five years, these subjects were within the jurisdiction of the states, but through the actions of the court, without constitutional amendment, and through reinterpretation of the clauses, the national government acquired significant power over these issues.

The fear that a powerful national government would dominate constituent state governments and increase its power relative to them was apparent in *The Federalist Papers*. James Madison wrote:

The powers delegated by the proposed Constitution to the federal government are few and defined. The former will be exercised principally on external objects, as war, peace, negotiation, and foreign commerce, with which last the power of taxation will, for the most part, be connected. The powers reserved to the several states will extend to all the objects which, in the ordinary course of affairs, concern the lives, liberties, and properties of the people and the internal order, improvement, and prosperity of the state.[23]

Madison's assurances notwithstanding, the power of the national government has outstripped the original mold established in the Constitution. The intentions of the Founders have been reinterpreted. Structurally, American government retains most of its conservative features and tendencies that obstruct rapid change. Conceptually, however, key constitutional doctrines have been reinterpreted without constitutional amendment: the subsequent changes have been dramatic. The conservative political tradition is rooted in individual responsibility, best summarized by Samuel Eliot Morison:

> Puritanism was a cutting edge which hewed liberty, democracy, humanitarianism, and universal education out of the black forest of feudal Europe and the American wilderness.
>
> Puritan doctrine taught each person to consider himself a significant, if sinful, unit to whom God has given a particular place and duty, and that he must help his fellow men.
>
> Puritanism is an American heritage to be grateful for and not to be sneered at because it required everyone to attend divine worship and maintained a strict code of moral ethics.[24]

The conservative political tradition relies on a set of fixed rules written in the Constitution and on the hearts of its citizens. The political institutions operate within fixed parameters: the terms of the original agreement cannot be altered to suit changing circumstances.

The Conservative Economic Tradition

The conservative economic thought of today was known in the last century as either "laissez-faire" economics, classical economics or economic liberalism. Its central premise, which was an innovation in a time of powerful nation-states, was a bias against the state. The publication of

John Locke's *Second Treatise of Civil Government* in 1690 introduced a theory of the state which substituted constitutionalism and limited government for absolute rule and arbitrary power. In Locke's state of nature, individuals were endowed with rights that derive from natural law; collectively these rights were called "property" rights. The Lockean definition of property exceeds the purely economic sphere, and extends to the whole orbit of "life, liberty, and the pursuit of happiness." It is to enjoy this "property" that people mutually contract to institute a government.

For Locke, the legitimate powers of government were derived from that portion of a citizen's natural rights which were entrusted to its care, and its functions were regulated by the rights retained by the citizens. The scope of state activity should be confined to the limits set by the community; if the state passes out of bounds it becomes an invader of a domain where it has no right to enter. In Locke's treatise, only the people have rights: "The government as trustee has only duties, which are defined by the interests of the trustor and beneficiary, (i.e., the people) and not by those of the trustee (i.e., the government)."[25]

The next step in the process of economic thought and limited government was taken by a French school called the "Physiocrats." Their philosophy advocated economic and political governance "in keeping with the laws implanted in Nature by Providence." The Physiocrats were influential in France during the 1760s and 1770s. For them the prosperity of agriculture was the prime indicator of national wealth, and the interests of landowners overrode those of merchants. The school's key postulate was that only the productive class cultivating the land produced a net product: "Expansion of the economy and the population therefore depended upon expansion of the expenditure of the productive class and the resultant expansion of the net product," (i.e., prosperity in agriculture).[26] The Physiocrats wanted to curb the influence of the state and limit it within boundaries that left the agrarian economy to the operation of "nature." Their specific cry of protest to the state was "Laissez-faire"—leave us alone.

The final flowering of classical economic principles took place in Britain and the United States in the last quarter of the eighteenth century and the early part of the nineteenth century. Adam Smith's *Wealth of Nations,* published in 1776, set in motion a generation of work by English writers and economists like David Ricardo (*Principles of Political*

Economy (1917)) and T. R. Malthus. The permanent contribution of this scholarship was to be found in its general picture of how a social order can best function.

What was this picture? The classical economic model depicted the individual as the true unit, and society as the artificial aggregate of individuals in association. If all individuals desire their self-interest and each person is the best judge of the means appropriate to the goal of material enrichment, it follows that the larger the sphere of action left to the initiative of private persons the better. Individuals pursuing material enrichment reap the best rewards for themselves and for society as a whole. If the economic system were left to operate on its own, the interplay of complex, human exchange forces would be in accordance with set, harmonious natural laws. Certain of these were based on psychological assumptions of universal human egoism and the operation of physical factors rooted in nature. The analysis of these laws with their absolute inferences about human behavior formed the substance of economic science.

Where did the state fit into this order of thinking? Classical economic theory assumed a dichotomy between nature, with its own laws of supply and demand, and the artificial or man-made laws of the state. Natural laws were good; human laws were harmful. The only beneficial state policy was one that enlarged the sphere of private enterprise, which was always deemed superior to the public enterprise. In fact, classical theory placed on the state the onus of proving that its functions were justified. There was a distinct bias against the state.

Though the classical economists aspired to be scientific and independent of the particular social and political circumstances of their time, serious depressions in the English economy had the practical effect of discrediting their assumptions. The belief that the natural order was inherently simple, harmonious, beneficient, and devoid of ethical attributes was challenged by evidence of social and class tensions. Behind the wall of "leave us alone," laissez-faire industrialists in Britain and the United States during the nineteenth century used underpaid, overworked, and underfed manpower in factories, mines, railroads, and other workplaces. This fact did not escape the notice of Karl Marx, who criticized capitalism and the industrialized economies for their emphasis on surplus accumulation over consumption and misallocation of wealth.

The critique of Marxist economics and state interference in the economy was accomplished by a group of German economists who collectively became known as the "Austrian School." They expanded upon the classical assumptions to make them appropriate for industrial capitalism. The Austrians analyzed the origin and usefulness of money, concluding that its value is in helping to determine the distribution of scarce goods among competing uses. Simply put, people use money to make choices about what they want. Springing from this analysis in the 1870s is the logic of choice, or the "economic calculus" of modern economic theory.

It was just such a theory which proved that Marxist economies could not calculate economically, lacking as they did a true price system based on private ownership of produced goods. "It follows that socialism cannot successfully plan and operate a modern industrial economy," wrote Ludwig von Mises in his 1922 critique of socialism entitled *Socialism: An Economic and Sociological Analysis.* Mises's insights and theories were gradually used to articulate a consistent view of political economy which held that nothing was to be gained from various types of government intervention in the economy. In opposition to the doctrines of British economist John Maynard Keynes, who argued that it was necessary for social and political reasons for government to maintain full employment and prevent extreme fluctuations in the business cycle, Mises held that such intervention was unworkable. The disciples of the Austrian school emerged in the twentieth century as the most consistent, uncompromising defenders of laissez-faire.

In the United States the argument for minimal government interference in the economy is carried by the "public choice" school, of whom 1986 Nobel Prize winner James Buchanan is a leading proponent. This theory sees economic choices in the context of politics, with special interest groups dominating the legislative process of the welfare state and politicians responding to their requests with accommodating legislation. Since the 1930s, the modern democratic state has had an egalitarian impulse. Politicians seek reelection by making political calculations in accordance with a set of preferences designed to grant favors to some groups while denying special treatment to others.

Central to conservative economic theory since the eighteenth century is the value of the individual in the marketplace. Such an actor makes consistent choices to better himself; such a person behaves rationally within a consistent value system. In economic parlance, other things being equal, people always prefer more to less. The conservative economic position is that the state should not interfere with individual freedom to make decisions.

The Conservative Religious Tradition

Political scientist Kenneth W. Thompson has written that central to America's founding and history is a religious tradition:

> At the core of [America's] founding and history is a moral and political tradition representing what Walter Lippmann has called "the forgotten foundations of democracy." But if the foundations have been forgotten, they have never been lost . . . as the brilliant columnist James Reston has pointed out, "The liberties which all the spokesmen . . . talk about defending today, after all, were established by that remarkable group of eighteenth century American political leaders who took their conception of man from the central religious tradition of Western civilization."[27]

From the colonial period to the recent past, the Christian faith was the greatest single influence on American public institutions and daily life. Sociologist Robert N. Bellah has written, "The Bible was the one book that literate Americans in the 17th, 18th, and 19th centuries could be expected to know well. . . . Biblical imagery provided the basic framework for imaginative thought in America up until quite recent times and, unconsciously, its control is still formidable."[28]

Nowhere was the grip of Christian morality more apparent than in the conception of the nature of man held by the original founders of the American republic. After acknowledging that religion had a pervasive influence on the Constitution, American political historian Richard Hofstadter concludes that the Founders adhered to the conservative notion that man's nature was essentially evil:

> To them a human being was an atom of self-interest. They did not believe in man, but they did believe in the power of a good political constitution to control him. . . . From a humanistic standpoint there is a serious dilemma in the philosophy of the Fathers, which derives from their conception of man. They thought man was a creature of rapacious self-interest, yet they wanted him to be free—free, in essence, to contend to engage in

an umpired strife. . . . They had no hope and they offered none for any ultimate organic change in the way men conduct themselves. The result was that while they thought self-interest the most dangerous and un-brookable quality of man, they necessarily underwrote it in trying to con-trol it.[29]

Hofstadter's conclusions are substantiated by an examination of the views of human nature held by the Founders. James Madison spoke of the "degree of depravity in mankind which requires a certain degree of circumspection and distrust," the "caprice and wickedness of man," and the "infirmities and depravities of human character."[30] John Jay said man was governed by "dictates of personal interest," while Alexander Hamilton spoke of the "folly and wickedness of mankind."[31] Even Thomas Jefferson believed in the nether side of human nature when he wrote, "Free government is founded on jealousy, not in confidence; it is jealousy and not confidence which prescribes limited constitutions, to bind those we are obligated to trust with power. In questions of power, let no more be heard of confidence in man but bind him down to mischief by the chains of the constitution."[32]

The Judeo-Christian conception of man is that he is a creature with a dual nature, part beast and part angel. Man was cast by God in His image, yet fell into sin in the rebellious wish to be "as God." As a result man was estranged from the Creator and forever destined to be torn between the downward pull of his materialistic, self-indulgent, animal-self and his elevated, creative, and divine image. The object of education was to improve man by extolling the values central to his better nature. Michael Novak points out that Harvard College, founded in 1636 to train ministers, adopted as one of the rules and precepts for students that "everyone shall consider the main end of his life and studies to know God and Jesus Christ, which is eternal life."[33] Yale was constituted in 1701 in recognition of the fact that the colonies had been established "both to plant and under the Divine Blessing to propagate in this wilderness, the blessed reformed Protestant religion, in the purity of its order and worship, not only to their posterity, but also to the barbarous natives."[34]

The Christian influence pervaded early education, and its object was the improvement of man. Alexis de Tocqueville, concluding that this tradition was dominant in American society, said, "Religion exercises little influence upon the laws and upon the details of public opinion; but it directs the customs of the community, and by regulating domestic life, it regulates the state."[35] The ethic of the time emphasized service to a higher end, a desire to give God your best and enrich the society as a byproduct of such allegiance. De Tocqueville sums up the experience this way:

> It was religion that gave birth to the English colonies in America. One must never forget that. In the United States religion is mingled with all the national customs and all those feelings which the word evokes. For that reason it has peculiar power. . . . Christianity has kept a strong hold over the minds of Americans, and . . . its power is not just that of a philosophy which has been examined and accepted, but that of a religion believed in without discussion. . . . Christianity itself is an established and irresistible fact which seeks not to attack or defend.[36]

The Founding of a Nation

Nowhere is the religious imperative clearer than in the motivations of those who first founded the country and set its vision for the future.[37] Beginning with Queen Isabella's commission to Columbus, and continuing over several centuries, the evidence reinforces the religious basis for colonization and exploration. Columbus recorded in his diary that his purpose in finding "undiscovered worlds" was to "bring the Gospel of Jesus Christ to the heathens." He wrote, "It was the Lord who put into my mind . . . the fact that it would be possible to sail from here to the Indies . . . I am the most unworthy sinner, but I have cried out to the Lord of grace and mercy, and they have covered me completely . . . no one should fear to undertake any task in the name of the Saviour, if it is just and if the intention is purely for His holy service."[38]

What follows is a recitation of dates and documents which are largely, if not entirely, ignored in modern scholarship and textbook writing— but which bear immeasurably upon the establishment of a conservative religious heritage in America.[39]

1606. King James I in the Virginia Charter dedicates the founding of the colony "to the glory of his divine Majesty, in propagating the Christian religion to such people as yet live in ignorance of the true knowledge and worship of God. . . ."

1609. The second charter granted to Virginia states that "the principal effect which we can expect or desire of this action is the conversion and reduction of the people in those parts unto the true worship of God and the Christian religion."

1620. The Mayflower Compact records the covenant "for the glory of God and the advancement of the Christian faith."

1629. The First Charter of Massachusetts states its intention that the citizens "maie wynn and incite the Natives of County to the Knowledg and Obedience of the onlie true God and Savior of Mankinde, and the Christian Fayth. . . ."

1629. The inhabitants of Exeter, New Hampshire, "In the name of Christ and in the sight of God, combine ourselves together to erect and set up among us such government as shall be, to our best discerning, agreeable to the will of God."

1638. The Fundamental Orders of Connecticut declares that the people entered "into Combination and Confederation togather to mayntayne and presearve the liberty and purity of the Gospell of our Lord Jesus, which we now professe. . . ."

1644. The charter of New Haven colony specifies ". . . that the judicial laws of God, as they were delivered by Moses . . . be a rule to all the courts in this jurisdiction. . . ."

1649. The Maryland Toleration Act announces that "No person or persons whatsoever within this province . . . professing to believe in Jesus Christ shall . . . henceforth be any ways troubled, molested (or disapproved of) . . . in respect of his or her religion nor in the free exercise thereof. . . ."

1689. The Great Law of Pennsylvania proclaims, "Whereas the glory of Almighty God and the good of mankind is the reason and the end of government . . . therefore government itself is a venerable ordinance of God. . . ."

1752. Inscribed on the Liberty Bell in Philadelphia are these words from Leviticus 25:10, "Proclaim liberty through all the land and to all the inhabitants thereof."

1774. Meeting in Philadelphia, the Continental Congress authorizes payments to chaplains to open its sessions with prayer.

1776. In appointing a day of fasting and prayer, the Congress implores that they might "by sincere repentance and amendment of life, appease

God's righteous displeasure, and through the merits and mediation of Jesus Christ, obtain His pardon and forgiveness."

1776. The Virginia Bill of Rights asserts that "It is the mutual duty of all to practice Christian forbearance, love and dignity towards each other."

1777. Twenty thousand copies of the Bible are authorized for purchase by the Continental Congress because the domestic supply was short; the Congress also authorizes chaplains for the Continental Army.

1782. The Congress recommends to the people "the Holy Bible as printed by Robert Aiken of Philadelphia" as "a neat edition of the Holy Scriptures for the use of schools."

1786. The Virginia Statute of Religious Liberty declares that "Almighty God hath created the mind free; that all attempts to influence it by temporal punishments or burdens, or by civil incapacitations . . . are a departure from the plan of the Holy Author of our religion. . . ."

1787. The Northwest Ordinance states that "No person, demeaning himself in a peaceable and orderly manner, shall ever be molested on account of his mode of worshipping or religious sentiments. . . . Religion, morality, and knowledge being necessary to good government and the happiness of mankind, schools and the means of education shall be forever encouraged."

1788. Writing in *The Federalist Papers,* James Madison proclaims that "We have staked the future . . . upon the capacity of each and all of us to govern ourselves, to sustain ourselves, according to the Ten Commandments of God."

1821. John Quincy Adams maintains that "The highest glory of the American Revolution was this: it connected, in one indissoluble bond, the principles of civil government with the principles of Christianity." Adams also said, "From the day of the Declaration . . . they (the American people) were bound by the laws of God, which they all, and by the laws of The Gospel, which they nearly all, acknowledged as the rules of their conduct."

1828. The first edition of Webster's dictionary contains a large number of biblical definitions. Webster would subsequently write that "the religion which has introduced civil liberty, is the religion of Christ and his apostles . . . this is genuine Christianity, and to this we owe our free constitutions of government . . . the moral principles and precepts contained in the Scriptures ought to form the basis of all of our civil constitutions and laws."

1836. In the foreword to the first edition of *McGuffey's Reader,* which sold 122 million copies between 1836 and 1920, McGuffey says, "The Christian religion is the religion of our country. From it are derived our prevalent notions of the Character of God, the great moral governor of the universe. On it doctrines are founded the peculiarities of our free institutions."

1841. Alexis de Tocqueville writes in *Democracy in America* that "In the United States of America the sovereign authority is religious." He also notes that "there is no country in the world in which the Christian religion retains a greater influence over the souls of men than in America."

1851. In his *Commentaries on the Constitution of the United States,* Supreme Court Justice Joseph Story states: "Probably at the time of the adoption of the Constitution, and of the first amendment to it . . . the general if not the universal sentiment in America was, that Christianity ought to receive encouragement by the state so far as was not incompatible with the private rights of conscience and the freedom of religious worship. Any attempt to level all religions, and to make it a matter of state policy to hold all in utter indifference, would have created universal disapprobation, if not universal indignation."

1892. In *Church of the Holy Trinity v. United States,* the Supreme Court decides: "Our laws and our institutions must necessarily be based upon and embody the teachings of the Redeemer of mankind. It is impossible that it should be otherwise; and in this sense and to this extent our civilization and our institutions are emphatically Christian." The court continues by saying that "This is a religious people. This is historically true. From the discovery of this continent to the present hour, there is a single voice making this affirmation . . . we find everywhere a clear recognition of the same truth . . . this is a Christian nation."

This chronology of a Christian heritage, with its attendant absolute moral code, reveals two things. First, the original cultural values emphasized self-regulation and moral responsibilities rather than government rights and freedoms. There was not, and could never be, a barrier between the Christian religious heritage and the practice of democracy. Instead, the founding of the new nation and its political institutions were largely a result of the religious enterprise. Cultural practices stressed moral values in education, manners, and social behavior as being more important than governmental activity.

Christianity gave American culture the concept of the exalted individual, emphasizing almost limitless respect for human beings but wariness of society. The dignity and value of people was ensured by their destiny, which was bestowed in creation and restored and reformed in Christ. As Glenn Tinder has written, "The nobility granted in Christianity to even the most degraded individuals would have been incomprehensible to the ancient Greeks," who saw the aim of all relationships as the cultivation and sharing of a virtuous life. The cultural value of the exalted individual means that government must treat people with care. Because of the fallen human condition, the "just society" envisioned by Plato and subsequent philosophers is not realizable. Ideal utopias are impossible, and "To pursue the ideal of perfect justice is to ignore our fallenness." Christianity, therefore, taught a substitute less pure but more attainable.[40]

Second, by past and present standards, the Christian culture was exceptionally tolerant of minorities and dissent. Countless immigrants found a freedom from persecution on American shores which was unknown in Europe. To be sure, there was racial oppression and overt discrimination. Still, the Christian conscience condemned the excesses of slavery and was responsible for moderating and eventually eliminating that institution. In the communities of the new America, fundamental property and citizenship rights were available to all free men. The values of Christian love and forebearance had a social reality which often tolerated even the most odious outrage.

Writing on this point, Rabbi Joshua O. Haberman, former senior rabbi of the Washington Hebrew Congregation of reformed Judaism and later visiting professor at Washington Theological Union, offers several conclusions rooted in the premise that America's conservative religious tradition is, and was, a safeguard from the totalitarianism which he experienced as a young Jew in Vienna:

> The suspension of the Bible's moral "barriers" has made possible all the atrocities of Hitler, Stalin and other totalitarian rulers.
>
> The veneration of the Scriptures as supreme law, superior to the laws of kings, potentates, or magistrates, was the germ of the all-important political philosophy—the very heart of our democracy—which recognizes "a government of laws and not of men."

The Bible gave our nation its moral vision. And today, America's Bible belt is our safety belt, the enduring guarantee of fundamental rights and freedoms.[41]

The contribution Christianity made to the culture was to set an absolute standard, aside from the democratic majority, by which the rights and wrongs of government could be judged. As Rabbi Haberman points out, the bulwark against totalitarianism is the absolute standards given in the Bible. While many of those involved in the founding and development of the United States were not believing Christians, they were still operating on the consensus Christianity gave to cultural values. The effect of their work was to create institutions which reflected that consensus.

The conservative tradition emphasizes and seeks to maintain this consensus. Conservatives may not agree about specific religious doctrines, but they would agree that human nature is constant and flawed. There are certain fundamental aspects of a human being that are unchanging and unchangeable regardless of time or place. Modern man has much to learn about himself from the writings of Plato, the confessions of Augustine, and the values of Churchill. Because conservatives believe there is an objective moral order of real, immutable, and eternal truths by which man must measure his conduct, they oppose laws which limit or restrict the practice of the Christianity.[42]

American Political Theology

The dimensions of liberalism and conservatism along ideological and theological lines are shown in Figure 6-1. The relationship between religious conviction and political ideology is clearly seen in George McGovern's autobiographical book *Grassroots*:

The study of these men (Hegel and Marx) forced me to think seriously about the political process, but neither of them captured my interest with anything approaching the enthusiasm I experienced in discovering "the social gospel." This effort to find in the New Testament and the Hebrew prophets an ethical imperative for a just social order strongly appealed to me. To know that long years of familiarity with the Bible and the idealism nurtured in my public school years were resources that I could direct to humane political and economic ends was a satisfying discovery. Religion was more than a search for personal salvation, more than an instantaneous expression of God's grace; it could be the essential moral underpinning for a life devoted to the service of one's time. Indeed, one's own salvation depended upon service to others.[43]

Figure 6-1 shows how someone like former Senator Barry Goldwater and Senator Robert Dole could both be considered ideologically conservative, but theologically liberal. Both come from liberal, mainstream Protestant backgrounds in the Episcopal and Methodist churches, respectively. Goldwater openly opposed the policy agenda of religious groups who so zealously supported Ronald Reagan. Dole's 1988 campaign for the Republican presidential nomination was damaged because he did not champion conservative religious causes. President George Bush was outside the conservative religious orbit until pragmatic political considerations led him to make peace with leading conservatives, many of whom were skeptical of his allegiance to their cause.

To develop Figure 6-1, each political personality's background and beliefs were compared to the liberal and conservative ideas in Figure

FIGURE 6-1
Theological and Political/Ideological Relationships

Liberal
Ideology

Liberal Theology		Conservative Theology
Bill Clinton Gary Hart George McGovern Mario Cuomo Edward Kennedy Jesse Jackson Walter Mondale		John Anderson Richard Gephardt Mark Hatfield
George Bush Robert Dole Barry Goldwater Lamar Alexander Phil Gramm Newt Gingrich		Jesse Helms Ronald Reagan Jack Kemp Pat Robertson Dan Quayle Pat Buchanan Bill Buckley

Conservative
Ideology

2-1 in Chapter Two. Personalities like Walter Mondale, Jesse Jackson, Gary Hart, and George McGovern come from liberal backgrounds, both ideologically and theologically. Edward M. Kennedy and William F. Buckley, Jr., illustrate the contrast between Roman Catholics of liberal and conservative persuasions, both ideologically and theologically. Senator Mark Hatfield and former 1980 presidential candidate John Anderson reflect a theologically conservative but ideologically liberal perspective. Hatfield and Anderson have advocated numerous liberal policy initiatives in both domestic and foreign affairs; Anderson even left the Republican Party in 1980 to run for president as an independent, receiving much of his support from ideological liberals, especially in the Jewish community. Yet both of these men claimed to be orthodox theological conservatives.

Other politicians like Ronald Reagan, Strom Thurmond, and Jesse Helms are conservative in both an ideological and theological sense. One of President Jimmy Carter's problems was his apparent waffling among the quadrants on Figure 6-1. At one time or another, he could have been classified in all four quadrants. He campaigned for the nomination as an ideological and theological conservative, professing to be "born again" and opposed to big government in Washington. But during his administration he permitted liberal interest groups access to power, lost public support with his signing of the Panama Canal treaty, and failed to curtail the expansion of worldwide Soviet military power.

George Herbert Walker Bush is in many ways the epitome of conservative noblesse oblige. Born of a Brahmin family on the East Coast, he attended the best schools and attained early wealth in the high-stakes oil business. His public service has been marked by a concern for results and an unspoken acceptance of traditional values. In the 1988 presidential election Bush was embarrassed by the constant questioning of his religious beliefs. His political theology is classically liberal Episcopalian, but in the crisis of the Iraq War Bush asked Billy Graham to accompany him to Camp David for a prayer service. His conservative theology is reflected in his call for a Day of Prayer on the Sunday before Operation Desert Storm was concluded.

So often the mistake is made of looking at great events, movements, or personalities in isolation, failing to see them in context. Just as in a symphony the prelude announces the main movement, so too in politics religious debates foreshadow major events. Franklin D. Roosevelt's New

Deal was not new, it only stated the principles which had been discussed, debated, and decided several decades before the 1932 campaign. The Methodist Social Creed of 1908, for example, embodied many of the New Deal's public policy principles, and it was drafted when Roosevelt's much older namesake was still president. Similarly, Ronald Reagan's conservative agenda was not new, it merely reflected the historical development of conservative ideas, many of which were rooted in the debates of Christian denominations during the 1960s and 1970s.

Conclusion

In 1959 John Steinbeck wrote a letter to Adlai Stevenson in which he said that Americans were strangely afflicted, "having too many things they spend their hours and money on the couch searching for a soul."[44] The essence of the American conservative tradition is that the soul is the key to a rediscovery of American uniqueness. The nation has a special tradition with economic, political, and religious roots.

These tripartite traditions do not conflict with one another. The Bible teaches a fallen man; economic theory holds that such a person seeks material gain whenever possible; and the political tradition holds that governmental power should be divided to protect against the exploitation of the people by those in authority. Each of these conservative premises substantiates the other two, but the ideas of religion are most important in defining the texture of a culture.

These traditions have been overlooked by mainstream academia. *The Times Literary Supplement* once lamented the entrusting of the Greco-Roman, Judeo-Christian inheritance to intellectuals, because they were prone to appeal to imaginary utopias. "The survival of intellectual, indeed of spiritual and ethical activity is dependent on a refusal to accept political slogans that are not tested by the touchstone of historic experience."[45] Paul Johnson is more pointed in his critique: "One of the principal lessons of our tragic century, which has seen so many millions of innocent lives sacrificed in schemes to improve the lot of humanity is—beware [of] intellectuals. Not merely should they be kept well away from the levers of power, they should also be objects of particular suspicion when they seek to offer collective advice."[46] It comes as no surprise to discover that the ideas of conservatism are dismissed as unimportant in much of the academic literature.

While the conservative tradition remains strong, its strength has been weakened through efforts, beginning in the New Deal, to dismiss the religious base of the social order as unimportant, redefine the meaning of the Constitution, and assert that government guidance of the economy is a desirable thing. Conservative solutions to the dilemmas of modern man tend to be anchored in absolute values and principles, and their view of the future lacks the compelling vision of liberal rhetoric. Instead, conservatives offer the past as prologue to future problems and solutions.

Notes

1. Paul Johnson, *Modern Times* (New York: Harper & Row, 1983), p. 4.

2. Paul Johnson, *Modern Times*, p. 4.

3. Ronald W. Clark, *Einstein* (New York: Avon Books, 1971), p. 422.

4. Barbara Tuchman, *The Guns of August* (New York: Macmillan, 1962), p. 310.

5. David R. Contosta and Robert Muccigrosso, *The World in the Twentieth Century* (New York: Harper & Row, 1988), p. 92.

6. Alexander I. Solzhenitsyn, *A World Split Apart* (New York: Harper & Row, 1978), pp. 9, 29–30, 53–61.

7. "Russia's Prophet in Exile," *Time*, July 24, 1989, pp. 56–60.

8. "The Most Amazing 60 Years," *Time*, Vol. 122, October 3, 1983, p. 26.

9. Charles Wallis (ed.), *Our American Heritage* (New York: Harper & Row, 1970), p. 51.

10. John Locke, "An Essay Concerning the True Original, Extent and End of Civil Government," in J. A. St. John (ed.), *Works*, Vol. 5 (London: G. Bell, 1908), pp. 1–13.

11. John Locke, "The Reasonableness of Christianity as Defined in the Scriptures," in *Works*, Vol. 7. William Ebenstein, *Great Political Thinkers* (New York: Holt, Rinehart and Winston, 1969), pp. 390–400. Sir Ernest Barker (ed.), *Social Contract: Essays by Locke, Hume and Rousseau* (New York: Oxford University Press, 1947), pp. 1–145.

12. William Blackstone, "Of Laws in General," in *Commentaries on the Laws of England* (Chicago: University of Chicago Press, 1979), pp. 3–62.

13. Daniel J. Elazar, "Political Theory of Covenant: Biblical Origins and Development," Paper presented to the American Political Science Association, 1980.

14. Louis I. Bredvold and Ralph G. Ross (eds.), *The Philosophy of Edmund Burke* (Ann Arbor, Mich: University of Michigan Press, 1960), p. 157.

15. Rexford Guy Tugwell, quoted in Howard Zinn (ed.), *New Deal Thought* (Indianapolis, Ind.: Bobbs-Merrill, 1966), p. 89.

16. Rexford Guy Tugwell, "Rewriting the Constitution," *The Center Magazine*,

publication of the Center of the Study of Democratic Institutions, I, 3 (March, 1968), pp. 18–25.

17. Samuel J. Ervin, Jr., and Ramsey Clark, *Role of the Supreme Court: Maker or Adjudicator* (Washington, D.C.: American Enterprise Institute for Public Policy Research, 1970), p. 52.

18. Felix Frankfurter, quoted in Carl Brent Swisher, *The Growth of Constitutional Power in the United States* (Chicago: University of Chicago Press, 1963), p. 77.

19. Oliver Wendell Holmes, quoted in Alpheus T. Mason, *The Supreme Court From Taft to Warren* (New York: Norton, 1964), p. 15.

20. *United States v. Butler* (1936).

21. *National Labor Relations Board v. Jones & Laughlin Corp.* (1937).

22. *Wickard v. Filburn* (1942).

23. Clinton Rossiter (ed.), *The Federalist Papers* (New York: New American Library, 1964), pp. 292–293.

24. Charles Wallis (ed.), *Our American Heritage*, p. 53.

25. William Ebenstein, *Great Political Thinkers* (4th ed.; New York: Holt, Rinehart and Winston, 1969), p. 396.

26. "Economic Thought," *International Encyclopedia of the Social Sciences*, Vol. 4, p. 444.

27. Kenneth W. Thompson, *The Moral Issue in Statecraft* (Baton Rouge, La.: Louisiana State University Press, 1966), p. xii.

28. Robert N. Bellah, *The Broken Covenant: American Civil Religion in Time of Trial* (New York: The Seabury Press, 1975), p. 12.

29. Richard Hofstadter, *The American Political Tradition* (New York: Knopf, 1948), p. 16.

30. Clinton Rossiter (ed.), *The Federalist Papers*, pp. 231, 346, 353. The essays quoted are from papers No. 38, 55, and 57.

31. Clinton Rossiter (ed.), *The Federalist Papers*, p. 471.

32. Thomas Jefferson, "Resolution Relative to the Alien and Sedition Laws," 1798, in Philip S. Faver (ed.), *Basic Writings of Thomas Jefferson* (New York: Willey Book Co., 1944), p. 330.

33. Michael Novak, *Choosing Our King* (New York: Macmillan, 1974), pp. 114–115.

34. Michael Novak, *Choosing Our King*, pp. 114–115.

35. Alexis de Tocqueville as cited in Robert S. Alley, *So Help Me God* (Richmond, Va.: John Knox Press, 1972), p. 21.

36. Alexis de Tocqueville as cited in Ellis Sandoz, "Classical and Christian Dimensions of American Political Thought," *Modern Age*, Vol. 25, p. 21.

37. For conservative studies on this theme see M. E. Bradford, *A Worthy Company: Brief Lives of the Framers of the United States Constitution* (Plymouth, Mass.: Plymouth Rock Foundation, 1982). *American Historical Documents* (New York: Barnes & Noble, 1960). R. J. Rushdoony, *This Independent Republic* (Tyler, Tex.: Thoburn Press, 1964). Alice M. Baldwin, *The New England Clergy and the American Revolution* (New York: Frederick Ungar, 1928). John W. Whitehead, *The Separation Illusion* (Milford, Mich.: Mott Media, 1977). John W. Whitehead, *The Second American Revolution* (Elgin, Ill.:

David C. Cook, 1979). Verna Hall, *The Christian History of the Constitution of the United States of America* (San Francisco, Calif.: Foundation for American Christian Education, 1960). Verna Hall, *The Christian History of the American Revolution* (San Francisco, Calif.: Foundation for American Christian Education, 1976). Rus Walton, *Fundamentals for American Christians* (Plymouth, Mass.: Plymouth Rock Foundation, 1978). Rus Walton, *One Nation Under God* (Washington, D.C.: Third Century Publishers, 1975).

38. Harold C. Syrett (ed.), *American Historical Documents* (New York: Columbia University Press, 1960), Chapter 1, pp. 110–113.

39. For many other quotations and points of analysis, see the sources cited in footnote 37. The printing of these and related quotations in one source may be found in "Letter From Plymouth Rock," (Plymouth, Mass.: The Plymouth Rock Foundation, 1983), pp. 1–8.

40. Glenn Tinder, *The Political Meaning of Christianity* (Baton Rouge, La.: Louisiana State University Press, 1989), pp. 23–95.

41. Joshua O. Haberman, "America's Safety Belt in the Bible Belt," *World*, October 19, 1987, p. 8.

42. Melvin J. Thorne, *American Conservative Thought Since World War Two* (New York: Greenwood Press, 1990), pp. 1–53.

43. George McGovern, *Grassroots* (New York: Random House, 1977), p. 34.

44. Elaine Steinbeck and Robert Wallsten (eds.), *Steinbeck: A Life in Letters* (New York: Viking Press, 1976), p. 652.

45. *The Times Literary Supplement*, September 17, 1954, as printed in Peter Viereck, *Conservatism Revisited* (New York: Greenwood Press, 1978), pp. 8–9.

46. Paul Johnson, *Intellectuals* (New York: Harper & Row, 1988), p. 342.

CHAPTER SEVEN

The Directions of Contemporary American Conservatism

*If we achieve full employment and greater economic
growth—if we have cities of gold and alabaster—but our
children have not learned how to walk in goodness, justice and
mercy, then the American experiment, no matter how gilded,
will have failed.*

WILLIAM BENNETT[1]

In September of 1863 Abraham Lincoln dedicated a cemetery in Gettysburg, Pennsylvania, and asked: "Can this nation, or any nation so conceived and so dedicated, long endure?" Questions about the national character lie at the heart of the future of the American experiment. Today, many observers believe that the nation's greatest weaknesses are in the civic, cultural, and moral domain where government is often deficient and unworkable. Jack Kemp has written: "A society that is indifferent to its moral and spiritual life is indifferent to its future."[2]

William Bennett, under the auspices of the Heritage Foundation, released an "index of leading cultural indicators," in 1993. It showed that since 1960 there had been a 560 percent increase in violent crime, a more than 400 percent increase in illegitimate births, a quadrupling of divorces, a tripling of the percentage of children living in single-parent homes, a more than 200 percent increase in the teenage suicide rate, and a drop of seventy-five points in the SAT scores of high school students. The statistics showed that 30 percent of all births in the United States, and 68 percent of Black births, were in fatherless homes.[3]

Public opinion confirms the cultural concerns summarized by Bennett, with much of the blame attributed to government. Shortly before the 1994 election a Times Mirror Center poll found that only 33 percent of the public believed that elected officials care about their beliefs, and only 41 percent believe government benefits all of the people. Nearly 70 percent said that dealing with the federal bureaucracy wasn't worth the trouble, and only 41 percent said government should help the needy.[4] Paradoxes abound. The public wants their fellow citizens to live more responsibly but finds that the public schools fail to teach children right from wrong. Society wants to stop the spiral of illegitimate births but recoils on learning that schools dispense condoms more than moral advice. Polls show Americans want law and order, but the criminal justice system regularly releases violent criminals to the streets.

What Americans seem to want above all else is civic revitalization grounded in the precepts of morality. A cultural renaissance must come from local communities, whose strengths rest upon the pillars of family, neighborhood, church, and synagogue. For conservatives the "tripod of character, community and culture" are central building blocks of the conservative worldview.[5]

Conservatives believe that government has its limitations and that there are many things in life more important than politics, among them "religion, art, study, family, friends, music, fun, duty."[6] In the eyes of American conservatives, these intermediary institutions, which stand between the citizen and his government, are the womb of culture. Government should leave well enough alone and let these institutions nourish society.

Conservatism suffered massive defeats during the 1960s and 1970s when government programs began to interfere with the pillars of society's strength, damaging the coherence and cohesion of community. Events on public school and college campuses dramatically illustrate the impact on these intermediary institutions.

In 1983 a blue-ribbon government commission studying the educational system of the United States declared the country to be "a nation at risk." At a time when conservative values were acceptable on campus, students were not studying the right subjects, working hard enough, or learning enough. Schools suffered from slack and uneven standards, with teachers ill-prepared to teach even if their classroom materials were adequate—and most were not. "If an unfriendly foreign power had attempted to impose on America the mediocre educational performance that exists today," the panel said, "we might well have viewed it as an act of war."[7]

Campus unrest was not a response to conservative principles: they were practically nonexistent among college faculties. Instead, the revolt was a reaction to the frustrated aspirations of New Deal liberalism. Allan Bloom wrote about campus turmoil that "universities were offering them [students] every concession other than education. . . . They [were] unified only in their relativism and their allegiance to equality."[8] The traditional emphasis in American education on values and moral knowledge had diminished to the vanishing point.

In the 1980s the situation was the reverse: students exchanged political activism and protest for a business suit of establishment values. No alienation was greater in college classrooms than that between leftist faculty members and conservative students.

Why has education failed in the United States? In 1852 John Henry Cardinal Newman analyzed the problem in a remarkably prescient essay entitled "On the Scope and Nature of University Education." Arguing that what was missing was the unity between knowledge and religious conviction, Newman asked, "Is it logically consistent in a seat of learning to exclude theology from the number of its studies?" Theology, Newman said, "meets us with a profession and a proffer of the highest truths of which the human mind is capable," and only a superficial approach to education could ignore the ethical and religious foundations of culture.[9] At the root of the educational crisis, say many conservative critics, is the appalling loss of traditional values in the curriculum.

Conservatives carefully point out that the problem of learning in schools is but a by-product of the dramatic change in American family life and values. The basic ties of the family are the heart of society, they argue, and the very nursery of civic virtue. Since the 1960s divorce has been breaking up families more rapidly than death did in the early years of the twentieth century. An article in *Current Problems in Pediatrics* concluded that "the American family is in a period of crisis and transition."[10] The alarm over education is but an aftershock of the dissolution of stability in the home. In the first study on the effects of divorce on men, women, and children a decade after divorce, the authors conclude that America is now "a world in which marriage is freely terminable at any time . . . [and] we lack the psychological theory that we need to predict the consequences."[11] The evidence points to fewer marriages and more children unwilling or unable to make lasting commitments to one another. The children of divorced parents and the parents of divorced children often look to the state to supply basic needs such as housing, child care, education supplements, and economic assistance.

For much of their history, Americans could count on other Americans who shared similar values, standards, and principles, but today social institutions possess a dwindling core of commonly accepted cultural values. Impossible to overlook in the modern lexicon of social research are such words as *disorganization, disintegration, decline, insecurity, breakdown, instability,* and *dysfunctional.* The intrusion of government programs and power interfered with the community's intermediary institutions, leading to the collapse of the moral order. "The family, religious association, and local community—these, the conservatives insist, cannot be regarded as the external products of man's thought and behavior; they are essential prior to the individual and the indispensable supports of belief and conduct."[12]

Traditionally, religion provided the core values, symbols, stories, and language for the legitimation of the social order. In America the Judeo-Christian tradition was the source of moral values in the society; various legal concepts, accepted beliefs about family and education, and governmental ideas about shared power and the nature of man were all rooted in this heritage. There is a venerable pedigree for this idea of a "civil religion," which was best summed up by Robert Bellah in the 1960s.[13] The legacy of this broad religious tradition is seen in the use of God on the nation's coinage and invocations to the Almighty in the last line of political speeches. Approximately 96 percent of the American people continue to believe in God, 72 percent believe in heaven, and 53 percent believe in hell.[14]

In the late 1980s, Robert Wuthnow of Princeton University argued that this underlying consensus for American civil life was rapidly disintegrating.[15] The postwar expansion of the state into every corner of the society resulted, said Wuthnow, in a liberal and conservative realignment of religious communities without regard to denominational distinctions. Two opposing camps have emerged, which James Hunter called the "orthodox" and the "progressive," each giving followers the assurance that they represent the cause of authentic biblical religion.[16]

What is worrisome in any picture of the national future is that such issues as illegitimate births, abortion, prayer in the public schools, and the regard given the symbols of American culture such as the flag are really a battle over conflicting constructions of reality. In dispute are the meaning of the world and God's relationship to it, the definition of human nature, the basis of moral judgments, and the divine purpose of history. Unfortunately, the terms *liberal* and *conservative* often fail to capture the depth of the differences between the two camps. What is sure, however, is the depth of dissimilarity between the worldviews of those who oppose one another on these cultural issues.

"Perhaps the most remarkable non-event of modern times," writes Paul Johnson, "is the failure of religious beliefs to disappear."[17] Governor John Winthrop of Massachusetts described the original vision of America in biblical words as a "city upon a hill, [with] the eyes of all people upon us."[18] Even the American Revolution was, in the minds of some, little more than a political expression of the religious revivals of the Great Awakening. In the twentieth century the secular winds of atheism and agnosticism which gradually removed the Reformation's heritage from Europe are sweeping America, and replacing the notion of a transcendent personal god with one made in the image of man. This crisis, more than any other, is causing the deep divisions within the nation.

The prospect that such a secular legacy has now split the nation into feuding factions with alternative explanations of reality is not comforting to conservatives familiar with the civic culture that guided the earlier American experience. They worry that the loss of guiding values will promote the growth of government power. What all this means is that diverse religious camps will continue to wage war with one another for the spiritual soul of American life, while the culture slides into relativism.

The dark side of American culture is that it is decidedly materialistic. While church attendance remains high, there has been a liberalizing trend in theology, with Protestant clergymen funding revolutionary terrorist groups and Catholics advocating liberation theology while attempting a dialogue with Marxist-Leninist rebels. Michael Novak states that any such behavior is a betrayal of the very foundations of Christianity and endangers the church by making it a political actor.[19] Glenn Tinder argued in the *Atlantic Monthly* that Christianity has played an important part in the definition of Western democracies: "The absorption of Americans in the pleasures of buying and consuming, of mass entertainment and sports, suggest [an] erosion of the grounds of political health and impairment of personal being." The Western religious belief in the provisions of God and the reliance of man on him are being replaced by a materialistic philosophy that makes man an evolutionary pawn buffeted by forces of a history and society that he can neither understand nor change. Tinder concluded, "If we turn away from transcendence, from God, what will deliver us from a politically fatal fear and faintheartedness?"[20]

Conservatives fear that the ways of thinking, living, and behaving have now changed the nation to the point where it has little of its original community spirit and purpose. They argue that there must be some concept of "the sacred" because the greatest of human duties is "Thy will be done." It is impossible to discuss political and social duty unless there is an awareness of some truth to which one is selfless and loyal. America possesses a great and widely distributed wealth, as well as social mobility and education on an unprecedented scale. For the most part, the world is at peace in spite of deep passions; yet, there can be no radiance or happiness until individuals and society realize their purposes and duties.

The conservative message is that the deepest longing of the human heart is for transcendent truth, to be able to give oneself to a cause larger than the moment. What the nation needs is something it has lost: a sense of the good and an awareness of the permanent things. Until this need is satisfied, any discussion of rights, duties, and the human spirit is pointless. Is it possible in the twenty-first century to recapture lost spiritual anchors? Or must we say, with Lewis Carroll, that "all the king's horses and all the king's men couldn't put Humpty Dumpty together again?"

Rekindling the Democratic Spirit

The renewal of democracy begins with a realization that religious faith is more fundamental to the good society than government action. As long as people are told that there are no absolutes and that they are not responsible for their own behavior, they will rely on the government to define what is wholesome and good. There has never been a case in history in which a society survived for long without a strong moral code, and that code has always been informed by a religious truth.

In such books as *Mere Christianity* and *The Abolition of Man*, the twentieth-century British Christian apologist C. S. Lewis refuted Immanuel Kant and other secular writers who had worked to remove God from public discourse. His essay "Men Without Chests" drew an analogy between the spiritual life and the body, which he used to critique the rationalism of the Enlightenment and the soul of Christianity. Lewis argues that the head of reason cannot control the stomach of passion without the chest—which was spirit—to restrain the base appetites of human beings. Commenting on a society that had no sense of the spiritual, Lewis wrote: "We make men without chests and we expect of them virtue and enterprise. We laugh at honor and we are shocked to find traitors in our midst."[21]

A first principle of national renewal demands a remembrance of past American values. Foremost among such recollections is the realization that faith, self-control, and limited government undergird democracy. The French Revolution in 1789 sought not only liberty, but also equality and fraternity. The Jacobins esteemed human reason and equality. The French Declaration of the Rights of Man and Citizen asserted Rousseau's basic axiom that all men were born equal and had been separated from that natural equality by "arbitrary socializing institutions that were invested with arbitrary force."[22]

The American Revolution stood, in contrast to the French, for values regulated by the rule of law. American colonists wanted to protect the traditional liberties that were theirs as British subjects. Those liberties included the rights to bring legal cases before truly independent judges rather than ones subordinate to the king; to be free of having British troops quartered in their homes; to engage in trade without burdensome restrictions; and not to pay taxes voted by the British parliament in which they had no representation. In sum, the liberties for which the colonists fought were based on freedom from arbitrary control by a government in which they had no voice.

These liberties were widely understood, and there was agreement as to the concept of equality. When the Founders said "all men are created equal," they were making a statement about equality of opportunity, not equality of results. The American concept differed from the French: the pride of colonial liberty was to allow freedom within the bounds of law.

Conservative thought holds that the essence of this original vision for the nation was a limited, representative government restrained by laws that were difficult to alter and nullify. A nation forged in reaction to tyranny and arbitrary power wrote a Constitution to secure for its people every right wrested from autocratic kings, priests, and nobles in Europe.

History taught that a government of laws was the only insurance against arbitrary, uncertain, and inconstant wills of impatient men hungry for power.

The conservative legacy emphasizes that the Founding Fathers framed and ratified a document intended to last for the ages; they recognized and applied a truth derived from years of European history. Simply put, that rule was: "Freedom is political power divided into small fragments."[23] The American interpretation of that maxim was separation of powers among the three branches of government and federalism, the division of power between the state and national governments. In contrast to England and most European states, where political authority was centralized in the national government, the American system diffused power.

Avoiding the concentration of power is a centerpiece of conservative thought. The principles of separation and division of powers, the use of judicial review, and the limitations on government authority are fundamental to conservatives. Dispersion of governmental power enables the intermediary institutions to flourish.

Since the adoption of the Constitution, these principles have been the object of debate over how they should be improved. The early part of this century found America heir to the cultural legacy of Britain and the Western democracies. The lifestyle and values of the United States were exported abroad, and European ideas and immigrants flooded American shores. Today the opposite is the case. Higher education curricula emphasize multiculturalism and diversity, demanding the reduction and elimination of Eurocentric and patriarchal biases in the American political system. Limited representative government retards participation by ethnic minorities, say modern reformers. They demand that there be less separation of powers, that the central government be given more authority at the expense of local governments, and that judicial activism be adopted as a remedy for compelling social problems.

America, dominated by Western European ancestry and culture, will be challenged in the twenty-first century when white Americans may become a minority group. The question already asked is whether it is good to esteem such a history. At the college level the traditional canon of Greek, Latin, and Western European humanities has been challenged. Books once seen as classics of culture are now scorned as examples of racial imperialism and ethnic oppression.

Conservatives argue that every society needs a set of universally accepted values and that immigrants should be willing to adopt them. Such was the case until recent years. Without these traditional values and institutions to moderate and shape the dynamic energy of democratic government, society may degenerate into tyranny. The modern emphasis, however, is on the racism and sexism of the past, in contrast to the self-evident virtues of American pluralism. A balkanized society of cultural groups, each objecting to the other and agreeing on no central values, will characterize the future unless the customs and traditions of America's past rekindle the democratic spirit.

Restoring the Economic Spirit

The American economic experiment is the most glittering, most astonishing, most inventive, most organized, and greatest wealth-producing enterprise the world has ever known. In material terms, capitalism works well for most people most of the time. Year after year, individuals go into the marketplace and end up richer at the end of the year than when they began. Billions of private decisions by individuals and by firms to buy, sell, save, store, invest, or scrap guide the invisible hand that Adam Smith lauded two centuries ago.

The rough and tumble of the capitalist marketplace is the best way for lifting a country's population out of poverty, yet as the Western democracies head into the twenty-first century, persistent questions plague the conservative defense of unfettered free markets. The conflict between economic growth and environmental health is the most important issue facing capitalism in the next century. More and more evidence shows that today's smoke and fumes will lead to cataclysmic ecological problems in the future. Conservatives, devoted fans of free markets and unbridled capitalistic expansion, are often seen as opposed to environmental controls. The ecological crisis could tame the dynamism of capitalism and open the door for government regulation of the economy.

The sheer size of the problem presents a challenge to any economic theory. In 1800 one billion human beings lived on the planet; that number doubled by 1930 and doubled again by 1975. If current birthrates hold, the world's present population will double again shortly after the turn of the century.[24] The Third World is envious of Western affluence, and the prospects of terrorism for food increase as the gulf between rich and poor widens. Technological advances have upset nature's equilibrium. Smokestacks have disgorged gases into the atmosphere, factories have dumped toxic wastes into rivers and streams, and automobiles have guzzled irreplaceable fossil fuels and fouled the air with their exhausts. Forests have been denuded, lakes poisoned, and pesticides dispensed without much thought of the future. The fault for much of this is laid at the doorsteps of the defenders of capitalism.

Conservatives argue that the market mechanisms that stimulated capitalism can be used to make sure prices reflect the social costs of energy and waste. They contend that government should enforce taxes and permits instead of legislating quotas and bans on production.[25] Conservative solutions emphasize free-market economies for health care and education; it is reasonable to think that such market devices could also ensure that economic development would be both clean and orderly.[26]

Newt Gingrich firmly believes that the lessons of American history are the key to solving future challenges. Western civilization is in the midst of a transformation, says Gingrich, quoting such futurists as Alvin and Heidi Toffler, from an Industrial Age to an Information Age. American innovation, a renewed commitment to quality, and capitalistic freedom are the building blocks for the next century. In the future Gingrich sees political power devolving to citizens who are the building blocks of a new "semi-direct democracy," innovating on the local level and passing information around. The next century will see government connected to citizens through the traditional means of political parties, voting, and the media but also utilizing technology to tap resources on other planets and in cyberspace.[27]

The assumption is that government should play a smaller role in the lives of citizens. Despite the intuitive appeal and proven record of accomplishment inherent in market alternatives, in the last half of the twentieth century such options have taken a backseat to calls for federal regulation and intervention. Polls regularly show that most Americans want government to address a problem rather than allow the private market to offer a solution. As a result, growth in the public sector has been the rule during the past three decades. Public spending in the seven largest Western nations rose from 29 percent of the gross national product in 1960 to about 39 percent in 1990.[28] During much of this time, especially the decade of the 1980s, these developed nations were led by conservative governments.

Government interference in free markets quashes individual creativity and discovery. The spirit of invention and discovery that characterized American capitalism has been rendered impotent by federal rules and regulations.[29] Compared to its pre-1932 history, the American national government has much more power in numerous areas of American life, including increased influence over the affairs of individual entrepreneurs.

Over time, the nationalization of politics found conservatives generally accepting an enlarged federal government with minimal protest as long as the government entitlements benefited all classes of people. The higher income people, who might have been expected to support conservative causes in opposition to enlarged social welfare measures, were themselves coopted by programs such as Medicare, Medicaid, and the farm subsidy allocation that made them beneficiaries. Middle- and upper-class people found that they liked their entitlements to the national government's largesse almost as much as lower-class people do. What might have been a natural conservative constituency in opposition to these entitlements did not emerge until the entire structure faced bankruptcy.

A fundamental human desire for security enabled the national government to expand and provide programs to meet social needs. Health, safety, retirement income, and savings protection spawned many other programs, revealing that conservatism is easier to support in the abstract than in the concrete. Philosophically, much of today's business elite is more comfortable with welfare-state liberalism than with the competitive rawness of economic free markets.

The great democratization of American politics that accompanied the New Deal, Fair Deal, New Frontier, and Great Society strengthened the role of the national government in domestic affairs. The federal programs created an upper-class as well as a lower-class constituency, making it difficult for elected leaders to resist public opinion. The result of these forces is that conservatives have generally accepted the social welfare programs, even speaking at times of a public policy of social welfare conservatism. Some conservatives were critical of the Reagan presidency for precisely this reason: despite rhetoric to the contrary, there was no shrinkage of the size and scope of government in any real sense. Robert

Nisbet charged that Reagan (1) had a motivation more in keeping with the New Deal liberal Democrat experience than any genuine conservative Republican era since he spoke frequently of revolution and quoted liberal Democrats, such as Franklin D. Roosevelt and John F. Kennedy, as precedents for his actions more than he did conservative presidents; (2) had a passion for crusades both domestic and international, which led to a larger and more powerful government; and (3) retained, rather than abolished, the Departments of Education and Energy and the National Endowments for the Arts and Humanities, all established under liberal Democratic presidents.[30]

By 1994 the chorus for change at the national level grew into a howl, but no consensus emerged as to what should be eliminated. Efforts to shrink the size and scope of government were met by entrenched constituencies decrying the inhumanity of cutting school lunch programs and reducing federal expenditures for the poor and elderly. After the election, the halls of Congress filled with lobbyists, lawyers, and career officials defending their programs against the threat of a federal carving knife.

The presence and popularity of social welfare conservatism means an acceptance of government intervention in the economy even when the canons of conservatism argue otherwise. Given the widespread familiarity and acceptance of greater public spending, another challenge for conservatism is to balance economic growth with a reduction of social programs to help those displaced by periodic economic realignments. Unemployed steel workers, the homeless in urban settings, and racial minorities beset with poverty make regular demands on the economic and political system.

In such an environment, conservatism has proven to be both strong and weak. Its strength rests in the ideas that even its opponents accept as necessary if society is to be stable: respect for authority, a reduced role for government, and a high regard for tradition. Its weakness rests in the difficulty of popularizing ideas whose very existence denies the promises of economic, political, and social progress embodied in the New Deal, Fair Deal, New Frontier, and Great Society. The fundamental impulse of conservatism is toward restraint, even when cutting the size of establishment government. By contrast, liberalism moves toward action. The needs of the urban poor and the unemployed are readily addressed by liberalism, where conservative solutions appear cold and aloof. The liberal hour in American politics came during the Great Depression, after President Hoover's conservative remedies failed to provide the type and level of action people demanded. Conservatives find their moment at the end of the century, as they face the failed solutions of central government.

Conclusion

"In America," writes Robert Heineman, "conservative thought has been a much misunderstood and heavily stereotyped form of intellectual activity."[31] Even in triumph, conservatism never achieved widespread popular support until the late 1970s and 1980s; yet, many of its ideas significantly influenced American society throughout its history. It has exercised this influence because conservative leaders found arenas of politics in which to battle for the achievement of their goals. This accomplishment is more important than the fact that conservatism was misunderstood and never enjoyed wide acceptance throughout society. The recent popularity of conservatism as an economic, political, religious, and social movement was made possible by society's reaction to liberalism more than by an undying allegiance to the conservative banner.

While the breadth of conservatism may encompass differing schools of thought, that strength is also a weakness when it comes to maintaining balance among its ideas and respect among its advocates. These differences affect how the various advocates view the role of government, religion, and speech. On the one hand, an economic conservative, especially one with libertarian tendencies, wants to have a very small government that interferes as little as possible in the lives of Americans; but such a person is unlikely to support religious freedoms. A traditional or religious conservative, on the other hand, may appreciate a larger government in order to protect moral values as the norm of societal behavior. Such differences are seen in the disagreement between conservative columnist William F. Buckley, Jr., and former secretary of education and drug czar William Bennett over solutions to the drug crisis in American cities. Buckley favors the libertarian solution of legalization, while Bennett advocates the more traditionally conservative argument of stiffer sentences and better enforcement. Both of these conservative

spokesmen have impeccable ideological credentials, yet they see the solution to the problem differently.

The Republican Party of the 1990s reveals these divisions. Younger
conservatives in their twenties, attracted to the Republican Party in the
years of the Reagan presidency, are interested in the economic aspects
of conservatism and favor the ideas of minimal governmental restraints
on the achievement of economic success. Another strong group in the
Republican Party comprises the religious conservatives, who argue that
government must stop abortion and restore prayer and Bible reading in
the public schools. Midwestern conservatives, such as the late senators
Robert Taft and Everett M. Dirksen, former president Gerald Ford, and
Senator Robert Dole, are pragmatic conservatives. Unlike those who
adhere to economic and religious conservatism, they are not sorely both-
ered by either government regulation or morality questions. Their pragmatic position seeks to prevent excesses of government regulation and
the growth of government.

Still another division occurs with the idea of the military and military
service. Should military service be voluntary or conscriptive? How large
should the military be? Staunch conservatives argue that the first responsibility of government is the safety of citizens and that the military should
be large in order to protect the nation's political and economic interests
around the world. This position means a larger government, more taxes,
and higher spending. Conservatives who value individual freedom oppose conscription while other strongly patriotic conservatives do not.

There are many varieties of conservatives who collectively identify
with the election and presidency of Ronald Reagan and the subsequent
triumph of conservative policies in the early 1990s. Some of these loyal-
ists were motivated by the social and moral agenda of the religious right;
others were moved by the conviction that American foreign policy had
weakened and foundered in the 1970s; still others came to the "Reagan
Revolution" because they shared a passion to cut taxes and reduce the
powers of the federal government. In the 1990s these reformers found
themselves in power and at odds with one another. For much of its
history American conservatism has been on the outside looking in; its
viable policies were developed in opposition to liberal policies. Now the
ideological shoe is on the other foot.

The resolution of tensions within the ranks of conservatism is important because conservatism has been prone to factionalism throughout its

history. After dominating presidential politics for most of the decades since 1950, the conservative monolith cracked following the election of George Bush in 1988. The return of a liberal to the White House in 1992 signaled the end of the conservative resurgence to some. The basic division within the movement remains between two strains: the mostly urban, ethnic, and economic free-market neoconservatives and the traditional, small-town, agrarian conservatives who stress cultural values over economics. The former group was influential in popularizing the economic agenda of conservatism early in the Reagan administration. The latter group, alarmed by the secular drift of society away from the native values of religion and community, worked for the defeat of liberal ideas in the 1994 midterm election.

The Bush presidency will be remembered as an example of pragmatism over ideology. Irving Kristol warned in the beginning of the last decade of the twentieth century that "the Republican Party [was] a defective vehicle for the mobilization of conservative energies and the formulation of even a minimally coherent conservative agenda."[32] He was right, and the future of conservatism will hang on the ability of adherents to mobilize and persuade their peers, absent parties and elections.

Western culture is presently going through a monumental change. As the world enters the twenty-first century a new postmodern worldview is gaining dominance in American universities and culture. This impulse emphasizes indeterminacy, chance, anarchy, and the silence of meaning and knowledge in the world. Postmodernists base their new relativism on the view that all meaning is socially constructed on a particular conviction of language, so words cannot render truths about the world in any coherent way.[33]

During the twentieth century Western civilization had to survive powerful assaults from without: socialism, fascism, and secular nihilism. In the next century the threat will come from the very people who render the values and virtues to a free people. The postmodern ethic is regnant in the media and entertainment industries. In his acceptance speech of the Templeton Prize in 1994, Michael Novak described this threat of postmodernism as the most "Insidious and invidious attack from within: There is no such thing as truth. . . . Truth is bondage, believe what seems right to you, there are as many truths as there are individuals. Follow your feelings, do as you please, get in touch with yourself [and] do what feels comfortable."[34]

In the next century the belief in truth will be equated to acceptance of authoritarian control. The American impulse is internal, for self-government, self-esteem, and self-actualized individuals with personal peace and affluence. In such an environment no individual wants to bend to the dictates of church, community, or tradition, especially when it cannot be known if anything is true.

The future of conservatism is tied to how significant cultural values are related to the propagation of a political idea. Traditional conservatives believe that religious and community values are the bedrock of societal stability, arguing that there is a causal relationship between traditional Western, Judeo-Christian values and the political order. Still other conservatives emphasize the ideas of economic stability and pragmatic opposition to foreign threats as being more important than native values. In the next century the morality of a free society will determine its future.

Conservatism's divergent factions allow it to reach to more people, but such differences make the achievement of common goals difficult. The conservative movement must have tension to be successful, but respect needs to be maintained between its competing factions. Will the future find conservatism broadening its base of support or splintering into divergent factions in the struggle to rule? To improve the marketability of conservatism, it will need to attract Blacks and other minorities. Roman Catholics and the South will also be crucial to the continued viability of the movement.

The values of the family, church, and neighborhood school are the major issues of political debate in the decade ahead. The Reagan administration left a legacy of conservative concern for such institutions that was embraced by the new conservative majority in the nineties, but it remains to be seen whether cultural values will restore conservatism to its past glory.

To sustain power in America, an indictment of liberalism is not enough. In the final analysis, regnant conservatism requires those very qualities of the Western tradition that make civilization possible. The American Revolution, unlike the French, stood for values rooted in the biblical experience. History teaches us that an age wrong about God is almost certain to be wrong about man. The French Revolution of 1789 sought not only liberty, but also equality and fraternity. The French Revolution believed Rousseau's basic axiom that men were born free and everywhere they were in chains. By the end of the century dictatorship crushed democracy in France and much of Europe paid the price. The Russian Revolution in 1917 and the Chinese Revolution of 1949 echoed the quest for equality with the same result: the expansion of central government power and the extinction of the individual.

Walter Lippmann recounts an evening in the days before America's entry into World War II, when the U.S. ambassador to Britain, Joseph P. Kennedy, opined that if war came, the English would be defeated. Such a prognosis stirred Winston Churchill to magnificent oration, "I for one would willingly lay down my life in combat, rather than, in fear of defeat, surrender to the menaces of these most sinister men." Churchill went on to consider the possibility of the unthinkable, a world without British influence: "It will then be for you, for the Americans, to preserve and maintain the great heritage of the English-speaking peoples."[35] America came into the twentieth century as the youngest prodigy in the grown-up world of Western culture; it ends it as the heir apparent to that lineage. The constant struggle of free societies is to maintain three freedoms: economic, political, and cultural. Of these three, the cultural struggle, long neglected in the United States, is the place where the fate of free societies will rest in the twenty-first century.

Notes

1. William Bennett, "Commuter Massacre, Our Warning," *Wall Street Journal*, December 10, 1993.

2. Jack Kemp, "A Cultural Renaissance," *Imprimis* Vol. 23, No. 8 (August 1994).

3. William J. Bennett, "The Index of Leading Cultural Indicators," Washington, D.C.: Heritage Foundation. (March 1993).

4. "Americans Increasingly Bitter, Frustrated, Cynical, Poll Says," *The Greenville News*, October 13, 1994.

5. Don Eberly, "The Quest for a Civil Society," in Don Eberly, ed., *Building a Community of Citizens* (Lanham, Md.: University Press of America, 1994), pp. xvii–xviii.

6. Quintin Hoff, *The Case for Conservatism* (London: Macmillan Press, 1947), p. 47.

7. National Commission on Excellence in Education, *A Nation at Risk* (Washington, D.C.: U.S. Govt. Printing Office, 1983), pp. 1–10.

8. Allan Bloom, *The Closing of the American Mind* (New York: Simon and Schuster, 1987), pp. 25, 50.

9. John Henry Cardinal Newman, *The Scope and Nature of University Education* (London: Longman, Green, Longman, Roberts, 1859).

10. Carolyn M. Newberger et al., "The American Family in Crisis: Implications for Children," *Current Problems in Pediatrics*, Vol. 16 (December 1986), pp. 686–688, 713.

11. Judith S. Wallerstein and Sandra Blakeslee, *Second Chances* (New York: Ticknor & Fields, 1989), p. 297.

12. Robert Nisbet, *The Quest for Community*, 2d ed. (New York: Oxford University Press, 1970), p. 25.

13. Robert Bellah, *Beyond Belief* (New York: Harper & Row, 1970).

14. *The Economist*, May 20, 1989, p. 35.

15. Robert Wuthnow, *The Restructuring of American Religion* (Princeton, N.J.: Princeton University Press, 1989).

16. Charles W. Dunn, *American Political Theology* (New York: Praeger, 1984). James Davidson Hunter, *Culture Wars* (New York: The Free Press, 1991), p. 44.

17. Paul Johnson, *Modern Times* (New York: Harper & Row, 1983), p. 698.

18. Robert C. Winthrop, *Life and Letters of John Winthrop* (New York: Da Capo Press, 1971), pp. 18–19.

19. Michael Novak, *Liberation Theology and Liberal Society* (Washington, D.C.: American Enterprise Institute, 1987).

20. Glenn Tinder, "Can We Be Good Without God?" *Atlantic Monthly*, December 1989, p. 85.

21. C. S. Lewis, "Men Without Chests," in William J. Bennett, ed., *The Book of Virtues* (New York: Simon and Schuster, 1993), pp. 263–265.

22. Simon Schama, *Citizens* (New York: Knopf, 1989), p. 475.

23. Samuel J. Ervin, "Judicial Verbicide: An Affront to the Constitution," in George A. Panchias, ed., *Modern Age* (Indianapolis, Ind.: Liberty Press, 1988), pp. 455–464.

24. Richard J. Barnet, *The Lean Years* (New York: Simon and Schuster, 1980), pp. 15–20.

25. "The Vision Thing: Conservatism for the Nineties," *Policy Review*, Spring 1990, pp. 4–37.

26. Conrad P. Waligorski, *The Political Theory of Conservative Economists* (Lawrence, Kans.: University of Kansas Press, 1990).

27. Newt Gingrich, *To Renew America* (New York: Harper Collins, 1995). Alvin Toffler, *Future Shock* (New York: Random House, 1970). Alvin Toffler, *The Third Wave* (New York: Random House, 1983). Alvin and Heidi Toffler, *Creating a New Civilization* (Washington D.C.: Progress & Freedom Foundation, 1994).

28. *The Economist*, May 19, 1990, p. 11.

29. For a history of individual freedom in the world and the United States see: Daniel J. Boorstin, *The Discoverers* (New York: Vintage Books, 1983); *The Creators* (New York: Random House, 1992); *The Americans: Three Volumes* (New York: Vintage Books, 1958, 1965, 1973).

30. Robert Nisbet, *Conservatism* (Minneapolis, Minn.: University of Minnesota Press, 1986), pp. 104–105.

31. Robert Heineman, "Tradition and the American Conservative: Toward a Wider Political Dialogue," *Politics in Perspective*, Vol. 13 (Summer 1986), p. 174.

32. Irving Kristol, "Conservatives' Greatest Enemy May Be the GOP," *The Wall Street Journal*, February 20, 1990, p. A24.

33. David Harvey, *The Condition of Postmodernity* (Cambridge, Mass.: Basil Blackwell, 1989).

34. Michael Novak, "Awakening from Nihilism," The Templeton Address, Westminster Abbey, London, May 5, 1994.

35. William Manchester, *The Last Lion: Winston Spencer Churchill Alone* (Boston: Little Brown, 1988), pp. 439–440.

A Selected Topical Bibliography

On General Bibliographic Aids

Filler, Louis. *Dictionary of American Conservatism*. New York: Philosophical Library, 1987.

Intercollegiate Studies Institute. *ISI Bibliography*. Bryn Mawr, Pa.: 1994.

Vance, Mary. *Conservatism: Monographs, Nineteen Eighty to Nineteen Eighty-Seven*. Monticello, Ill.: Vance Bibliographies, 1988.

Wilcox, Laird. *Guide to the American Right: Directory and Bibliography*. Olathe, Kans.: Wilcox, Laird Editorial Research Service, 1989.

Wolfe, Gregory. *Right Minds: A Sourcebook of American Conservative Thought*. Chicago: Regnery, 1987.

On the Conservative Tradition in America

Blackstone, Sir William. *Commentaries on the Laws of England*. Chicago: University of Chicago Press, 1979.

Bloom, Allan. *The Closing of the American Mind*. New York: Simon & Schuster, 1987.

Bowen, Catherine Drinker. *Yankee from Olympus*. Boston: Little, Brown, 1944.

Brennan, Mary C. *Turning Right in the Sixties*. Chapel Hill, N.C.: University of North Carolina Press, 1995.

Buckley, William F., Jr., ed. *Up from Liberalism*. New York: Stein and Day, 1958.

———, ed. *Did You Ever See a Dream Walking? American Conservative Thought in the 20th Century*. Indianapolis, Ind.: Bobbs–Merrill, 1970.

Buckley, William F., Jr., and Charles R. Kesler, eds. *Keeping the Tablets: Modern American Conservative Thought*. New York: Harper & Row, 1987.

Calhoun, John C. *Discourse on the Constitution and Government of the United States*. New York: Russell & Russell, 1968.

Carey, George, ed. *Freedom and Virtue: The Conservative/Libertarian Debate*. Lanham, Md.: University Press of America/Intercollegiate Studies Institute, 1984.

Carey, George, and Willmoore Kendall. *The Basic Symbols of the American Political Tradition.* 2d ed. Washington, D.C.: Catholic University Press, 1995.

Chodorov, Frank. *One Is a Crowd.* New York: Devin-Adair, 1952.

"Conservatism and History." Special issue of *Continuity: A Journal of History* 4–5 (Spring, Fall, 1982).

Covell, Charles. *The Redefinition of Conservatism: Politics and Doctrine.* New York: St. Martin's, 1986.

Davidson, Donald. *The Attack on Leviathan: Regionalism and Nationalism in the United States.* Chapel Hill, N.C.: University of North Carolina Press, 1938.

East, John P. *The American Conservative Movement: The Philosophical Founders.* Chicago: Regnery, 1986.

Elshtain, Jean Bethke. *Democracy on Trial.* New York: Basic Books, 1996.

Evans, M. Stanton. *The Future of Conservatism.* New York: Holt, Rinehart and Winston, 1968.

Free Congress Research and Education Foundation. *Cultural Conservatism: Toward a New National Agenda.* Washington, D. C.: Free Congress, 1988.

Friedman, Milton. *Capitalism and Freedom.* Chicago: University of Chicago Press, 1962.

Frohnen, Bruce. *Virtue and the Promise of Conservatism.* Lawrence, Kans.: University of Kansas Press, 1993.

Fryer, Russell. *Recent Conservative Political Thought: American Perspectives.* Lanham, Md.: University Press of America, 1979.

"A Generation of the Intellectual Right." Special issue of *Modern Age* 26, no. 3–4 (Summer/Fall, 1982).

Genovese, Eugene. *The Southern Tradition: The Achievement and Limitations of an American Conservatism.* Cambridge, Mass.: Harvard University Press, 1994.

Goldwater, Barry M. *The Conscience of a Conservative.* Shepardsville, Ky.: Victor Publishing, 1960.

Goldwin, Robert, ed. *Left, Right and Center: Essays on Liberalism and Conservatism in the United States.* Chicago: Rand McNally, 1967.

Gottfried, Paul. *The Search for Political Meaning: Hegel and the Postwar American Right.* DeKalb, Ill.: Northern Illinois University Press, 1986.

Gottfried, Paul, and Thomas Fleming. *The Conservative Movement.* Boston: Twayne, 1988.

Guttman, Allan. *The Conservative Tradition in America.* New York: Oxford Press, 1967.

Hallowell, John. *The Moral Foundations of Democracy.* Chicago: University of Chicago Press, 1973.

Harbour, William R. *The Foundations of Conservative Thought.* Notre Dame, Ind.: University of Notre Dame Press, 1982.

Hart, Jeffrey. *The American Dissent.* Garden City, N.Y.: Doubleday, 1966.

Holmes, Stephen. *Passions and Constraint: On the Theory of Liberal Democracy.* Chicago: University of Chicago Press, 1995.

Horwitz, Robert. *The Moral Foundations of the American Republic*. Charlottesville, Va.: University of Virginia Press, 1977.

Kendall, Nellie D., ed. *Willmoore Kendall Contra Mundum*. New Rochelle, N.Y.: Arlington House, 1971. Reissued: Lanham, Md.: University Press of America, 1994.

Kendall, Willmoore. *The Conservative Affirmation*. Chicago: Regnery, 1985.

Kirk, Russell. *A Program for Conservatives*. Chicago: Regnery, 1954.

———. *The Roots of the American Order*. LaSalle, Ill.: Open Court, 1974.

———. *John Randolph of Roanoke*. Indianapolis, Ind.: Liberty Press, 1978.

———. *The Portable Conservative Reader*. New York: Viking Press, 1982.

———. *Reclaiming a Patrimony*. Washington, D.C.: Heritage Foundation, 1982.

———. *The Conservative Mind*. 7th. ed. Chicago: Regnery, 1989.

———. *Prospects for Conservatives*. Chicago: Regnery, 1989.

———. *The Conservative Constitution*. Washington, D.C.: Regnery Gateway, 1990.

———. *America's British Culture*. New York: Transaction, 1993.

———. *The Politics of Prudence*. Bryn Mawr, Pa.: Intercollegiate Studies Institute, 1993.

———. *The Sword of Imagination: Memoirs of a Half-Century of Literary Conflict*. Grand Rapids, Mich.: Eerdmans, 1995.

Kirk, Russell, and James McClellan. *The Political Principles of Robert A. Taft*. New York: Fleet, 1967.

Kristol, Irving. *On the Democratic Idea in America*. New York: Harper & Row, 1972.

———. *Two Cheers for Capitalism*. New York: Basic Books, 1978.

———. *Reflections of a Neoconservative*. New York: Basic Books, 1983.

Lora, Ronald. *Conservative Minds in America*. Westport, Conn.: Greenwood, 1976.

Meyer, Frank S. *In Defense of Freedom: A Conservative Credo*. Chicago: Regnery, 1962.

———. *The Conservative Mainstream*. New Rochelle, N.Y.: Arlington House, 1969.

———, ed. *What Is Conservatism?* New York: Holt, Rinehart and Winston, 1964.

Nash, George H. *The Conservative Intellectual Movement in America Since 1945*. New York: Basic Books, 1976. Reissued: Bryn Mawr, Pa.: Intercollegiate Studies Institute, 1995.

Nisbet, Robert. *The Quest for Community*. New York: Oxford University Press, 1953.

———. *The Twilight of Authority*. New York: Oxford University Press, 1975.

———. *The History of the Idea of Progress*. New York: Basic Books, 1980.

———. *Conservatism*. Minneapolis, Minn.: University of Minnesota Press, 1986.

Reinhard, David. *The Republican Right Since 1945*. Lexington, Ky.: University of Kentucky Press, 1983.

Rossiter, Clinton. *Conservatism in America*. 2nd ed. Cambridge, Mass.: Harvard University Press, 1982.

Schaeffer, Francis A. *The Complete Works of Francis Schaeffer*. Westchester, Ill.: Crossway Books, 1985.

Shain, Barry. *The Myth of American Individualism*. Princeton, N.J.: Princeton University Press, 1994.

Sigler, Jay A., ed. *The Conservative Tradition in American Thought*. New York: Putnam, 1969.

Sorman, Guy. *The Conservative Revolution in America*. Chicago: Regnery, 1985.

Sowell, Thomas. *Dissenting from Liberal Orthodoxy: A Black Scholar Speaks for the "Angry" Moderates*. Washington, D.C.: American Enterprise Institute, 1976.

Steinfels, Peter. *The NeoConservatives*. New York: Simon & Schuster, 1979.

Story, Joseph. *Commentaries on the Constitution*. Boston: Little, Brown, 1873.

Thorne, Melvin J. *American Conservative Thought Since World War II: The Core Ideas*. New York: Greenwood, 1990.

Tocqueville, Alexis de. *Democracy in America*. Garden City, N.Y.: Doubleday Anchor, 1969.

Viereck, Peter. *Conservatism Revisited*. New York: Viking Press, 1949.

———. *Conservatism*. Westport, Conn.: Greenwood, 1978.

Weaver, Richard. *Ideas Have Consequences*. Chicago: University of Chicago Press, 1948.

———. *Life Without Prejudice and Other Essays*. Chicago: Regnery, 1965.

———. *The Southern Tradition at Bay*. New Rochelle, N.Y.: Arlington House, 1968.

Whittaker, Robert, ed. *The New Right Papers*. New York: St. Martin's, 1982.

Will, George. *Statecraft as Soulcraft*. New York: Simon & Schuster, 1983.

Wilson, Francis G. *The Case for Conservatism*. Seattle, Wash.: University of Washington Press, 1951.

Winchell, Mark Royden. *Neo-Conservative Criticism*. Boston: Twayne, 1991.

On American Politics

Adams, Henry. *Democracy*. New York: Farrar, Straus and Young, 1952.

Adams, John. *A Defense of the Constitution of the United States*. New York: Da Capo, 1971.

Babbitt, Irving. *Democracy and Leadership*. Indianapolis, Ind.: Liberty Press, 1979.

Barber, James D. *The Pulse of Politics*. New York: Norton, 1980.

Barone, Michael. *Our Country: The Shaping of America from Roosevelt to Reagan*. New York: The Free Press, 1990.

Beichman, Arnold. *Nine Lies About America*. LaSalle, Ill.: Open Court, 1972.

Boorstein, Daniel. *The Genius of American Politics*. Chicago: University of Chicago Press, 1953.

———. *The Americans*. 3 vols. New York: Vintage Books, 1958, 1965, 1973.

————. *The Discoverers*. New York: Vintage Books, 1983.

————. *The Creators*. New York: Random House, 1992.

Bradford, M. E. *A Better Guide Than Reason*. LaSalle, Ill.: Sherwood Sugden, 1979.

————. *A Worthy Company: Brief Lives of the Framers of the United States Constitution*. Marlborough, N.H.: Plymouth Rock Foundation, 1982.

————. *Original Intentions*. Athens, Ga.: University of Georgia Press, 1994.

Brennan, Mary C. *Turning Right in the Sixties*. Chapel Hill, N.C.: University of North Carolina Press, 1995.

Brownson, Orestes. *The American Republic*. New Haven, Conn.: College and University Press, 1972.

Burnham, James. *Congress and the American Tradition*. Chicago: Regnery, 1965.

Calhoun, John C. *A Disquisition on Government*. New York: Liberal Arts Press, 1953.

Ceasar, James W. *American Government*. New York: McGraw-Hill, 1984.

Contosta, David R., and Robert Muccigrosso. *America in the Twentieth Century*. New York: Harper & Row, 1988.

Cooper, James Fenimore. *The American Democrat*. Indianapolis, Ind.: Liberty Press, 1981.

Diamond, Martin. *The Democratic Republic*. Chicago: Rand McNally, 1970.

————. *The Founding of the Democratic Republic*. Itasca, Ill.: F. E. Peacock, 1981.

Dunn, Charles W. *Constitutional Democracy in America*. Glenview, Ill.: Scott, Foresman, 1987.

Gentz, Friedrich von. *The Origins and Principles of the American Revolution Compared with the Origins and Principles of the French Revolution*. Delmar, N.Y.: Scholar's Press, 1977.

Hamilton, Alexander, James Madison, and John Jay. *The Federalist Papers*. New York: New American Library, 1964.

Hyneman, Charles, and Donald Lutz, eds. *American Political Writings during the Founding Era: 1760–1805*. Indianapolis, Ind.: Liberty Press, 1983.

Isaac, Rael Jean, and Erich Isaac. *The Coercive Utopians*. Chicago: Regnery, 1983.

Jaffa, Harry V. *Crisis of a House Divided*. Garden City, N.Y.: Doubleday, 1959.

————. *American Conservatism and the American Founding*. Chapel Hill, N.C.: Carolina Academic Press, 1984.

Kendall, Willmoore, and George Carey. *The Basic Symbols of the American Political Tradition*. Baton Rouge, La.: Louisiana State University Press, 1970.

Kilpatrick, James Jackson. *The Sovereign States*. Chicago: Regnery, 1957.

Kristol, Irving. *On the Democratic Idea in America*. New York: Harper & Row, 1972.

Lipset, Seymour Martin. *The First New Nation*. Garden City, N.Y.: Doubleday, 1963.

McClay, Wilfred M. *The Masterless: Self and Society in Modern America*. Chapel Hill, N.C.: University of North Carolina Press, 1994.

McDonald, Forrest. *The American Presidency*. Lawrence, Kans.: University of Kansas Press, 1994.

Mansfield, Harvey. *Statesmanship and Party Government*. Chicago: University of Chicago Press, 1965.

———. *Taming the Prince*. New York: Free Press, 1989.

Morgan, Richard E. *Disabling America: The Rights Industry in America*. New York: Harper & Row, 1972.

Murray, John Courtney. *We Hold These Truths*. New York: Doubleday Image, 1964.

Navarro, Peter. *The Policy Game: How Special Interests and Ideologues Are Stealing America*. New York: John Wiley, 1984.

Novak, Michael. *Choosing Our King*. New York: Macmillan, 1974.

———. *The Spirit of Democratic Capitalism*. New York: Simon & Schuster, 1982.

Nye, Joseph S. *Bound to Lead: The Changing Nature of America Power*. New York: Basic Books, 1990.

Ransom, John Crowe, et al. *I'll Take My Stand*. Baton Rouge, La.: Louisiana State University Press, 1977.

Schlesinger, Arthur M. *The Cycles of American History*. Boston: Houghton Mifflin, 1986.

Stephenson, D. Grier, et al. *American Government*. New York: Harper & Row, 1988.

Storing, Herbert. *The Anti-Federalists*. Chicago: University of Chicago Press, 1981.

Wallis, Charles. *Our American Heritage*. New York: Harper & Row, 1970.

White, John Kenneth. *The New Politics of Old Values*. Hanover, N.H.: University Press of New England, 1988.

White, L. D. *The Jacksonian Persuasion*. Palo Alto, Calif.: Stanford University Press, 1957.

Wilson, James Q. *American Government*. Lexington, Mass.: D. C. Heath, 1989.

Winthrop, John. *History of New England, 1630–1649*, ed. James Savage. 2 vols. Boston: Little, Brown, 1853.

On Religion and American Politics

Allitt, Patrick. *Catholic Intellectuals and Conservative Politics in America, 1950–1985*. Ithaca, N.Y.: Cornell University Press, 1993.

Atkins, Stanley, and Theodore McConnell eds. *Churches on the Wrong Side*. Chicago: Regnery, 1986.

Bainton, Roland. *The Reformation of the Sixteenth Century*. Boston: Beacon Press, 1952.

Berger, Peter. *The Sacred Canopy*. Garden City, N.Y.: Doubleday, 1967.

———. *A Rumor of Angels*. Garden City, N.Y.: Doubleday, 1970.

Brown, Harold O. J. *Heresies: The Image of Christ in the Mirror of Heresy and Orthodoxy: From the Apostles to the Present*. Garden City, N.Y.: Doubleday, 1984.

Chadwick, Owen. *The Reformation*. New York: Penguin, 1964.

Dannhauser, Werner J. "Religion and the Conservatives." *Commentary* (December 1985).

Dunn, Charles W. *American Political Theology*. New York: Praeger, 1984.

———, ed. *Religion in American Politics*. Washington, D.C.: Congressional Quarterly Press, 1989.

Eidsmoe, John. *Christianity and the Constitution*. Grand Rapids, Mich.: Baker Books, 1987.

Eliot, T. S. *Christianity and Culture*. New York: Harcourt, Brace & World, 1968.

Evans, M. Stanton. *The Theme Is Freedom*. Washington, D.C.: Regnery Publishing, 1994.

Fowler, Robert Booth. *Religion and Politics in America*. Metuchen, N.J.: American Theological Association, 1985.

———. *Unconventional Partners*. Grand Rapids, Mich.: Eerdmans, 1989.

Goldberg, George. *Church, State and the Constitution*. Chicago: Regnery, 1987.

Hart, Benjamin. *Faith and Freedom*. Dallas, Tex.: Lewis & Stanley, 1988.

Herberg, Will. *Protestant, Catholic, Jew*. Garden City, N.Y.: Doubleday Anchor, 1960.

Hitchcock, James. *Catholicism and Modernity*. New York: Seabury Press, 1979.

Jaki, Stanley L. *Cosmos and Creator*. Chicago: Regnery, 1982.

———. *The Savior of Science*. Chicago: Regnery, 1987.

———. *The Only Chaos and Other Essays*. Bryn Mawr, Pa.: Intercollegiate Studies Assoc. Press, 1990.

———. *Patterns and Principles and Other Essays*. Bryn Mawr, Pa.: Intercollegiate Studies Assoc. Press, 1995.

Kilpatrick, William K. *Psychological Seduction: The Failure of Modern Psychology*. Nashville, Tenn.: Thomas Nelson, 1983.

Lawler, Philip F. *The Ultimate Weapon*. Chicago: Regnery, 1984.

Lefever, Ernest W. *Amsterdam to Nairobi: The World Council of Churches and the Third World*. Washington, D.C.: Ethics and Public Policy Center, 1979.

Lewis, C. S. *Mere Christianity*. New York: Macmillan, 1960.

———. *The Abolition of Man*. New York: Macmillan, 1965.

———. *God in the Dock: Essays on Theology and Ethics*. Grand Rapids, Mich.: Eerdmans, 1970.

Marsden, George. *Fundamentalism and American Culture*. New York: Oxford University Press, 1980.

Marty, Martin. *Pilgrims in Their Own Land*. New York: Penguin Books, 1984.

Muggeridge, Malcolm. *Jesus Rediscovered*. Garden City, N.Y.: Doubleday, 1969.

———. *Christ and the Media*. Grand Rapids, Mich.: Eerdmans, 1977.

Nash, Ronald H. *Social Justice and the Christian Church*. Milford, Mich.: Mott Media, 1983.

————, ed. *Liberation Theology*. Milford, Mich.: Mott Media, 1984.

Neuhaus, Richard John. *The Naked Public Square*. Grand Rapids, Mich.: Eerdmans, 1984.

Novak, Michael. *The Spirit of Democratic Capitalism*. New York: Simon & Schuster, 1982.

————. *Freedom with Justice: Catholic Social Thought and Liberal Institutions*. San Francisco: Harper & Row, 1984.

Reichley, A. James. *Religion in American Public Life*. Washington, D.C.: Brookings Institution, 1985.

Rice, Charles W. *Beyond Abortion: The Theory and Practice of the Secular State*. Chicago: Franciscan Herald Press, 1978.

Schaeffer, Francis A. *The Complete Works of Francis Schaeffer*. Westchester, Ill.: Crossway Books, 1985.

Schall, James V. *Liberation Theology*. San Francisco: Ignatius Press, 1982.

————. *The Politics of Heaven and Hell*. Lanham, Md.: University Press of America, 1984.

————, ed. *Out of Justice, Peace and Winning the Peace*. San Francisco: Ignatius Press, 1984.

Scully, Michael. *The Best of This World*. Lanham, Md.: University Press of America, 1986.

Stanmeyer, William. *Clear and Present Danger*. Ann Arbor, Mich.: Servant Press, 1983.

Wald, Ken. *Religion and Politics in the United States*. New York: St. Martin's, 1987.

Wuthnow, Robert. *The Restructuring of American Religion*. Princeton, N.J.: Princeton University Press, 1988.

Vitz, Paul C. *Psychology as Religion: The Cult of Self Worship*. Grand Rapids, Mich.: Eerdmans, 1977.

On Liberalism

Buckley, William F., Jr. *Up from Liberalism*. Briarcliff Manor, N.Y.: Stein & Day, 1985.

Burnham, James. *Suicide of the West*. Chicago: Regnery, 1985.

Coser, Louis A., and Irving Howe, eds. *The New Conservatives: A Critique from the Left*. New York: New American Library, 1976.

Crick, Bernard. *In Defense of Politics*. Chicago: University of Chicago Press, 1962.

Evans, M. Stanton. *The Liberal Establishment*. New York: Devin-Adair, 1965.

George, Robert P. *Making Men Moral*. London: Oxford University Press, 1993.

Gitlin, Todd. *Years of Hope, Days of Rage*. New York: Bantam, 1987.

Griffin, Bryan F. *Panic Among the Philistines*. Chicago: Discipleship Books, 1985.

Hampson, Norman. *The Enlightenment*. New York: Penguin, 1968.

Hartz, Louis. *The Liberal Tradition in America*. New York: Harcourt, Brace, 1955.

Hayek, Friedrich A. von. *The Road to Serfdom*. Chicago: University of Chicago Press, 1956.

Johnson, Paul. *Modern Times*. New York: Harper & Row, 1982.

————. *The Intellectuals*. New York: Harper & Row, 1988.

Liebowitz, Nathan, and Daniel Bell. *The Agony of Modern Liberalism*. New York: Greenwood, 1985.

Mallock, William Hurrell. *A Critical Examination of Socialism*. New Brunswick, N.J.: Transaction, 1991.

Mansfield, Harvey. *The Spirit of Liberalism*. Cambridge, Mass.: Harvard University Press, 1978.

McGovern, George. *Grassroots*. New York: Random House, 1977.

Minogue, Kenneth. *The Liberal Mind*. New York: Random House, 1963.

Oakeshott, Michael. *On Human Conduct*. London: Oxford University Press, 1975.

————. *On History and Other Essays*. London: Basil Blackwell, 1983.

Peters, Charles. *New Road for America: The Neoliberal Movement*. Lanham, Md.: Madison Books, 1985.

Reich, Robert B. *The Resurgent Liberal*. New York: Times Books, 1989.

Rothbard, Murray. *Egalitarianism as a Revolt Against Nature*. Washington, D.C.: Libertarian Review Press, 1974.

Spitz, David. *The Real World of Liberalism*. Chicago: University of Chicago Press, 1982.

Spragens, Thomas A. *The Irony of Liberal Reason*. Chicago: University of Chicago Press, 1981.

Strauss, Leo. *Liberalism, Ancient and Modern*. New York: Basic Books, 1968.

Trilling, Lionel. *The Liberal Imagination*. New York: Viking, 1950.

Tyrrell, Emmet. *The Liberal Crack-Up*. New York: Simon & Schuster, 1984.

Weaver, Richard. *Ideas Have Consequences*. Chicago: University of Chicago Press, 1948.

Zinn, Howard. *New Deal Thoughts*. Indianapolis, Ind.: Bobbs-Merrill, 1966.

On Conservatism in Personal Life

Bradford, M. E. *Against the Barbarians*. Lawrence, Kans.: University of Kansas Press, 1992.

Buckley, James. *If Men Were Angels: A View of the Senate*. New York: Putnam, 1975.

Buckley, William F., Jr. *God and Man at Yale*. 2d ed. Chicago: Regnery, 1977.

————, ed. *Odyssey of a Friend: The Letters of Whittaker Chambers to William F. Buckley, Jr., 1954–1961*. New York: Putnam, 1970.

Chamberlain, John. *A Life with the Printed Word*. Chicago: Regnery, 1981.

Chamberlain, William Henry. *The Evolution of a Conservative*. Chicago: Regnery, 1959.

Chambers, Whittaker. *Witness*. Chicago: Regnery, 1978.

Feulhner, Edwin. *Conservatives Stalk the House*. Ottawa, Ill.: Green Hill, 1983.

Goldwater, Barry, with Jack Casserly. *Goldwater*. New York: Doubleday, 1988.

Himmelfarb, Gertrude. *Lord Acton: A Study in Conscience and Politics*. Chicago: University of Chicago Press, 1952.

Kristol, Irving. *Reflections of a Neoconservative*. New York: Basic Books, 1983.

Lyons, Eugene. *Assignment in Utopia*. Westport, Conn.: Greenwood, 1971.

Morley, Felix. *For the Record*. Chicago: Regnery, 1979.

Nock, Albert J. *Memoirs of a Superfluous Man*. Chicago: Regnery, 1964.

Podhoretz, Norman. *Breaking Ranks*. New York: Harper & Row, 1979.

————. *Making It*. New York: Harper & Row, 1980.

Regnery, Henry. *Memoirs of a Dissident Publisher*. New York: Harcourt, Brace, Jovanovich, 1979.

Rozell, Mark, and James F. Pontuso, eds. *American Conservative Opinion Leaders*. Boulder, Colo.: Westview, 1989.

Rusher, William. *The Rise of the Right*. New York: Morrow, 1984.

Santayana, George. *Persons and Places*. New York: Scribners, 1944.

Toledano, Ralph de. *Lament for a Generation*. New York: Farrar, Straus, Giroux, 1960.

Viguerie, Richard. *The Establishment vs. the People*. Chicago: Regnery, 1983.

On Political Thought

Arendt, Hannah. *On Revolution*. New York: Viking, 1963.

————. *Origins of Totalitarianism*. New York: Harcourt, Brace & World, 1966.

Babbitt, Irving. *Democracy and Leadership*. Indianapolis, Ind.: Liberty Press, 1979.

Bishirjian, Richard. *A Public Philosophy Reader*. New Rochelle, N.Y.: Arlington House, 1978.

Bradford, M. E. *Remembering Who We Are: Observations of a Southern Conservative*. Athens, Ga.: University of Georgia Press, 1985.

Burke, Edmund. *Works*. Boston: Little, Brown, 1865.

Carey, George, and James V. Schall, eds. *Essays on Christianity and Political Philosophy*. Lanham, Md.: University Press of America, 1984.

Crick, Bernard. *The American Science of Politics*. London: Routledge & Kegan Paul, 1959.

East, John P. "Leo Strauss and American Conservatism." *Modern Age* 21 (Winter 1977): 2–19.

Ebenstein, William. *Great Political Thinkers.* New York: Holt, Rinehart and Winston, 1969.

Germino, Dante. *Beyond Ideology: The Revival of Political Philosophy.* New York: Harper & Row, 1967.

———. *Machiavelli to Marx.* Chicago: University of Chicago Press, 1979.

Hayek, Friedrich A. von. *The Constitution of Liberty.* Chicago: University of Chicago Press, 1956.

———. *The Road to Serfdom.* Chicago: University of Chicago Press, 1956.

Jouvenel, Bertrand de. *On Power.* New York: Viking, 1949.

Kirk, Russell. *Enemies of the Permanent Things.* La Salle, Ill.: Sherwood Sugden, 1984.

———, ed. *Orestes Brownson.* New Brunswick, N.J.: Transaction, 1991.

Kravchenko, Victor A. *I Chose Justice.* New Brunswick, N.J.: Transaction, 1991.

Lane, Rose Wilder. *Discovery of Freedom.* New York: John Day, 1943.

Lippman, Walter. *The Public Philosophy.* Boston: Little, Brown, 1965.

Lipson, Leslie. *The Great Issues of Politics.* Englewood Cliffs, N.J.: Prentice-Hall, 1981.

McAllister, Ted V. *Revolt Against Modernity: Leo Strauss, Eric Voegelin, and the Search for a Post-Liberal Order.* Lawrence, Kans.: University of Kansas Press, 1995.

Molnar, Thomas. *Utopia: The Perennial Heresy.* New York: Sheed & Ward, 1967.

———. *The Decline of the Intellectual.* New Rochelle, N.Y.: Arlington House, 1973.

Monogue, Kenneth. *Alien Powers: The Pure Theory of Ideology.* New York: St. Martin's, 1985.

Munson, Thomas J. *The Essential Wisdom of George Santayana.* New York: Columbia University Press, 1962.

Niemeyer, Gerhart. *Between Nothingness and Paradise.* Baton Rouge, La.: Louisiana State University Press, 1971.

Nisbet, Robert. *The Present Age.* New York: Harper & Row, 1988.

Nozick, Robert. *Anarchy, State and Utopia.* New York: Basic Books, 1974.

Oakeshott, Michael. *Rationalism in Politics and Other Essays.* New York: Methuen, 1981.

Orwell, George. *1984.* New York: Harcourt, Brace, 1949.

Ryn, Claes G. *Democracy and the Ethical Life.* Baton Rouge, La.: Louisiana State University Press, 1978.

Sabine, George, and Thomas L. Thorson. *A History of Political Theory.* Hinsdale, Ill.: Dryden Press, 1973.

Schaeffer, Francis A. *The Complete Works of Francis Schaeffer.* Westchester, Ill.: Crossway Books, 1985.

Strauss, Leo. *Natural Right and History.* Chicago: University of Chicago Press, 1953.

————. *Thoughts on Machiavelli*. Seattle, Wash.: University of Washington Press, 1958.

————. *What Is Political Philosophy?* Glencoe, Ill.: Free Press, 1959.

————. *On Tyranny*. Glencoe, Ill.: Free Press of Glencoe, 1963.

————. *Liberalism, Ancient and Modern*. New York: Basic Books, 1968.

Strauss, Leo, and Joseph Cropsey, eds. *History of Political Philosophy*. Chicago: Rand Mc-Nally, 1982.

Talmon, J. L. *The Origins of Totalitarian Democracy*. New York: Praeger, 1968.

Vivas, Eliseo. *Contra Marcuse*. New York: Dell, 1971.

Voeglin, Eric. *The New Science of Politics*. Chicago: University of Chicago Press, 1952.

————. *Science, Politics, and Gnosticism*. Chicago: Regnery, 1968.

Weaver, Richard. *Ideas Have Consequences*. Chicago: University of Chicago Press, 1984.

————. *Visions of Order*. Baton Rouge, La.: Louisiana State University Press, 1964; 2d ed., Bryn Mawr, Penn.: Intercollegiate Studies Institute, 1995.

Wilhelmsen, Frederick. *Christianity and Political Philosophy*. Athens, Ga.: University of Georgia Press, 1978.

On the Constitution and the Courts

Anastaplo, George. *The Constitutionalist: Notes on the First Amendment*. Dallas, Tex.: Southern Methodist University Press, 1971.

Bastiat, Frederic. *The Law*. New York: Foundation for Economic Education, 1984.

Berger, Raoul. *Government by Judiciary: The Transformation of the Fourteenth Amendment*. Cambridge, Mass.: Harvard University Press, 1977.

————. *Federalism: The Founders' Design*. Norman, Okla.: University of Oklahoma Press, 1987.

Berns, Walter. *Freedom, Virtue and the First Amendment*. Chicago: Regnery, 1965.

Bickel, Alexander. *The Least Dangerous Branch*. Indianapolis, Ind.: Bobbs-Merrill, 1962.

————. *The Supreme Court and the Idea of Progress*. New Haven, Conn.: Yale University Press, 1978.

Blackstone, Sir William. *Commentaries on the Laws of England*. Chicago: University of Chicago Press, 1979.

Bork, Robert. *The Tempting of America*. New York: Free Press, 1989.

Bozell, L. Brent. *The Warren Revolution*. New Rochelle, N.Y.: Arlington House, 1966.

Canavan, Francis. *Freedom of Expression*. Durham, N.C.: Carolina Academic Press, 1985.

Carey, George. *In Defense of the Constitution*. New York: Liberty Fund, 1995.

Clor, Harry. *Obscenity and Public Morality*. Chicago: University of Chicago Press, 1969.

Corwin, Edwin S. *Court Over Constitution*. Princeton, N.J.: Princeton University Press, 1938.

———. *The Higher Law Background of American Constitutional Law*. Ithaca, N.Y.: Cornell University Press, 1955.

———. *The Presidency: Office and Powers*. New York: New York University Press, 1964.

———. *Presidential Control of Foreign Relations*. New York: Johnson Reprint Corporation, 1970.

Dreisbach, Daniel L. *Real Threat and Mere Shadow: Religious Liberty and the First Amendment*. Westchester, Ill.: Crossway Books, 1987.

Epstein, Richard. *Takings: Private Property and the Power of Eminent Domain*. Cambridge, Mass.: Harvard University Press, 1986.

Goldberg, George. *Reconsecrating America*. Grand Rapids, Mich.: Eerdmans, 1984.

Kurland, Philip. *Politics, The Constitution and the Warren Court*. Chicago: University of Chicago Press, 1970.

Kurland, Philip, and Ralph Lerner. *The Founders' Constitution*. Chicago: University of Chicago Press, 1987.

Mason, Alpheus T. *The Supreme Court from Taft to Warren*. New York: Norton, 1964.

McClellan, James. *Joseph Story and the American Constitution*. Norman, Okla.: University of Oklahoma Press, 1971.

McDonald, Forrest. *A Constitutional History of the U.S.* New York: Franklin Watts, 1982.

———. *Novus Ordo Seclorum*. Lawrence, Kans.: University of Kansas Press, 1985.

McDowell, Gary. *Equity and the Constitution*. Chicago: University of Chicago Press, 1982.

McGuigan, Patrick B., and Randall R. Rader, eds. *A Blueprint for Judicial Reform*. Washington, D.C.: Free Congress Research & Education Foundation, 1981.

Mead, Lawrence. *Beyond Entitlement*. New York: Free Press, 1986.

Ostrom, Vincent. *The Political Theory of a Compound Republic*. Blacksburg, Va.: Public Choice, 1971.

Rabkin, Jeremy. *Judicial Compulsions*. New York: Basic Books, 1989.

Rushdoony, R. J. *This Independent Republic*. Tyler, Tex.: Thoburn Press, 1964.

Ryan, Thomas. *Orestes A. Brownson*. Huntington, Ind.: Our Sunday Visitor, 1976.

Siegan, Bernard. *Economic Liberties and the Constitution*. Chicago: University of Chicago Press, 1980.

Story, Joseph. *Commentaries on the Constitution*. Boston: Little, Brown, 1973.

Swisher, Carl Brent. *The Growth of Constitutional Power in the United States*. Chicago: University of Chicago Press, 1963.

Whitehead, John. *The Separation Illusion*. Milford, Mich.: Mott Media, 1977.

On Criminal Justice

Berns, Walter. *For Capital Punishment.* New York: Basic Books, 1979.

Carrington, Frank. *Neither Cruel Nor Unusual: The Case for Capital Punishment.* New York: Crown, 1978.

Carrington, Frank, and William Lambie. *The Defenseless Society.* Ottawa, Ill.: Green Hill, 1976.

McGuigan, Patrick, and Randall Rader, eds. *Criminal Justice Reform.* Chicago: Regnery, 1983.

Vanden Haag, Ernest. *Punishing Criminals.* New York: Basic Books, 1975.

————. *The Death Penalty: A Debate.* New York: Plenum Books, 1983.

Wilson, James Q., and Richard Herrstein. *Thinking about Crime.* New York: Basic Books, 1975.

————. *Crime and Human Nature.* New York: Simon and Schuster, 1985.

Wilson, James Q., ed. *Crime and Public Policy.* San Francisco: Institute for Contemporary Studies, 1983.

On Political Economy

Bauer, P.T. *Equality, The Third World, and Economic Delusion.* Cambridge, Mass.: Harvard University Press, 1981.

————. *Reality and Rhetoric: Studies in the Economics of Development.* Cambridge, Mass.: Harvard University Press, 1984.

Brookes, William T. *The Economy in Mind.* New York: Universe Books, 1982.

Brozen, Yale. *Concentration, Mergers, and Public Policy.* New York: Macmillan, 1982.

Buchanan, James M. *The Limits of Liberty: Between Anarchy and Leviathan.* Chicago: University of Chicago Press, 1977.

Buchanan, James M., and Gordon Tullock. *The Calculus of Consent: Logical Foundations of Constitutional Democracy.* Ann Arbor, Mich.: University of Michigan Press, 1962.

Buchanan, James M., and Richard E. Wagner. *Democracy in Deficit: The Political Legacy of Lord Keynes.* New York: Academic Press, 1977.

Chamberlain, John. *The Enterprising Americans: A Business History of the United States.* New York: Harper & Row, 1963.

————. *The Roots of Capitalism.* Indianapolis, Ind.: Liberty Press, 1976.

Davenport, John. *The U.S. Economy.* Chicago: Regnery, 1964.

Dietze, Gottfried. *In Defense of Property.* Baltimore: Johns Hopkins University Press, 1971.

Fink, Richard H., ed. *Supply-Side Economics.* Frederick, Md.: University Publications of America, 1982.

Friedman, Milton. *An Economic Protest*. Englewood Cliffs, N.J.: Prentice-Hall, 1972.

Friedman, Milton, and Rose Friedman. *Free to Choose*. New York: Harcourt, Brace, Jovanovich, 1980.

Friedman, Milton, Rose Friedman, and Anna Schwartz. *A Monetary History of the United States*. Princeton, N.J.: Princeton University Press, 1963.

Gilder, George. *Wealth and Poverty*. New York: Basic Books, 1981.

Goodman, John, ed. *Privatization*. Dallas, Tex.: National Center for Policy Analysis, 1985.

Gwartney, James, and Richard Stroup. *Economics: Public and Private Choice*. New York: Academic Press, 1980.

Hayek, Friedrich A. von. *The Road to Serfdom*. Chicago: University of Chicago Press, 1944.

————. *Individualism and Economic Order*. Chicago: University of Chicago Press, 1948.

Hazlitt, Henry. *The Failure of the "New Economics."* Princeton, N.J.: Van Nostrand, 1959.

————. *Economics in One Lesson*. New Rochelle, N.Y.: Arlington House, 1979.

————, ed. *The Critics of Keynesian Economics*. New Rochelle, N.Y.: Arlington House, 1977.

Hessen, Robert. *In Defense of the Corporation*. Stanford, Calif.: Hoover Institution Press, 1979.

Hutt, William H. *The Strike-Threat System: The Economic Consequences of Collective Bargaining*. New Rochelle, N.Y.: Arlington House, 1973.

————. *The Theory of Idle Resources*. Indianapolis, Ind.: Liberty Press, 1977.

Jouvenel, Bertrand de. *The Ethics of Redistribution*. Cambridge: Cambridge University Press, 1951.

Kirzner, Israel M. *The Economic Point of View: An Essay in the History of Economic Thought*. New York: New York University Press, 1976.

————. *Competition and Entrepreneurship*. Chicago: University of Chicago Press, 1978.

Knight, Frank H. *Ethics of Competition and Other Essays*. New York: Harper and Brothers, 1935.

Kristol, Irving. *Two Cheers for Capitalism*. New York: Basic Books, 1978.

Lepage, Henri. *Tomorrow, Capitalism: The Economics of Economic Freedom*. La Salle, Ill.: Open Court, 1978.

McKenzie, Richard B. *Bound to be Free*. Stanford, Calif.: Hoover Institution, 1983.

Mises, Ludwig von. *Human Action*. Chicago: Regnery, 1966.

————. *Omnipotent Government*. New Haven, Conn.: Yale University Press, 1969.

————. *A Critique of Interventionism*. New Rochelle, N.Y.: Arlington House, 1977.

————. *Socialism*. Indianapolis, Ind.: Liberty Press, 1981.

————. *Bureaucracy*. Cedar Falls, Iowa: Center for Future's Education, 1983.

North, Douglas C., and Robert Paul Thomas. *The Rise of the Western World: A New Economic History.* Cambridge: Cambridge University Press, 1973.

Novak, Michael. *The Spirit of Capitalism.* New York: Simon & Schuster, 1982.

Nutter, G. Warren. *Political Economy and Freedom.* Indianapolis, Ind.: Liberty Press, 1983.

Roberts, Paul Craig. *The Supply-Side Revolution.* Cambridge, Mass.: Harvard University Press, 1984.

Roepke, Wilhelm. *The Humane Economy: The Social Framework of the Free Market.* Chicago: Regnery, 1960.

————. *Economics of the Free Society.* Chicago: Regnery, 1983.

————. *The Social Crisis of Our Time.* New York: Transaction, 1995.

Schuettinger, Robert, and Eamonn F. Butler. *Forty Centuries of Wage and Price Controls.* Washington, D.C.: Heritage Foundation, 1979.

Schumpeter, Joseph. *Capitalism, Socialism and Democracy.* New York: Harper & Row, 1962.

Sowell, Thomas. *Race and Economics.* New York: McKay, 1975.

————. *Knowledge and Decisions.* New York: Basic Books, 1979.

————. *Marxism: Philosophy and Economics.* New York: William Morrow, 1985.

Stigler, George. *The Intellectual and the Marketplace.* Glencoe, Ill.: Free Press, 1963.

————. *The Economist as Preacher and other Essays.* Chicago: University of Chicago Press, 1982.

Tullock, Gordon. *The Politics of Bureaucracy.* Washington, D.C.: Public Affairs Press, 1964.

Vanden Haag, Ernest, ed. *Capitalism: Sources of Hostility.* New Rochelle, N.Y.: Epoch Books, 1979.

Waligorski, Conrad P. *The Political Theory of Conservative Economists.* Lawrence, Kans.: University of Kansas Press, 1990.

On Social Welfare Policy

Anderson, Martin. *Welfare: The Political Economy of Welfare Reform in the United States.* Stanford, Calif: Hoover Institution Press, 1978.

Anderson, Terry, and P. J. Hill. *The Birth of a Transfer Society.* Stanford, Calif.: Hoover Institution Press, 1980.

Blum, Walter, and Harvey Kalben, Jr. *The Uneasy Case for Progressive Taxation.* Chicago: University of Chicago Press, 1953.

Gilder, George. *Wealth and Poverty.* New York: Basic Books, 1981.

Hazlitt, Henry. *The Conquest of Poverty.* New Rochelle, N.Y.: Arlington House, 1973.

Himmelfarb, Gertrude. *The Idea of Poverty*. New York: Knopf, 1984.

Jouvenel, Bertrand de. *The Ethics of Redistribution*. Cambridge: Cambridge University Press, 1952.

Moynihan, Daniel P. *Maximum Feasible Misunderstanding*. New York: Free Press, 1969.

Murray, Charles. *Losing Ground: American Social Policy, 1950–1980*. New York: Basic Books, 1984.

Nock, Albert J. *Our Enemy the State*. New York: Arno Press, 1972.

Nozick, Robert. *Anarchy, State and Utopia*. New York: Basic Books, 1974.

Olasky, Marvin. *The Tragedy of American Compassion*. Washington, D.C.: Regnery Gateway, 1992.

Sowell, Thomas. *Markets and Minorities*. New York: Basic Books, 1982.

Tullock, Gordon. *The Economics of Income Redistribution*. Boston: Kluwer-Nijhoff, 1983.

Will, George. *Statecraft as Soulcraft*. New York: Simon & Schuster, 1983.

Williams, Walter. *The State Against Blacks*. New York: New Press, 1982.

On Foreign Policy and International Politics

Beilenson, Laurence B. *Survival and Peace in a Nuclear Age*. Chicago: Regnery, 1980.

Crozier, Brian, et al. *This War Called Peace*. New York: Universe Books, 1985.

DeMuth, Christopher C., et al. *The Reagan Doctrine & Beyond*. Washington, D.C.: American Enterprise Institute, 1988.

Eidelberg, Paul. *Beyond Detente: Toward an American Foreign Policy*. La Salle, Ill.: Sherwood Sugden, 1977.

Falcoff, Mark, and Robert Royal, eds. *Crisis and Opportunity: U.S. Policy in Central America and the Caribbean*. Washington, D.C.: Ethics and Public Policy Center, 1984.

Francis, Samuel. *Soviet Strategy of Terror*. Washington, D.C.: Heritage Foundation, 1981.

Graham, Daniel. *High Frontier: A New National Strategy*. Washington, D.C.: Heritage Foundation, 1981.

Gray, Colin. *The Soviet-American Arms Race*. Lexington, Mass.: Lexington Books, 1976.

Kelly, J. B. *Arabia, the Gulf and the West*. New York: Basic Books, 1980.

Kirkpatrick, Jeane J. *Dictatorship and Double Standards: Rationalism and Reason in Politics*. New York: Simon & Schuster, 1982.

Lawler, Philip E., ed. *Justice and War in the Nuclear Age*. Lanham, Md.: University Press of America, 1983.

Lefever, Ernest W. *Amsterdam to Nairobi: The World Council of Churches and the Third World*. Washington, D.C.: Ethics and Public Policy Center, 1979.

Lefever, Ernest W., and E. Stephen Hunt. *The Apocalyptic Premise: Nuclear Arms Debated*. Washington, D.C.: Ethics and Public Policy Center, 1982.

Luttwak, Edward N. *The Grand Strategy of the Soviet Union.* New York: St. Martin's, 1983.

Pipes, Richard. *Survival Is Not Enough: Soviet Realities and America's Future.* New York: Simon & Schuster, 1984.

Podhoretz, Norman. *The Present Danger.* New York: Simon & Schuster, 1980.

Scott, Otto. *The Other End of the Lifeboat.* Chicago: Regnery, 1985.

Staar, Richard F., ed. *Arms Control: Myth versus Reality.* Stanford, Calif.: Hoover Institution Press, 1984.

Thompson, Kenneth. *The Moral Issue in Statecraft.* Baton Rouge, La.: Louisiana State University Press, 1966.

Thompson, W. Scott, ed. *National Security in the 1980s: From Weakness to Strength.* San Francisco: Institute for Contemporary Studies, 1980.

Turner, Robert. *The War Powers Resolution.* Philadelphia: Foreign Policy Research Institute, 1983.

Ulam, Adam. *The Rivals: America and Russia Since World War II.* New York: Penguin, 1972.

———. *Expansion and Coexistence: Soviet Foreign Policy: 1917–1973.* New York: Holt, Rinehart and Winston, 1974.

Whelan, James P. *Catastrophe in the Caribbean: The Failure of America's Human Rights Policy in Central America.* Ottawa, Ill.: Jameson Books, 1984.

———. *The Soviet Assault on America's Southern Flank.* Washington, D.C.: Regnery, 1988.

———. *Out of Ashes: Life, Death and Transfiguration of Democracy in Chile.* Washington, D.C.: Regnery, 1989.

On the Ideology of Communism

Baron, John. *KGB: The Secret Work of Soviet Secret Agents.* New York: Bantam, 1974.

Burnham, James. *The Coming Defeat of Communism.* New York: John Day, 1950.

———. *Containment or Liberation?* New York: John Day, 1954.

———. *The Web of Subversion.* New York: John Day, 1954.

Chambers, Whittaker. *Witness.* Chicago: Regnery, 1978.

Conquest, Robert. *The Great Terror.* New York: Macmillan, 1968.

Cranston, Maurice, ed. *Prophetic Politics: Critical Interpretations of the Revolutionary Impulse.* New York: Simon & Schuster, 1970.

Deucher, Isaac. *Stalin.* London: Oxford University Press, 1949.

Hollander, Paul. *Political Pilgrims: Travels of Western Intellectuals to the Soviet Union.* New York: Oxford University Press, 1981.

Huntford, Roland. *The New Totalitarians*. New York: Stein & Day, 1980.

Koestler, Arthur. *Darkness at Noon*. London: J. Cape, 1965.

Koestler, Arthur, et al. *The God That Failed*. New York: Harper & Row, 1950.

Kuehnelt-Leddihn, Erik von. *Leftism: From De Sade and Marx to Hitler and Marcuse*. New Rochelle, N.Y.: Arlington House, 1974.

Leys, Simon. *Chinese Soldiers*. New York: Viking, 1974.

Lyons, Eugene. *The Red Decade: The Stalinist Penetration of America*. Indianapolis, Ind.: Bobbs-Merrill, 1961.

Mosher, Stephen. *Broken Earth: The Rural Chinese*. New York: Free Press, 1983.

Niemeyer, Gerhard. *An Inquiry into the Soviet Mentality*. New York: Praeger, 1956.

———. *The Communist Ideology*. Washington, D.C.: Government Printing Office, 1959.

———. *A New Look at the Soviet Threat*. New Rochelle, N.Y.: Arlington House, 1971.

Pipes, Richard. *Survival Is Not Enough*. New York: Simon & Schuster, 1984.

Shelton, Judy. *The Coming Soviet Crash*. New York: Free Press, 1989.

Sterling, Claire. *The Terror Network: The Secret War to International Terrorism*. New York: Holt, Rinehart and Winston, 1981.

Strausz-Hupe, Robert, et al. *The Protracted Conflict*. New York: Harper & Row, 1959.

Tucker, Robert C. *Stalin as Revolutionary, 1879–1929*. New York: Norton, 1973.

Turner, Robert. *Vietnamese Communism: Its Origins and Development*. Stanford, Calif.: Hoover Institution Press, 1975.

On Urban Social Policy

Anderson, Martin. *The Federal Bulldozer*. New York: McGraw-Hill, 1967.

Arkes, Hadley. *The Philosopher in the City: The Moral Dimensions of Urban Politics*. Princeton, N.J.: Princeton University Press, 1981.

Banfield, Edward. *The Unheavenly City*. Boston: Little, Brown, 1970.

———. *The Unheavenly City Revisited*. Boston: Little, Brown, 1974.

Butler, Stuart. *Enterprise Zones: Greening the Inner Cities*. New York: Universe Books, 1981.

Glazer, Nathan. *Ethnic Dilemma*. Cambridge, Mass.: Harvard University Press, 1983.

———. *The Limits of Social Policy*. Cambridge, Mass.: Harvard University Press, 1988.

———, ed. *Cities in Trouble*. Chicago: Quadrangle, 1970.

Glazer, Nathan, and William Gorham, eds. *The Urban Predicament*. Washington, D.C.: Urban Institute, 1976.

Glazer, Nathan, and Daniel P. Moynihan. *Beyond the Melting Pot*. Cambridge, Mass.: MIT Press, 1970.

Jacobs, Jane. *The Death and Life of Great American Cities.* New York: Random House, 1961.

———. *The Economy of the Cities.* New York: Random House, 1970.

Pride, Richard A., and J. David Woodard. *The Burden of Busing.* Knoxville, Tenn.: University of Tennessee Press, 1985.

On Authority, Family, Community, and Society

Berger, Peter, and Richard John Neuhaus. *To Empower the People: The Role of Mediating Structures in Public Policy.* Washington, D.C.: American Enterprise Institute, 1981.

Dexter, Midge. *The New Chastity and Other Arguments Against Women's Liberation.* New York: Coward, McCann & Geoghegan, 1972.

———. *Liberal Parents, Radical Children.* New York: Coward, McCann & Geoghegan, 1975.

Gilder, George. *Sexual Suicide.* New York: Quadrangle, 1973.

———. *Naked Nomads: Unmarried Men in America.* New York: Quadrangle, 1974.

———. *Men and Marriage.* Gretna, La.: Pelican, 1986.

Horan, Dennis J., and David Mall, eds. *Death, Dying and Euthanasia.* Frederick, Md.: University Publications of America, 1982.

Horan, Dennis J., and Eugene F. Diamond, eds. *Infanticide and the Handicapped Newborn.* Provo, Utah: Brigham Young University, 1982.

Howard, John A., ed. *The Family: America's Hope.* Rockford, Ill.: The Rockford Institute, 1979.

Krason, Stephen. *Abortion: Politics, Morality and the Constitution.* Lanham, Md.: University Press of America, 1984.

Kreeft, Peter. *The Unaborted Socrates.* Downers Grove, Ill.: InterVarsity Press, 1983.

Nathanson, Bernard. *Aborting America.* New York: Doubleday, 1979.

Nisbit, Robert. *The Quest for Community.* New York: Oxford University Press, 1953.

———. *The Sociological Tradition.* New York: Basic Books, 1966.

———. *Social Change and History: Aspects of Western Theory and Development.* New York: Oxford University Press, 1969.

———. *The Twilight of Authority.* New York: Oxford University Press, 1975.

Noonan, John T., Jr. *A Private Choice.* New York: Free Press, 1979.

———, ed. *The Morality of Abortion.* Cambridge, Mass.: Harvard University Press, 1970.

Rice, Charles E. *The Vanishing Right to Live.* Garden City, N.Y.: Doubleday, 1969.

Wallerstein, Judith, and Sandra Blakeslee. *Second Chances: Men, Women and Children a Decade after Divorce.* New York: Ticknor & Fields, 1989.

On Minorities

Capaldi, Nicholas. *Out of Order: Affirmative Action and the Crisis of Doctrinaire Liberalism.* Buffalo, N.Y.: Prometheus Books, 1985.

Eastland, Terry, and William J. Bennett. *Counting by Race: Equality from the Founding Fathers to Baake.* New York: Basic Books, 1979.

Gilder, George. *Visible Man: A True Story of Post-Racist America.* New York: Basic Books, 1979.

Glazer, Nathan. *Affirmative Action: Ethnic Inequality and Public Policy.* New York: Basic Books, 1978.

Novak, Michael, and Peter Rossi, eds. *The Rise of the Unmeltable Ethnics.* New York: Macmillan, 1971.

Roche, George. *The Balancing Act: Quota Hiring in Higher Education.* LaSalle, Ill.: Open Court, 1974.

Sowell, Thomas. *Affirmative Action: Was It Necessary in Academia?* Washington, D.C.: American Enterprise Institute, 1975.

———. *Ethnic America: A History.* New York: Basic Books, 1981.

———. *Civil Rights: Rhetoric or Reality?* New York: William Morrow, 1984.

Steele, Shelby. *The Content of Our Character: A New Vision of Race in America.* New York: St. Martin's, 1991.

Storing, Herbert. *What Country Have I?* New York: St. Martin's, 1970.

Williams, Walter. *Youth and Minority Unemployment.* Stanford, Calif.: Hoover Institution Press, 1977.

———. *America: A Minority Viewpoint.* Stanford, Calif.: Hoover Institution Press, 1982.

Wortham, Anne. *The Other Side of Racism: A Philosophical Study of Black Race Consciousness.* Columbus, Ohio: Ohio State University Press, 1981.

On American History: Revisionist Perspectives

Berthoff, Rowland. *An Unsettled People: Social Order and Disorder in American History.* New York: Harper & Row, 1971.

Handlin, Oscar. *The Distortion of America.* Boston: Little, Brown, 1981.

Hayek, Friedrich A. von., ed. *Capitalism and the Historians.* Chicago: University of Chicago Press, 1963.

Jaki, Stanley L. *The Origin of Science and the Science of Origin.* Chicago: University of Chicago Press, 1978.

———. *The Road of Science and the Ways to God.* Chicago: University of Chicago Press, 1978.

Johnson, Paul. *Modern Times: The World from the Twenties to the Eighties.* New York: Harper & Row, 1983.

Klehr, Harvey. *The Heyday of American Communism.* New York: Basic Books, 1984.

Kraditor, Aileen S. *The Radical Persuasion, 1890–1917.* Baton Rouge, La.: Louisiana State University Press, 1981.

Lewy, Guenter. *America in Vietnam.* New York: Oxford University Press, 1978.

Lukacs, John. *A History of the Cold War.* Garden City, N.Y.: Doubleday, 1966.

———. *Outgrowing Democracy: A History of the United States in the Twentieth Century.* New York: Doubleday, 1984.

———. *Historical Consciousness, Or The Remembered Past.* New York: Schocken Books, 1985.

Lynn, Kenneth, S. *The Air-Line to Seattle.* Chicago: University of Chicago Press, 1983.

Maddox, Robert James. *The New Left and the Origins of the Cold War.* Princeton, N.J.: Princeton University Press, 1973.

McDonald, Forrest. *We the People: The Economic Origins of the Constitution.* Chicago: University of Chicago Press, 1958.

———. *E Pluribus Unum: The Formation of the American Republic.* Indianapolis, Ind.: Liberty Press, 1979.

———. *Alexander Hamilton: A Biography.* New York: Norton, 1979.

———. *A Constitutional History of the United States.* New York: Franklin Watts, 1982.

———. *Novus Ordo Seclorum: The Intellectual Origins of the Constitution.* Lawrence, Kans.: University of Kansas Press, 1985.

McWhiney, Grady. *Southerners and Other Americans.* New York: Basic Books, 1964.

Morgan, H. Wayne, ed. *The Gilded Age: A Reappraisal.* Syracuse, N.Y.: Syracuse University Press, 1963.

Nash, George. *The Life of Herbert Hoover, The Engineer, 1874–1914.* New York: Norton, 1984.

Nock, Albert Jay. *Jefferson.* New York: Hill & Wang, 1960.

Podhoretz, Norman. *Why We Were In Vietnam.* New York: Simon & Schuster, 1982.

Radosh, Ronald, and Joyce Milton. *The Rosenberg File.* New York: Holt, Rinehart and Winston, 1983.

Russell, Francis. *Sacco & Vanzetti: The Case Resolved.* New York: Harper & Row, 1986.

Scott, Otto J. *The Secret Six: John Brown and the Abolitionist Movement.* New York: Times Books, 1979.

Shapiro, Edward S. *Clio from the Right: Essays of a Conservative Historian.* Lanham, Md.: University Press of America, 1983.

Silver, Thomas. *Coolidge and the Historians.* Durham, N.C.: Carolina Academic Press, 1982.

Ulam, Adam. *A History of Soviet Russia*. New York: Holt, Rinehart and Winston, 1976.

Weinstein, Allan. *Perjury: The Hiss-Chambers Trial*. New York: Random House, 1978.

On Cultural and Literary Criticism

Aron, Raymond. *Politics and History*. New Brunswick, N.J.: Transaction, 1988.

Bellow, Saul. *The Dean's December*. New York: Harper & Row, 1982.

Berman, Ronald. *Culture and Politics*. Lanham, Md.: University Press of America, 1984.

Bradbury, Ray. *Dandelion Wine*. New York: Bantam, 1969.

Brooks, Cleanth. *The Well Wrought Urn*. New York: Harcourt, Brace, Jovanovich, 1956.

Cather, Willa. *Death for the Archbishop*. New York: Random House, 1971.

Cowen, Louise. *The Fugitive Group*. Baton Rouge, La.: Louisiana State University Press, 1959.

Crunden, Robert M. *The Superfluous Men: Conservative Critics of American Culture, 1900–1945*. Austin, Tex.: University of Texas Press, 1977.

Davidson, Donald. *Still Rebels, Still Yankees*. Baton Rouge, La.: Louisiana State University Press, 1957.

De Vries, Peter. *I Hear America Swinging*. Boston: Little, Brown, 1976.

Dos Passos, John. *District of Columbia*. Boston: Houghton, Mifflin, 1952.

Eliot, T. S. *Selected Essays, 1917–1932*. New York: Harcourt, Brace, 1932.

Fleming, Thomas. *Politics of Human Nature*. New Brunswick, N.J.: Transaction, 1991.

Frost, Robert. *Poetry & Prose*. New York: Holt, Rinehart and Winston, 1973.

Griffin, Bryan. *Panic of the Philistines*. Chicago: Regnery, 1983.

Hawthorne, Nathaniel. *The Blithedale Romance*. New York: Norton, 1977.

Hazard, Paul. *European Thought in the Twentieth Century*. Cleveland, Ohio: World Publishers, 1963.

Hirsch, E. D. *Cultural Literacy*. Boston: Houghton Mifflin, 1987.

Hollander, Paul. *The Survival of the Adversary Culture*. New Brunswick, N.J.: Transaction, 1988.

James, Henry. *The Bostonians*. New York: New American Library, 1980.

Kenner, Hugh. *Wyndham: A Critical Guidebook*. New York: New Directions, 1954.

———. *The Pound Era*. Berkeley, Calif.: University of California Press, 1971.

Kirk, Russell. *Eliot and His Age*. La Salle, Ill.: Sherwood Sugden, 1984.

Koestler, Arthur. *Darkness at Noon*. New York: Bantam, 1970.

Lewis, C. S. *An Experiment in Criticism*. Cambridge: Cambridge University Press, 1961.

———. *The Discarded Image*. Cambridge: Cambridge University Press, 1961.

Lipman, Samuel. *The House of Music*. Boston: David R. Godine, 1984.

Lytle, Andrew. *Stories: Alchemy and Others*. Sewanee, Tenn.: University of the South Press, 1983.

McInerny, Ralph. *The Noonday Devil*. New York: Atheneum, 1985.

Mencken, H. L. *Notes on Democracy*. New York: Octagon, 1976.

Montgomery, Marion. *The Prophetic Poet and the Spirit of the Age*, 3 vols.: *Why Flannery O'Connor Stayed Home; Why Poe Drank Liquor; Why Hawthorne Was Melancholy*. La Salle, Ill.: Sherwood Sugden, 1981, 1983, 1984.

O'Connor, Flannery. *The Complete Stories of Flannery O'Connor*. New York: Farrar, Straus, and Giroux, 1971.

Panichas, George. *Irving Babbitt: Representative Writings*. Lincoln, Neb.: University of Nebraska Press, 1971.

———. *The Reverent Discipline: Essays in Literary Criticism & Culture*. Knoxville, Tenn.: University of Tennessee Press, 1974.

———. *The Courage of Judgment: Essays in Criticism, Culture & Society*. Knoxville, Tenn.: University of Tennessee Press, 1982.

Pei, Mario. *Double Speak in America*. New York: Hawthorn Books, 1975.

Percy, Walker. *Lost in the Cosmos: The Last Self-Help Book*. New York: Farrar, Straus, and Giroux, 1983.

Podhoretz, Norman. *The Bloody Crossroads: Where Literature and Politics Meet*. New York: Simon & Schuster, 1986.

Repplier, Agnes. *Times and Tendencies*. Freeport, N.Y.: Books for Libraries Press, 1971.

Simon, John. *Singularities: Essays on the Theater, 1964–1974*. New York: Random House, 1976.

———. *Paradigms Lost: Literacy and Its Decline*. New York: Penguin, 1981.

———. *Reverse Angle: American Film, 1970–1980*. New York: Crown, 1981.

Solzhenitsyn, Alexander. *A World Split Apart*. New York: Harper & Row, 1978.

Tate, Allen. *Essays of Four Decades*. Chicago: Swallow, 1969.

Trilling, Lionel. *The Middle of the Journey*. New York: Harcourt, Brace, Jovanovich, 1980.

Warren, Austin. *Rage for Order*. Ann Arbor, Mich.: University of Michigan Press, 1948.

Warren, Robert Penn. *All the King's Men*. New York: Harcourt, Brace, Jovanovich, 1946.

Wilder, Thornton. *The Eighth Day*. New York: Avon, 1976.

Wolfe, Tom. *Radical Chic and Mau-Mauing the Flak Catchers*. New York: Farrar, Straus, and Giroux, 1970.

———. *The Purple Decades*. New York: Farrar, Straus, and Giroux, 1984.

On Education

Babbitt, Irving. *Literature and the American College*. Clifton, N.J.: Augustus Kelly, 1972.

Barzun, Jacques. *The House of Intellect*. New York: Harper & Row, 1959.

———. *Teacher in America*. Indianapolis, Ind.: Liberty Press, 1981.

Bloom, Allan. *The Closing of the American Mind*. New York: Simon & Schuster, 1987.

Blumenfeld, Samuel. *NEA: Trojan Horse in American Education*. Boise, Idaho: Paradigm, 1984.

Bunzel, John H., ed. *Challenge to American Schools: The Case for Standards and Values*. New York: Oxford University Press, 1985.

Burleigh, Anne Husted, ed. *Education in a Free Society*. Indianapolis, Ind.: Liberty Press, 1973.

Chalmers, Gordon Keith. *The Republic and the Person*. Chicago: Regnery, 1952.

D'Souza, Dinesh. *Illiberal Education*. New York: The Free Press, 1991.

Ericson, Edward E. *Radicals in the University*. Stanford, Calif.: Hoover Institution Press, 1975.

Everhart, Robert B. *The Public School Monopoly: A Critical Analysis of Education and the State of American Society*. San Francisco: Pacific Institute, 1984.

Glazer, Nathan, ed. *Bureaucrats and Brainpower: Government Regulation of Universities*. San Francisco: Institute for Contemporary Studies, 1979.

Hart, Benjamin. *Poisoned Ivy*. New York: Stein & Day, 1984.

Jaspers, Karl. *The Idea of the University*. Boston: Beacon Press, 1959.

Kirk, Russell. *Academic Freedom*. Chicago: Regnery, 1955.

———. *Decadence and Renewal in Higher Learning*. Chicago: Regnery, 1978.

Ladd, Everett Carl, Jr., and Martin Seymour Lipset. *The Divided Academy: Professors & Politics*. New York: McGraw-Hill, 1975.

Lawler, Philip F. *Coughing in Red Ink*. Lanham, Md.: University Press of America, 1983.

Martin, William Oliver. *Order and Integration of Knowledge*. Ann Arbor, Mich.: University of Michigan Press, 1957.

Nisbet, Robert. *The Degradation of the Academic Dogma: The University in America, 1945–1970*. New York: Basic Books, 1971.

Phenix, Philip. *Education and the Common Good: A Moral Philosophy of the Curriculum*. New York: Harper & Row, 1961.

Powers, Richard. *The Dilemma of Education in a Democracy*. Chicago: Regnery, 1984.

Ravitch, Diane. *The Troubled Crusade: American Education, 1945–1980*. New York: Basic Books, 1983.

Roche, George. *Education in America*. Hillsdale, Mich.: Hillsdale College, 1969.

Sewall, Gilbert. *Necessary Lessons*. New York: Free Press, 1983.

Sowell, Thomas. *Black Education: Myths and Tragedies*. New York: McKay, 1972.

————. *Education: Assumptions Versus History.* Stanford, Calif.: Hoover Institution Press, 1986.

Tonsor, Stephen. *Tradition and Reform in Education.* La Salle, Ill.: Open Court, 1974.

On the Mass Media

Bethell, Tom. *Television Evening News Covers Inflation: 1978–79.* Washington, D.C.: Media Institute, 1980.

Bozell, L. Brent, III, and Brent H. Baker. *And That's the Way It Isn't: A Reference Guide to Media Bias.* Alexandria, Va.: Media Research Center, 1990.

Braestrup, Peter. *Big Story: How the American Press & Television Reported & Interpreted the Crises of TET 1968 in Vietnam and Washington.* Boulder, Colo.: Westview Press, 1977.

Braley, Russell. *Bad News: The Foreign Policy of the New York Times.* Chicago: Regnery, 1984.

Efron, Edith. *The News Twisters.* Los Angeles: Nash Publishing, 1971.

Efron, Edith, and Clytia Chambers. *How CBS Tried to Kill a Book.* Los Angeles: Nash Publishing, 1972.

Kowet, Don. *A Matter of Honor: General William C. Westmoreland versus CBS.* New York: Macmillan, 1984.

Lawler, Philip F. *The Alternative Influence: The Impact of Investigative Reporting on America's Media.* Washington, D.C.: Media Institute, 1984.

Lichter, S. Robert, Stanley Rothman, and Linda Lichter. *The Media Elite: America's New Powerbrokers.* Bethesda, Md.: Adler & Adler, 1986.

Muravchik, Joshua. *News Coverage of the Sandinista Revolution.* Washington, D.C.: American Enterprise Institute, 1988.

Phillips, Kevin P. *Mediacracy: American Parties and Politics in the Communications Age.* New York: Doubleday, 1975.

Rothman, Stanley, and S. Robert Lichter. *The Media Elite and American Values.* Washington, D.C.: Ethics and Public Policy Center, 1982.

Theberge, Leonard J., ed. *Crooks, Conmen and Clowns: Businessmen in TV Entertainment.* Washington, D.C. Media Institute, 1981.

————. *TV Coverage of the Oil Crises: How Well Was the Public Served?* New York: Pergamon, 1982.

Wattenberg, Ben. *The Good News Is the Bad News Is Wrong.* New York: Simon & Schuster, 1984.

Index